D0242570

Citizenship and National Identity

The Library
Stranmillis University College
Belfast

This item must be returned or renewed by the latest date shown or fines may be charged. It is also subject to earlier recall if in demand.

Renewals
   Online: 'My account' in StranCat
   Phone: **028 9038 4310**
   Email: **library@stran.ac.uk**

STRANMILLIS
UNIVERSITY COLLEGE
BELFAST

For Don Fowler
whose warmth and friendship I shall miss so much
and also for Peta

Citizenship and National Identity

David Miller

Polity Press

Copyright © David Miller 2000

The right of David Miller to be identified as author of this work has been asserted in accordance with the Copyright, Designs and Patents Act 1988.

First published in 2000 by Polity Press in association with Blackwell Publishers Ltd.

Editorial office:
Polity Press
65 Bridge Street
Cambridge CB2 1UR, UK

Marketing and production:
Blackwell Publishers Ltd
108 Cowley Road
Oxford OX4 1JF, UK

Published in the USA by
Blackwell Publishers Inc.
Commerce Place
350 Main Street
Malden, MA 02148, USA

All rights reserved. Except for the quotation of short passages for the purposes of criticism and review, no part of this publication may be reproduced, stored in a retrieval system, or transmitted, in any form or by any means, electronic, mechanical, photocopying, recording or otherwise, without the prior permission of the publisher.

Except in the United States of America, this book is sold subject to the condition that it shall not, by way of trade or otherwise, be lent, re-sold, hired out, or otherwise circulated without the publisher's prior consent in any form of binding or cover other than that in which it is published and without a similar condition including this condition being imposed on the subsequent purchaser.

Library of Congress Cataloging-in-Publication Data

Miller, David.
    Citizenship and national identity/David Miller.
        p. cm.
    Includes bibliographical references and index.
    ISBN 0–7456–2393–X—ISBN 0–7456–2394–8
    1. Citizenship. 2. Nationalism. I. Title

JF801 M55 2000
323'.04—'de21   99–058780

A catalogue record for this book is available from the British Library.

Typeset in 10 on 12 pt Sabon by Kolam Information Services Pvt. Ltd., Pondicherry, India
Printed in Great Britain by T.J. International, Padstow, Cornwall

This book is printed on acid-free paper.

Contents

Acknowledgements

I should like to thank the editors and publishers of the following essays for permission to reprint them in this book.

'Deliberative Democracy and Social Choice', *Political Studies*, 40 (1992), Special Issue on Prospects for Democracy, 54–67.

'In Defence of Nationality', *Journal of Applied Philosophy*, 10 (1993), 3–16.

'Citizenship and Pluralism', *Political Studies*, 43 (1995), 432–50.

'Group Identities, National Identities and Democratic Politics' in J. Horton and S. Mendus (eds), *Toleration, Identity and Difference* (London, Macmillan, 1999).

'Bounded Citizenship' in K. Hutchings and R. Dannreuther (eds), *Cosmopolitan Citizenship* (London, Macmillan, 1999).

'Communitarianism: Left, Right and Centre' in D. Avnon and A. de-Shalit (eds), *Liberalism and its Practice* (London, Routledge, 1999).

'Secession and the Principle of Nationality' in J. Couture, K. Nielsen and M. Seymour (eds), *Rethinking Nationalism* (Calgary, University of Calgary Press, 1998) (*Canadian Journal of Philosophy*, Supplementary Volume 22).

'Nationality in Divided Societies' in A. Gagnon and J. Tully (eds), *Struggles for Recognition in Multinational Societies* (Cambridge, Cambridge University Press, 2000).

Introduction

The essays collected in this book were all written during the last ten years, and together represent my attempt to throw some light on two central issues: what citizenship can mean in today's world, and whether nationality remains a defensible principle around which to organize our politics. I regard these issues as closely connected, in the sense that the form of citizenship that I advocate, which I call republican, is feasible only where it can call upon the ethical resources of a national community. So the defence of republican citizenship and the defence of nationality are closely linked, and I therefore believe that the essays included here, although composed for separate occasions, set out a coherent political theory.

Politically speaking, the position from which they are written is broadly social democratic. A concern for social justice, and the conditions under which it can be achieved, is never far below the surface, and indeed during the period in question I have been working in parallel on a restatement of my views on that topic, which has now appeared in book form as *Principles of Social Justice* (Cambridge, Mass., Harvard University Press, 1999). But the 1990s have been a difficult decade for those who share my general stance (the spate of electoral victories by social-democratic parties in Europe and elsewhere notwithstanding). Three developments in particular have appeared to threaten the idea of social justice pursued by democratic means within national boundaries, which I believe stands at the heart of social democracy as a political project.

The first of these is economic and cultural globalization – the set of processes which, it is argued, entail that the state is losing the capacity to control economic activity within its borders, and also the capacity to determine the cultural make-up of its citizens. Free international movement of both capital and labour means that all states are forced to pursue essentially similar economic policies internally if they are not to scare away investors or lose skilled labour to other states, while flows of information of all kinds across borders mean that citizens everywhere are increasingly exposed to the same barrage of cultural messages – they watch the same television shows, listen to the same news programmes, see the same advertisements, buy the same commodities and so on. As a result of all this, the argument goes, the power of the state is ebbing away, and it matters less to individual citizens what character their state has, or where its boundaries are drawn. So the effect of globalization is on the one hand to make social justice as it is usually understood harder to pursue, and on the other to make traditional concerns about citizenship and nationality increasingly marginal to the lives of ordinary people.

The second tendency runs in a sense directly counter to the first, but it too has disturbing implications for the nation-state in its traditional form. This is the emergence, in many parts of the globe, of sub-state nationalisms that challenge the legitimacy of existing states. Whether the challenge is violent or peaceful, the claim made is that established states are unable to satisfy the interests and the cultural demands of smaller, more local communities. Unfortunately, however, these claims may be very difficult to meet, not least because of territorial disputes between different national groups of the kind we have witnessed in former Yugoslavia, Sri Lanka, Israel and many other places. So the problem here is not that people are becoming economically or culturally cosmopolitan, but that they are engaging in forms of politics (and political violence) that bring to mind Isaiah Berlin's image of nationalism as a bent twig that when released lashes back uncontrollably at those who are seen as the oppressors and tormentors of the minority nations.

The third tendency has something in common with each of the first two. This is the appearance, within liberal democracies, of new forms of identity politics, whereby groups formed on the basis of shared ethnicity, religion, gender or sexuality enter political arenas in search of recognition and a remoulding of citizenship so that it comes to reflect these more fractionalized forms of personal identity. The message appears to be that political identity does indeed matter in politics, but that the identities that count are not the old identities stemming from nationhood and common citizenship, but new, more fragmented identities that are often shared with others outside the boundaries of the state. So identity politics appears in part to reflect the transmission of different cultures across national borders, and in part to reflect the desire for stronger, more direct forms of political identity that sub-state nationalisms also embody.

That these three tendencies are proceeding apace has been more or less the received wisdom of the last decade, and as with received wisdom generally, we ought to look carefully and critically at how far these claims are borne out by the facts. But even if they turn out to be exaggerated, it remains true that in many quarters the ideas of nationhood and common citizenship are under attack – whether on the grounds that they were flawed from the very start or on the grounds that they may once have been valuable, but have now been sidelined by historical change. So I have tried to bring out some of their virtues, and also some of the ways in which they can be adapted to respond to the trends outlined above. I accept, in other words, that the claims made about globalization, sub-state nationalism and identity politics are at least partly true; they reflect changes in the political landscape that are real enough, even if the arguments made about them are overstated. But how we should respond, normatively, to these changes, is another question. The argument here is that we should reassert the underlying values of republican citizenship as a form of politics and nationhood as a form of political identity, while simultaneously thinking creatively about how best to implement these values in the contemporary world.

I explain what I mean by republican citizenship in chapter 3, where I contrast the republican conception of the citizen as someone who is actively involved in shaping the future direction of his or her society with two other views: the liberal view, which understands citizenship as a set of rights and obligations enjoyed equally by everyone who is a full member of the political community in question, and the libertarian view, which represents the citizen as someone who chooses between different bundles of (public) goods and services, in the same way as the consumer chooses between different sets of commodities in the market. At first sight it might appear that these two latter ideas are better adapted to the circumstances of culturally plural societies than the republican idea, which in its traditional form emerged from the experience of relatively small and homogeneous city-states, such as Athens and Florence. I argue, however, that republican citizenship is actually better able to respond to cultural diversity than these other versions, by virtue of its ability to draw groups who initially have very different priorities into public debate, and to find compromise solutions to political issues that members of each group can accept.

This argument relies upon a model of democratic decision-making that has come to be called 'deliberative democracy'. A democratic system is deliberative to the extent that the decisions it reaches reflect open discussion among the participants, with people ready to listen to the views and consider the interests of others, and modify their own opinions accordingly. The contrast here is with forms of democracy in which people simply pursue their own interests or preferences when deciding how to vote. In a deliberative democracy, the final decision taken may not be wholly consensual, but it should represent a fair balance between the different views expressed in the course of the discussion, and to the extent that it does, even those who would prefer some other outcome can recognize the decision as legitimate. If republican citizenship is to function successfully among people with very different styles of life and cultural values, it is essential that decision-making bodies, at whatever level they operate, should come as close as possible to this deliberative ideal.

I describe deliberative democracy in greater detail in chapter 1, whose main aim is to defend the model against problems thrown up by social choice theory. Social choice theorists such as William Riker have argued that democratic procedures are always liable to produce arbitrary results, essentially because where there are several options to choose between, and people's preferences differ significantly, it may be impossible to identify one of these options as the unique democratic choice. I respond to this argument by suggesting that deliberation itself may in a variety of ways alter the political preferences of those who engage in it, so that the final decision reached does genuinely represent the majority will, at least, of the participants.

In chapter 4 I consider another challenge to republican citizenship and deliberative democracy, that represented by new forms of identity politics, or what is sometimes called 'the politics of recognition'. Advocates of politics in this mode argue that a primary aim of democratic politics should be to endorse and promote, both symbolically and materially, the group identities of historically disadvantaged groups, such as women and ethnic minorities. In order for this to occur, republican forms of citizenship, as traditionally understood, must be replaced by a new style of politics in which group identities are given formal recognition, for instance by reserving places on political bodies for group members, or giving them rights of veto over policies that affect them directly.

I believe that this perspective both misconceives the nature of group identities in contemporary societies and is potentially damaging to the interests of the groups it is meant to serve. I present evidence that these identities are very much more open and fluid than defenders of identity politics recognize, and maintain that because of this instability proposals to give them formal recognition in political arenas will simply have the effect of fixing and privileging some identities at the expense of others. I also argue that by turning their backs on forms of identity, particularly national identities, that can bond citizens together in a single community, advocates of identity politics would destroy the conditions under which disparate groups in a culturally plural society can work together to achieve social justice for all groups. Minority groups are likely to have little bargaining power, so they must rely on appeals to the majority's sense of justice and fairness, and these will be effective only to the extent that majority and minorities sympathize and identify with each other.

I develop this argument further in chapter 9, which returns to deliberative democracy and considers the charge, brought by some recent advocates of identity politics, that deliberative procedures are not neutral, but biased in favour of white, middle-class males and against women and disadvantaged minorities. These critics claim that the interests of these groups are best served not by deliberation as normally understood, but by new forms of political communication – greeting, rhetoric and storytelling – that are better able to convey their distinct perspectives and distinct interests. I argue in reply that this critique of deliberation rests on an unnecessarily restrictive view of the kind of reasoning that is required in deliberative settings, while the proposed alternatives have serious defects of their own. A political system governed by the ideal of deliberative democracy still seems to offer the best prospect of combating the injustices suffered by disadvantaged groups.

The question whether republican citizenship requires citizens to share a common identity is taken up again in chapter 5, which takes the form of a critique of cosmopolitan theories of citizenship: that is, theories advocating forms of citizenship that transcend conventional political boundaries, particularly boundaries between nation-states. To assess these theories, I look more closely at the virtues required by republican citizens, and argue that these virtues are likely to be cultivated only within national borders. If this argument is correct, transnational forms of citizenship must be either parasitic on national forms or else not genuine forms of citizenship at all. This I try to show by looking briefly first at European citizenship, and second at what is sometimes called 'global civil society', or the idea that people can act as citizens through participating in international political movements of various kinds.

The defence of republican citizenship I have offered in these essays might in a broad sense be called communitarian. However, I regard this label as potentially very misleading if it is left unqualified, and in chapter 6 I draw some distinctions that I hope clarify the position that I want to defend. Specifically, I contrast right, liberal and left versions of communitarianism, and align myself with the third. In doing so, I reject the idea that 'liberalism' and 'communitarianism' stand as two opposed political philosophies, as is so often assumed. I also criticize communitarianism as a political movement for its unwillingness to choose between the different versions, leaving itself open to the charge that it tries to be all things to all people, and ends up lacking any distinctive political programme.

All of the arguments so far outlined rely on the premise that nationality is a primary source of identity for citizens in contemporary democratic states, and the remaining essays in the book focus more directly on this issue. Chapter 2 presents a concise statement of the arguments in favour of nationality that were later spelt out at greater length in my book *On Nationality* (Oxford, Clarendon Press, 1995). The principle of nationality as I understand it comprises three interlinked propositions: that a national identity is a defensible source of personal identity, that nations are ethical communities that impose reciprocal obligations on members which are not owed to outsiders, and that nations have a good claim to be politically self-determining. The essay explains what distinguishes national identities from identities of other kinds, and attempts to rebut a number of criticisms that are frequently levelled at the principle of nationality just outlined.

In chapter 7 I focus on a particular issue that is often thought to raise insurmountable problems for the principle of nationality, namely demands by national minorities within existing states that they should be permitted to secede and form independent states of their own. The spectre that appears here is of a host of conflicting secessionist claims which are impossible to satisfy simultaneously, and whose political expression is liable to take a violent form. I argue in this chapter that the nationality principle dictates a discriminating response to such demands, one that balances the claims of would-be secessionists against the equally strong claims of minority groups whose interests and identities would be less adequately protected if a secession were to occur. So although secession is sometimes justified, in many other cases the demands of minority groups are better met by dispersing political authority through federalism, regional devolution and other such means.

The following chapter examines the particular case of states whose members have dual-level national identities, thinking of themselves as belonging both to a smaller nation and to a larger, more inclusive one (Belgium, Canada, Spain, Switzerland and the United Kingdom are the examples I have particularly in mind). These I describe as states with 'nested nationalities' and I contrast them both with ethnically plural states and with states composed of rival nations. Using the Anglo-Scottish relationship as my main example, I explore the processes through which such nested identities have arisen, and I argue that in such cases constitutionally protected devolution, rather than independence, is the appropriate way to respect the national identities of the smaller nations.

Taking these three chapters together, what I hope to have shown is that the principle of nationality is not only philosophically defensible, but also politically viable, in the sense that it can guide us towards solutions to the problems created by the existence of sub-state nationalisms and other movements that challenge the nation-state in its traditional form. My argument is that we cannot in general hope to preserve or create simple, culturally homogeneous nation-states, given the multi-layered array of national identities that we encounter in today's world, but that the nation-state model can be creatively adapted to deal with this complexity.

The final chapter in the book examines the claim that national self-determination must always yield to the demands of global justice: national communities are never justified in pursuing projects and goals that fail to give equal weight to the needs and interests of human beings world-wide, so the scope of self-determination must be construed quite narrowly. My view is that such claims misunderstand the demands of global justice. In particular, they overlook the fact that notions of *social* justice vary from one community to the next, so that justice at the global level must be interpreted in a way that respects these differences. I suggest that it imposes three core requirements on political communities: an obligation to respect and safeguard basic human rights everywhere, an obligation not to exploit other communities and individuals, and an obligation to help create the conditions under which all nations have the chance to achieve their own regimes of justice internally. Understood in this way, global justice sets certain limits on what nation-states can decide to do, but still leaves them with a wide range of options.

All of the essays assembled here, and especially perhaps the last, raise as many questions as they answer, and there is a great deal more to be said about each of the main topics of the book – nationality, republican citizenship, identity politics, democracy, global justice and so forth. My hope is that the perspective developed in the book is sufficiently clear and coherent that those who disagree with me on one topic will see that their disagreement must extend to other areas too. I have learnt a great deal from friendly critics – I have recorded individual debts of gratitude in the notes to each chapter – and I look forward to further lively exchanges now that the full extent of my heresies is revealed.

1

Deliberative Democracy and Social Choice

If we are in the business of thinking about liberal democracy and possible alternatives to it, we must begin by drawing a distinction between institutions and their regulative ideals. Liberal democracy may be taken to refer to the set of institutions – free elections, competing parties, freedom of speech – that make up the political system with which we are familiar in the West; or it may refer to the conception of democracy that underlies and justifies that system. The relationship between institutions and regulative ideals is not necessarily simple or one-to-one. The same institution may be justified from different points of view, although characteristically those who favour contrasting regulative ideals will aim to shape the institution in different ways. Thus, to take a familiar case, the practice of electing representatives to a legislative assembly may be seen as a way of subjecting legislators to popular control; alternatively, it may be seen simply as a means of removing visibly corrupt legislators from office. Which of these views you take will affect your preferences as to the form of the practice. (How frequent should elections be? Should the voting system be first-past-the-post or something else? And so forth.)

The argument that follows has mainly to do with competing regulative ideals of democracy. In comparing liberal democracy with what I shall call deliberative democracy, my aim is to contrast two basic ways of understanding the democratic process. In favouring deliberative democracy, therefore, I am not recommending wholesale abolition of the present institutions of liberal democracy, but rather a reshaping of those institutions in the light of a different regulative ideal from that which I take to be prevalent now. I shall only address the institutional questions briefly. My main aim is to bring out what is at stake between liberal and deliberative democracy, particularly in the light of social choice theory, which appears to challenge the cogency of anything beyond the most minimal of democratic ideals.

Liberal democracy and deliberative democracy

Let me now sketch the contrast between liberal and deliberative democracy as regulative ideals. In the liberal view, the aim of democracy is to aggregate individual preferences into a collective choice in as fair and efficient a way as possible.[1] In a democracy there will be many different views as to what should be done politically, reflecting the many different interests and beliefs present in society. Each person's preferences should be accorded equal weight. Moreover, preferences are sacrosanct because they reflect the individuality of each member of the political community (an exception to this arises only in the case of preferences that violate the canons of liberal democracy itself, such as racist beliefs that deny the equal rights of all citizens). The problem then is to find the institutional structure that best meets the requirements of equality and efficiency. Thus liberal democrats may divide on the question of whether majoritarian decision-making is to be preferred, or whether the ideal is a pluralist system which gives various groups in society different amounts of influence over decisions in proportion to their interest in those decisions. This, however, is a family quarrel in which both sides are guided by the same underlying ideal, namely how to reach a fair and efficient compromise given the many conflicting preferences expressed in the political community.

The deliberative ideal also starts from the premise that political preferences will conflict and that the purpose of democratic institutions must be to resolve this conflict. But it envisages this occurring through an open and uncoerced discussion of the issue at stake with the aim of arriving at an agreed judgement.[2] The process of reaching a decision will also be a process whereby initial preferences are transformed to take account of the views of others. That is, the need to reach an agreement forces each participant to put forward proposals under the rubric of general principles or policy considerations that others could accept. Thus even if initially my aim is to support the claims of a particular group to which I belong or which I represent, I cannot in a general discussion simply say 'I claim that group A – farmers, say, or policemen – should get more money'. I have to give reasons for the claim. These might be that the group in question has special needs, or that it is in the common interest to improve the living standards of the group. By giving these reasons, however, I am committing myself to a general principle, which by implication applies to any other similarly placed group. Thus I am forced to take a wider view, and either defend the claim I am making when applied not only to my group but to groups B, C and D which are like A in the relevant respects or else to back down and moderate the claim to something I am prepared to accept in these other cases too. Although finally when a decision has to be reached there may still need to be a vote taken between two or more options, what participants are doing at that point is something like rendering a judgement or a verdict on the basis of what they have heard. They are expressing an opinion about which policy best meets the various claims that have been advanced, or represents the fairest compromise between the competing points of view that have been expressed.

The deliberative view clearly rests on a different conception of 'human nature in politics' from the liberal view. Whereas the latter stresses the importance of giving due weight to each individual's distinct preferences, the former relies upon a person's capacity to be swayed by rational arguments and to lay aside particular interests and opinions in deference to overall fairness and the common interest of the collectivity. It supposes people to be to some degree communally-oriented in their outlook. It also seems to be more vulnerable to exploitation, in the sense that the practice of deliberative democracy can be abused by people who pay lip-service to the ideal of open discussion but actually attempt to manipulate their colleagues to reach decisions that serve private interests.[3] We shall shortly see, however, that liberal-democratic procedures are themselves vulnerable to political manipulation. At this stage, therefore, we must take it as an open question which of the two democratic ideals is more likely to be subverted by manipulative individuals or groups.

In presenting my account of deliberative democracy, I mean to distinguish it not only from liberal democracy but from what has been called 'epistemic' democracy.[4] The epistemic conception of democracy sees the aim of democratic procedures as being to arrive at a correct answer to some question facing the political community. It is assumed here, in other words, that there is some objectively right or valid answer to the question that has been posed, but because there is uncertainty as to what the answer is, a decision-procedure is needed, and democracy, in the form of majority voting, is the procedure most likely to produce the right answer. This was, for instance, the view of Condorcet,[5] and it has also been attributed to Rousseau,[6] although my own belief is that Rousseau's view is ambiguous as between deliberative and epistemic conceptions of democracy.[7]

I believe the epistemic conception sets an unrealistically high standard for political decision-making. Although occasionally a political community may have to decide on some question to which it is plausible to

suppose a correct answer exists (say some scientific question in circumstances where there is complete consensus on the ends which the decision
should serve), it is much more likely that the issue will concern competing
claims which cannot all be met simultaneously in circumstances where no
resolution of the competition can be deemed objectively right. In the
deliberative conception, the aim is to reach agreement, which might be
achieved in different ways. One way is for the participants to agree on a
substantive norm, which all concur in thinking is the appropriate norm
for the case in hand. Another way is to agree on a procedure, which
abstracts from the merits of the arguments advanced by particular claimants. (Thus suppose the question is how an available resource such as a
tract of land should be allocated as between several groups that lay claim
to it. One possibility would be to agree on a principle such as that the
resource should go to the group which needs it most or which could use it
most productively, and then on the basis of the arguments advanced
decide which group that was. Alternatively the deliberating body might
feel that it was not competent to make such a judgement, and opt instead
for a procedural solution, such as sharing the resource out equally
between the groups, rotating it between them, or deciding by lot.) In
either case, the outcome is a decision which all the parties involved may
feel to be reasonable, but this does not entail that it reflects any transcend-
ent standard of justice or rightness. The emphasis in the deliberative
conception is on the way in which a process of open discussion in
which all points of view can be heard may legitimate the outcome when
this is seen to reflect the discussion that has preceded it, not on deliberation as a discovery procedure in search of a correct answer.[8]

Social choice theory and the democratic models

My aim in this chapter is to see whether deliberative democracy may be
less vulnerable than liberal democracy to the problems posed by social
choice theory for democracy in general. In arguing in this way, I am
apparently reversing a common opinion which is that social choice
obliges us to abandon 'populist' models of democracy in which democratic decisions are represented as expressions of 'the people's choice' or
the 'popular will' in favour of 'liberal' models in which democratic
elections are construed merely as a safeguard against the emergence of
tyrannical rulers. Democracy on this view is a matter of the voters having
the right, at periodic intervals, to remove from office governments which
they have come to dislike. Any notion that the voters should in some more
positive way determine public policy is misguided. This argument plays
some role in the classical defences of liberal democracy by Schumpeter

and Dahl[9] and has recently been developed at length and with great intellectual force by William Riker.[10]

From my perspective, however, both liberalism and populism as understood by Riker count as variants on the liberal ideal of democracy. For populism is the view that individuals' preferences should be amalgamated, by voting, to yield a general will which then guides policy. Liberalism in Riker's sense is less ambitious in that it sees the purpose of elections in negative terms as involving the removal of unpopular leaders. Both views see democracy as a matter of aggregating voters' preferences: they differ over the question whether policy can be chosen in this way, or only the personnel of government. The idea that democratic decisions are not a matter of aggregating preferences at all but of reaching agreed judgements is foreign to both.

Let me now remind readers of the challenge which social choice theory poses for these liberal views of democracy. Suppose a voting public has to decide between a number of policy options – suppose, to take a concrete case, that the issue is how Britain should generate its electricity, and the public has to choose between coal-fired, oil-fired, gas-fired and nuclear power stations. The message of social choice theory, and in particular its most celebrated constituent, Arrow's general possibility theorem,[11] is that one cannot devise a mechanism for making such decisions which simultaneously meets a number of quite weak and reasonable-sounding conditions that we might want to impose, such as monotonicity or the requirement that if a voter raises the position of one option in his own personal ranking, this cannot have the effect of lowering it in the social ranking.

This, one might say, is *the* problem posed by social choice for democracy – that is, in general there is no fair and rational way of amalgamating voters' preferences to reach a social decision – but it entails two more specific problems. The first is the arbitrariness of decision rules and the second is the near-unavoidability of strategic voting, or more strictly of opportunities for strategic voting. Decision rules fall broadly speaking into two classes, which following Riker we may call majoritarian and positional methods of selecting a preferred outcome. Majoritarian rules proceed by offering voters a series of binary choices and, depending on which option wins which encounters, identify an overall winner. So, in our example, voters would be asked to choose between coal and oil for generating electricity, between coal and gas, and so forth. There would be a series of majorities on the questions asked, and then some rule for discovering the overall choice. Positional rules ask voters to rank the available options and then compute a winner using all or part of this fuller information. Thus voters might be asked to rank order the energy options from 1 to 4 on their ballot papers and then a winner might be found by some rule such as giving an option two points each time it is someone's first choice and one point each time it comes second.

The problem of arbitrariness arises because it is not clear which of the many possible rules best matches our intuitive sense of 'finding the option which the voters most prefer' or to put the point another way, for any given rule it is possible to give examples where using that rule produces an outcome that seems repugnant to our sense of what a democratic decision should be. Among majoritarian rules, a strong contender is the Condorcet rule that any option which beats all the others in a series of binary choices should be the social choice. But there is no guarantee in any particular case that such a Condorcet winner can be found, so the rule is incomplete. Thus gas might beat coal and oil but lose to nuclear power, which in turn was beaten by one of the other options. If the rule is to be complete it has then to be extended to cope with this possibility, but there is no extension that is obviously the right one.[12] Among positional rules, the one most often favoured is the Borda count, which scores each option according to the place it holds in each voter's ranking, so that my top option gets n points, my second option $n - 1$ points and so on right the way down. One problem with this is that it may make the decision among quite popular options depend upon the way some voters rank way-out or eccentric options if these are on the ballot paper. Finally, it is an embarrassment that the Condorcet and Borda rules do not necessarily converge; that is, a Condorcet winner may exist, but a different option may be selected by use of the Borda count. This might occur where the Condorcet winner – nuclear power, let's say – was the first choice of a fair number of people but tended to be ranked very low by those who were against it, whereas another option – gas, let's say – was the first preference of just a few, but ranked second by quite a lot. Here it is not at all clear which way we should jump. There is a case for the option with most first preferences, and a case for the compromise proposal which comes reasonably high in most people's rankings.

The second problem is strategic voting, which means misrepresenting your true preferences when you vote with the aim of increasing the chances of your favoured option. Obviously the success of this depends on your having some knowledge of the preferences of other voters. It can be shown that there is virtually no decision rule that is not vulnerable to strategic manipulation if some voters choose to act in this way.[13] Again a couple of examples may help to bring this out. Suppose we are using a majoritarian decision rule. It is possible by strategic voting to block the emergence of a Condorcet winner. Thus suppose in our example nuclear power is the Condorcet winner if everyone votes sincerely. I am not particularly averse to nuclear power, but I am very strongly committed to coal-fired stations. I cannot prevent nuclear power defeating coal in a run-off between these options, but if others think like me we can stop the nuclear power bandwagon by voting insincerely for gas when the choice between gas and nuclear power is posed, thus preventing the emergence of nuclear power as a Condorcet winner and triggering whatever subsidiary rule is being employed in the hope that coal will win. Equally, if a Borda count is being used and I know that gas, say, is the likely winner, then I can boost the chances of coal by insincerely pushing gas down into fourth place. There is of course no guarantee that my strategy will work, since my opponents may behave strategically too. But this only serves to underline the arbitrariness of the eventual decision which in these circumstances would have very little claim to be called anything like a popular will.

So the challenge posed by social choice to democratic theory can be reduced to two basic claims: that there is no rule for aggregating individual preferences that is obviously fair and rational and thus superior to other possible rules; and that virtually every rule is subject to strategic manipulation, so that even if it would produce a plausible outcome for a given set of preferences if everyone voted sincerely, the actual outcome is liable to be distorted by strategic voting.

Working from within the liberal view of democracy, pessimists such as Riker respond to this challenge by reducing the significance of the electoral process to that of providing a safeguard against what Riker calls 'tyranny'. But even this safeguard is quite weak, since if the outcome of elections is to some degree arbitrary (as the social choice analysis shows), it is not apparent why they should pick out for removal unpopular or 'tyrannical' leaders. Coleman and Ferejohn put this point well:

> Nonreasoned removal from office is precisely what follows if Riker is correct in interpreting the instability results of social choice theory as demonstrating the meaninglessness of voting. If outcomes are arbitrarily connected to the preferences of the electorate, we cannot infer from his removal from office that an officeholder's conduct was in fact disapproved of by the voters. This is hardly the ideal of officeholders being put at risk by elections that we associate with liberalism.[14]

Social choice theory seems to undermine the liberal view of democracy in a systematic way, regardless of the precise function that is assigned to the act of voting in elections.

Deliberative processes and social choice

Can the problems of social choice be avoided altogether by switching to the deliberative ideal of democracy? Social choice theory postulates voters with given preferences over outcomes, and it is sometimes suggested that, once we allow that voters' preferences may alter in the course of decision-making, its results no longer apply.[15] But this response is too simple-minded. So long as there is a problem of amalgamating the voters' wishes at the point of decision – so long, to be more precise, as three or more policy outcomes are still in play and there is no unanimous preference for one of these outcomes – the social choice results apply. A decision rule must be found, and this is potentially vulnerable to the problems of arbitrariness and strategic manipulation. In my account of deliberative democracy, I indicated that, although full consensus was the ideal guiding discussion, it would be quite unrealistic to suppose that every instance of deliberation would culminate in unanimous agreement. Votes will still have to be taken, and where voting occurs so, potentially, will social choice problems.

Rather than sweeping away social choice theory at a stroke, my aim is the more limited one of showing that deliberative democracy has the resources to attenuate the social choice problems faced by the political community. The case I shall make has two main aspects. The first concerns the way in which deliberation may limit the range of preferences that have to be amalgamated in the final judgement. The second concerns the way in which knowledge of the structure of opinion in the deliberating body may influence the choice of decision rule.

The first part of the argument addresses one of the axioms of Arrow's original theorem, namely the requirement that the social choice procedure should be able to accommodate any possible set of individual rank orderings of outcomes. This axiom may indeed seem self-evident; it appears to pick up the liberal idea that each person is entitled to express whatever preferences he chooses, so that any limits on individual rank orderings would be discriminatory [as Riker puts the point, 'any rule or command that prohibits a person from choosing some preference order is morally unacceptable (or at least unfair) from the point of view of democracy'].[16] But rather than some external prohibition of possible ways of ranking alternatives, the possibility I wish to contemplate is that some initial sets of preferences might spontaneously be transformed through the process of deliberation, so that the final set of rankings from which a decision had to be reached was much smaller than the original set. If this were so, we could drop Arrow's unrestricted condition in favour of the weaker requirement that the social decision procedure should be able to cope with all possible sets of *post-deliberation* rankings.

I shall shortly suggest how this might help to resolve the social choice problems we have identified. But first we need to consider why some initial preferences might be eliminated in this way. The most straightforward case is that of preference orders that are irrational because they are based on false empirical beliefs. To use the energy policy example, someone might judge energy sources entirely on the basis of environmental soundness and begin with the rank order coal, gas, oil, nuclear power. However, in the course of debate strong evidence is produced about the atmospheric effects of coal-burning power stations which decisively pushes coal below gas and oil from an environmental point of view. This is not to say that the original rank order is completely untenable because there may be other value stances from which it remains appropriate. But then again it may be that no one or virtually no one holds these value stances, so the effect of debate is to crystallize the rank orderings into a smaller number of coherent patterns.

A second case is that of preferences that are so repugnant to the moral beliefs of the society within which the decisions are being made that no one is willing to advance them in a public context. This seems to be roughly the position with racist beliefs in contemporary Britain: a number of people hold them privately, but it is generally recognized that they cannot be articulated in political forums like Parliament. And this does constrain the set of policies that can be supported. You may favour immigration restrictions for racist reasons, but the fact that you cannot present these reasons publicly means that the policies you advocate have to be general in form; that is, they cannot explicitly discriminate between black and white immigrants.

The most important way in which deliberation may alter initial preferences, however, is that outlined in my original description of the deliberative ideal. Preferences that are not so much immoral as narrowly self-regarding will tend to be eliminated by the process of public debate. To be seen to be engaged in political debate we must argue in terms that any other participant could potentially accept, and 'It's good for me' is not such an argument. Or as Bob Goodin has put the point, when we adopt a public role, we must launder our preferences so that only public-oriented ones are expressed.[17] I discount here the possibility of people expressing one set of preferences in debate and voting according to another set at decision time. If voting is public, this could only occur at the cost of immediate loss of future credibility, and this may be a good reason for having an open voting system under conditions that approximate to deliberative democracy, as Brennan and Pettit have recently argued.[18] However, even under a secret ballot, it seems to me quite unlikely that we would witness widespread hypocrisy such as is involved in arguing for one position and then voting for another. This is a claim about human psychology: it says that if you have committed yourself to one position publicly, you would find it demeaning to retreat to a more selfish posture at the point of material decision.[19] I do not say this is universally true, but I think it is widely true.

Since this claim about the moralizing effect of public discussion is crucial to my argument about deliberative democracy, I would like at this point to illustrate it with some empirical evidence, although not alas drawn directly from the field of politics. The first piece of evidence comes from psychological experiments which try to simulate the behaviour of juries.[20] In these experiments, a number of subjects are shown a video recording of a trial in which the evidence for and against the accused is fairly evenly balanced. They are then asked to give their private guilty/not guilty verdict and on the basis of this formed into a number of mock juries divided evenly between the two views. The question is: which verdict will the jury eventually reach? *A priori* one would predict some hung juries, and then equal proportions of guilty and not-guilty verdicts. In fact, however, there is a marked tilt towards the not-guilty side, which the researchers attribute to the presence of a 'leniency norm'. That is, where the presence of conflicting opinions suggests that there is real doubt as to the guilt or innocence of the accused, you should give the accused the benefit of that doubt by returning a not-guilty verdict. Now the leniency norm is always present to some degree, but the point to which I want to draw attention is that allowing the 'jurors' a period of discussion before asking them to give their collective verdict shifted the outcome noticeably in the non-guilty direction. The best explanation seems to be that the effect of discussion was to activate the norm so that some participants who went in thinking 'Yes, he did it' ended up thinking 'We can't agree on this, so I'd better give him the benefit of the doubt'. In other words, the effect of discussion was to shift at least some people from a particular judgement to a general norm which people in liberal societies tend to apply to cases of this sort.

I want, however, to claim not only that discussion can activate norms but also that it can create norms by inducing participants to think of themselves as forming a certain kind of group. Broadly speaking, discussion has the effect of turning a collection of separate individuals into a group who see one another as co-operators. Perhaps I can again illustrate this with some experimental evidence, this time involving groups confronting a classic Prisoner's Dilemma. Each member is given a small sum of money and told that he can either keep it himself, or donate it to a common pool whereupon it will be doubled in value and shared equally among all members of the group. Obviously if everyone donates, everyone doubles their income, but the individually rational thing to do is to hold back the money. In the experiment I am describing, a ten-minute period of discussion more than doubled the rate of co-operation, from 37.5 per cent to 78.6 per cent.[21] Exactly what the normative mechanism at work here is may be open to question, but plainly the effect of debate was to generate a norm of co-operation within the group strong enough in the great majority of cases to override individual self-interest. A group of friends would have no difficulty extricating themselves from a Prisoner's Dilemma – they would trust one another already. Talking to one another appears to be a fairly effective way of simulating friendship in this case.

The upshot of this argument is that we have good reason to expect the deliberative process to transform initial policy preferences (which may be based on private interest, sectional interest, prejudice, and so on) into ethical judgements on the matter in hand; and this will sharply curtail the set of rankings of policy outcomes with which the final decision procedure has to deal. How does this help to eliminate the social choice problems we identified earlier? Take first the indeterminacy problem, and our observation that the Condorcet rule may be defeated by the existence of voting cycles (where, say, majorities favour gas over coal, coal over nuclear power, and nuclear power over gas in two-way comparisons). Here I wish to appeal to the well-known finding that cycles of this kind (and the Arrow problem more generally) can be avoided on condition that voters' rank orderings are 'single-peaked'.[22] That is to say, the alternatives can be arrayed on a continuum such that if, say, a voter ranks the alternative on the left the highest, he does not rank the alternative on the right above that in the centre.[23] Where preferences are single-peaked in this sense, one option must be the Condorcet winner and it would be possible to find this by repeated binary votes.

What does single-peakedness reveal about voters' preferences? It shows that they understand the choice before them in the same way, even though they adopt different positions on the spectrum. Thus suppose in the example we are using that coal is the cheapest of the three fuels but environmentally the most harmful; that oil is the most expensive but environmentally the best; and that gas stands between coal and oil in both respects. Then we might see the choice facing the voters as essentially that between economic cost and environmental soundness, and they would naturally divide into economizers (who put coal first but prefer gas to oil), greens (who put oil first but prefer gas to coal) and moderates, who favour gas as the best trade-off between the two values. A single dimension of choice underlies the various positions, and this is sufficient to guarantee that the rank orderings will be single peaked.

In many cases we may expect ethically-informed judgements to display this property: the policy options represent a choice between two values, and different groups of voters weight these values differently.[24] However, it is still possible for single-peakedness to fail even where ethical judgements are involved. For an example of this consider the following. Suppose nuclear power replaces oil as the third possible source of energy, and the facts about it are these: it is moderately cheap, it is environmentally sound in general, but it carries with it the risk of a major accident. We might then have three groups of voters: economizers, whose ranking is (1) coal, (2) nuclear power and (3) gas; pessimistic greens, whose ranking is (1) gas, (2) coal and (3) nuclear power; and a more optimistic group of greenish voters who believe that the risk of a nuclear accident can be borne in the light of the all-round benefits of nuclear power, and whose ranking is therefore (1) nuclear power, (2) gas and (3) coal. As a moment's inspection shows, if no group of voters forms a majority we have a voting cycle in which each energy option can defeat one of the others.

How has this come about? There are two dimensions of disagreement underlying the decision in this case. One is the balance to be struck between cost and environmental safety; the other is the relative weighting to be given to predictable pollution as against the risk of a nuclear accident *within* the fold of environmental concern. The economizers think the issue is only about costs; the out-and-out greens think it is only about environmental safety; the third group think it is about both, but they also disagree with the greens about what environmental safety consists in. It is this condition of cross-cutting disagreement that produces rank orders that are not single-peaked and threatens to produce a voting cycle.

Now consider how such a choice might be handled within the context of deliberative democracy. Participants in the debate, aiming to convince others to support the alternative that they favour, must inevitably give grounds for their preference. As the various views are articulated, one thing that will be revealed is whether there is just a single dimension of disagreement underlying the original set of alternatives, or more than one dimension. If there is more than one dimension, then it may be possible to split the original decision into components. I say 'may be' here because it is of course possible that the original alternatives were discrete and irreducible. Consider again the choice between types of power station. It looks as though this might be a case where the alternatives are discrete (a station must *either* be coal- or gas-fired, and so on) whereas many possible dimensions of disagreement underlie the choice: relative costs, levels of employment, issues of environmental safety, and so on. However, I do not think that the choice is really so discrete. For instance, coal-fired stations might in general be favoured on cost grounds, but there could be a separate issue as to whether they should be fitted with filters to reduce emissions of sulphur or carbon dioxide at the cost of some loss of output. If it became clear in the course of debate that the major reason why some speakers were opposing coal-fired stations was their polluting emissions, then the obvious solution would be to have two votes, or series of votes, one concerning the basic technology, another concerning the environment/efficiency trade-off given that technology.

Such a solution is obvious in the sense that it enables a final outcome to emerge that can reasonably be regarded as the majority's choice, even in cases where it is not a Condorcet winner.[25] Here one is taking an Olympian perspective and saying what ought to happen. From the point of view of the participants, some may have an incentive to prevent the issues being disaggregated because they envisage that the alternative they favour will lose when this is done.[26] Indeed they may have an incentive artificially to yoke issues together – I am not a student of Labour Party politics, but I suppose this is the art of compositing as practised at party conferences; that is, running together motions to create artificial majorities encompassing the particular position you are interested in. However, the conditions for this technique to work appear to be that there is a group of people who are in a privileged position to manipulate the agenda in the sense of deciding which decisions will be taken separately and which together; and that this group also has a better sense of the pattern of preferences among ordinary participants than those participants do themselves. In a deliberative democracy the pattern of opinion – the extent to which opinions on one issue correlate or fail to correlate with opinions on others – should become public knowledge as different speakers argue for and against the various composite proposals on the table. It would then be difficult to make a public argument against the disaggregation of decisions where it was clear that the original choice was multidimensional. In cases where it was not so clear, speakers might of course try to bamboozle their fellows into choosing simply between composite proposals in the hope that their favoured composite might win.

Let me try to summarize the point I have just made. I have suggested that the major reason apart from empirical error why preference orders are likely not to be single-peaked is that the issue under discussion amalgamates separate dimensions of choice to which different voters attach different weights. I am claiming that it is a virtue of deliberative democracy (unlike, say, simple opinion-polling) that it will reveal this to be the case. Unless a lot of people are prepared to behave strategically, there should be a general willingness to break the decision down along its several dimensions, on each of which we should expect to find a winning position. Putting the bits together again, we would have an overall result which can fairly be said to represent the will of the majority, since it follows the majority's judgement on each dimension of policy choice.

Choosing decision procedures

In the foregoing discussion the Condorcet criterion has been used as the test of a democratic choice. Starting with preference orders that produce cycles, we have looked at ways in which the process of discussion might be expected to change either the preference orders or the decision agenda so that non-cyclical majorities emerge. However, earlier in the chapter I observed that majoritarian methods of decision-making competed with positional methods as represented, for example, by the Borda count, and this particular dilemma has still to be addressed.

The Condorcet criterion invites us to look for the policy option that can win a majority vote against any other, if one can be found. The Borda count invites us to look at voters' complete rank orderings and to choose the alternative with the highest overall score. What is at stake in the choice between these potentially conflicting decision rules? I think the question can best be brought into focus by citing Michael Dummett's case for preferring the Borda count to majoritarian methods of decision-making:

> The question turns on whether it be thought more important to please as many people as possible or to please everyone collectively as much as possible. The latter is surely more reasonable. The rule to do as the majority wishes does not appear to have any better justification than as a rough-and-ready test for what will secure the maximum total satisfaction: to accord it greater importance is to fall victim to the mystique of the majority.[27]

What is noticeable about this is that it treats political decisions as delivering variable amounts of satisfaction to those who vote for them. Now some decisions approximate to this stereotype. If, say, we have to take a vote on what dish is to be served at the annual College feast, then Dummett's argument that it matters much more that overall satisfaction is maximized than that a majority's will prevails seems a good one, and it would be perfectly sensible to use a Borda count to decide this matter. Equally, though, many other decisions are better represented as judgements about what is the right thing to do – say a decision about whether to impose the death penalty for a particular crime – and here it would be very odd to defend the Borda count in the way that Dummett does. Indeed it seems here that the natural procedure would be to use one of the majoritarian methods, since what seems important is that whatever is done is done by the will of the majority – if possible what the majority wills in preference to all other options.[28]

If that intuition is right, then the best and fairest decision procedure to use will depend on the issue at hand. Now one virtue of deliberative democracy here is that the process of deliberation will reveal what sort of issue is at stake if indeed that is not obvious from the outset. In my presentation of the deliberative model, I focused on its most distinctive aspect, namely the process whereby individual preferences are transformed into ethically-based judgements about matters of common concern. However, in any real democracy there are going to be other issues that come closer to the College feast stereotype in the sense that personal preferences should reasonably play a large role in deciding them. This will be true of many ordinary public goods, for instance. If we have to make a budget allocation as between football pitches and the swimming pool in the local park, the main consideration is likely to be the general direction and strength of preference between these options. So here once the alternatives are identified, it would be sensible to use a Borda count to find the most satisfactory way of allocating funds, and if no other considerations intervene, the final decision would simply amount to ratifying that result. This is a case where the role of deliberation is to identify a procedure for making a decision rather than to arrive at a substantive agreed judgement.

Conclusion: is deliberative democracy feasible?

What we have seen here is that standard social choice theory invites us to pick a mechanism for aggregating preferences regardless of the content of those preferences; whereas deliberative democracy, precisely because the content of people's preferences emerges in the course of deliberation, can in theory select the decision procedure most appropriate to the case in hand. Now clearly once we allow that the decision procedure might be flexible in this way, we open the door to manipulation by those who opt for a procedure not on grounds of its appropriateness to the issue but because they believe it enhances the chances of their preferred policy being adopted. This highlights the point that, for deliberative democracy to work well, people must exercise what we might call democratic self-restraint: they must think it more important that the decision reached should be a genuinely democratic one than that it is the decision that they themselves favour. This depends in turn on the level of trust that exists in the deliberating body: people will tend to behave in a democratic spirit to the extent that they believe that others can be trusted to behave likewise. Here the evidence cited earlier, showing that discussion itself is a good way of building up trust among the participants, is relevant. But this evidence, obtained from research in small group contexts, does also raise the question of the scale on which deliberative democracy can be expected to operate.

It is a mistake to think that the deliberative ideal requires us to treat the citizens of a modern nation-state as a single deliberating body. Although it is a requirement of democracy that every citizen should have the opportunity to participate in collective decision-making in some way, this requirement can be met in a system embodying a high degree of pluralism. Pluralism may work in either or both of two ways: decisions may be parcelled out to the sub-constituencies that are best placed to make them, or most affected by the outcome; or else lower-level deliberating bodies may act as feeders for higher-level ones, with arguments and verdicts being transmitted from one to the other by representatives. Thus one might, for instance, envisage primary assemblies at town or city level making decisions on local matters, and at the same time debating issues of national concern in the presence of their parliamentary representatives: the latter would not be bound by the outcome, since they would themselves be involved in a deliberative process in which new arguments might be presented, but part of their job would be to convey the sense of the local meeting to the national body.[29]

For citizens to be directly involved in deliberation even at local level poses major problems of organization, although recent technological developments can help us see how relatively large bodies of people might be brought together to engage in something we would recognize as common debate.[30] Nor do I want to consider the question whether citizens will be sufficiently motivated to take part in debating assemblies if these are brought into existence. Clearly these are key issues when considering the extent to which the deliberative ideal can be realized in a large society. My focus here has been on what I take to be a key weakness in the liberal conception of democracy – the vulnerability of preference-aggregating procedures to problems of social choice – and the way in which deliberative democracy can overcome that weakness. If we take social choice seriously, as I do, then rather than retreating to a minimal form of liberalism, we can seek to shift democratic practice towards the deliberative ideal, encouraging people not merely to *express* their political opinions (through opinion polls, referendums, and the like), but to *form* those opinions through debate in public settings.

2

In Defence of Nationality

My story begins on the river bank of Kenneth Grahame's imagination.

> 'And beyond the Wild Wood again?' [asked the Mole]: 'Where it's all blue
> and dim, and one sees what may be hills or perhaps they mayn't, and
> something like the smoke of towns, or is it only cloud drift?'
>   'Beyond the Wild Wood comes the Wide World,' [said the Rat]. 'And
> that's something that doesn't matter, either to you or me. I've never been
> there, and I'm never going, nor you either, if you've got any sense at all.
> Don't ever refer to it again, please.'[1]

The Rat, so very sound in his opinions about most things, boats especially, seems in this moment to reveal exactly what so many people find
distasteful about national loyalties and identities. He displays no overt
hostility to foreign lands and their ways. But the combination of wilful
ignorance about places beyond the Wild Wood, and complete indifference
to what is going on there, seems particularly provoking. Aggressive
nationalism of the 'my country right or wrong' variety is something we
might at least argue with. But the narrowing of horizons, the contraction
of the universe of experience to the river bank itself, seems to amount to
the triumph of sentiment over reasoned argument.

Nationality under attack

Philosophers, especially, will have great difficulty in coming to grips with
the kind of national attachments for which I am using the Rat's river-

bankism as an emblem. Philosophers are committed to forms of reasoning, to concepts and arguments, that are universal in form. 'What's so special about this river bank?' a philosophical Mole might have asked in reply. 'Why is this river bank a better place than other river banks beyond the Wood?' To which the Rat could only have said, 'This is *my* place; I like it here; I have no need to ask such questions.'

The Rat, clearly, is no philosopher. Yet in contemplating his frame of mind we might be led to recall the words of one who was:

> there are in *England*, in particular, many honest gentlemen, who being always employ'd in their domestic affairs, or amusing themselves in common recreations, have carried their thoughts little beyond those objects, which are every day expos'd to their senses. And indeed, of such as these I pretend not to make philosophers.... They do well to keep themselves in their present situation; and instead of refining them into philosophers, I wish we cou'd communicate to our founders of systems, a share of this gross earthy mixture, as an ingredient, which they commonly stand much in need of, and which wou'd serve to temper those fiery particles, of which they are composed.[2]

Plainly the Rat is well supplied with gross earthy mixture, literally and metaphorically, and the question is whether any philosophical system can make use of what he has to offer. The sort that can is the Humean sort. By this I mean a philosophy which, rather than dismissing ordinary beliefs and sentiments out of hand unless they can be shown to have a rational foundation, leaves them in place until strong arguments are produced for rejecting them. The Rat's beliefs cannot be deduced from some universally accepted premise; but that is no reason for rejecting them unless the arguments for doing so seem better founded than the beliefs themselves. In moral and political philosophy, in particular, we build upon existing sentiments and judgements, correcting them only when they are inconsistent or plainly flawed in some other way. We don't aspire to some universal and rational foundation such as Kant tried to provide with the categorical imperative.

It is from this sort of stance (which I shall not try to justify) that it makes sense to mount a philosophical defence of nationality. There can be no question of trying to give rationally compelling reasons for people to have national attachments and allegiances. What we can do is to start from the premise that people generally do exhibit such attachments and allegiances, and then try to build a political philosophy which incorporates them. In particular we can do two things: we can examine the critical arguments directed against nationality – arguments trying to undermine the validity of national loyalties – and show that they are flawed; and we can try to assuage the tension between the ethical particularism implied by such commitments and ethical universalism, by showing why it may be advantageous, from a universal point of view, that people have national loyalties.[3]

Philosophers may protest that it is a caricature of their position to suggest that the only reasons for belief or action that they will permit to count are those that derive from an entirely impersonal and universal standpoint. It is common now to distinguish between agent-neutral and agent-relative reasons and to give each some weight in practical reasoning.[4] But what motivates this concession is mainly a concern for individuals' private goals and for their integrity: people must be given the moral space, as it were, to pursue their own projects, to honour their commitments, to live up to their personal ideals. National allegiances, and the obligations that spring from them, are harder to fit into this picture, because they appear to represent, not a different segment of moral life, but a competing way of understanding the concepts and principles that make up the impartial or agent-neutral standpoint (consider, for example, the different conceptions of distributive justice that emerge depending on whether you begin from a national or a universal starting-point). That is why such loyalties appear to pose a head-on challenge to a view of morality that is dominant in our culture, as Alasdair MacIntyre has argued.[5]

It is a curious paradox of our time that while nationalism is politically on the advance, its would-be defenders (in the West at least) find themselves on the defensive. I have just given one reason for this: the view that national allegiances cannot withstand critical scrutiny, so a rational person cannot be a nationalist. There is also a more mundane reason: nationality is widely felt to be a backward-looking, reactionary notion; it is felt to stand in the way of progress. In the European context, for instance, we are invited to look forward to a 'Europe of the regions' in which Catalonia, Brittany, Bavaria, Scotland and the rest co-exist harmoniously under a common administrative umbrella, free from the national rivalries which have plunged us into two world wars. Progress means the overcoming of nationality. In the Oxford branch of the Body Shop (and doubtless in the branches in Paris, Tokyo and elsewhere) you can buy a lapel badge that quotes H.G. Wells: 'Our true nationality is mankind.' H.G. Wells and the Body Shop in tandem epitomize the modern idea of progress, whose disciples were described by George Orwell in such a wonderfully acid way: 'all that dreary tribe of high-minded women and sandal-wearers and bearded fruit-juice drinkers who come flocking towards the smell of "progress" like bluebottles to a dead cat'.[6] If you are one of these bluebottles, and most of us are to some degree, then you will think that ordinary national loyalties amount to reactionary nostalgia and queue up to sport the H.G. Wells slogan.

What is a nation?

So the would-be nationalist has two challenges to meet: the philosophical challenge and the progressive challenge. And now it is time to spell out more precisely the notion of nationality that I want to defend.[7] Nationality as I shall understand it comprises three interconnected propositions. The first concerns personal identity, and claims that it may properly be part of someone's identity that they belong to this or that national grouping; in other words that if a person is invited to specify those elements that are essential to his identity, that make him the person that he is, it is in order to refer to nationality. A person who in answer to the question 'Who are you?' says 'I am Swedish' or 'I am Italian' (and doubtless much more besides) is not saying something that is irrelevant or bizarre in the same way as, say, someone who claims without good evidence that he is the illegitimate grandchild of Tsar Nicholas II. Note that the claim is a permissive one: national identity may, but need not, be a constitutive part of personal identity.

The second proposition is ethical, and claims that nations are ethical communities. They are contour lines in the ethical landscape. The duties we owe to our fellow-nationals are different from, and more extensive than, the duties we owe to human beings as such. This is not to say that we owe *no* duties to humans as such; nor is it to deny that there may be other, perhaps smaller and more intense, communities to whose members we owe duties that are more stringent still than those we owe to Britons, Swedes, etc. at large. But it is to claim that a proper account of ethics should give weight to national boundaries, and that in particular there is no objection in principle to institutional schemes that are designed to deliver benefits exclusively to those who fall within the same boundaries as ourselves.

The third proposition is political, and states that people who form a national community in a particular territory have a good claim to political self-determination; there ought to be put in place an institutional structure that enables them to decide collectively matters that concern primarily their own community. Notice that I have phrased this cautiously, and have not asserted that the institution must be that of a sovereign state. Historically the sovereign state has been the main vehicle through which claims to national self-determination have been realized, and this is not just an accident. Nevertheless national self-determination *can* be realized in other ways, and as we shall see there are cases where it must be realized other than through a sovereign state, precisely to meet the equally good claims of other nationalities.

I want to stress that the three propositions I have outlined – about personal identity, about bounded duties and about political self-determination – are linked together in such a way that it is difficult to feel the force of any one of them without acknowledging the others. It is not hard to see how a common identity can support both the idea of the nation as an ethical community and the claim to self-determination, but what is more subtle – and I shall try to bring this out as I go along – is the way in which the political claim can reinforce both the claim about identity and the ethical claim. The fact that the community in question is either actually or potentially self-determining strengthens its claims on us both as a source of identity and as a source of obligation. This interlinking of propositions may at times seem circular; and the fact that the nationalist case cannot be spelt out in neat linear form may confirm philosophical suspicions about it. But I believe that if we are to understand the power of nationality as an idea in the modern world – the appeal of national identity to the modern self – we must try to understand its inner logic.

So let me now begin to look more closely at national identities them-selves, and in particular ask what differentiates them from other identities – individual or communal – that people may have. What does it mean to think of oneself as belonging to a national community?

The first point to note, and it has been noted by most of those who have thought seriously about the subject, is that national communities are constituted by belief: a nationality exists when its members believe that it does. It is not a question of a group of people sharing some common attribute such as race or language. These features do not of themselves make nations, and only become important insofar as a particular nation-ality takes as one of its defining features that its members speak French or have black skins. This becomes clear as soon as one looks at the candid-ates that have been put forward as objective criteria of nationhood, as Ernest Renan did in his famous lecture on the subject:[8] to every criterion that has been proposed there are clear empirical counter-examples. The conclusion one quickly reaches is that a nation is in Renan's memorable phrase 'a daily plebiscite'; its existence depends on a shared belief that its members belong together, and a shared wish to continue their life in common. So in asserting a national identity, I assume that my beliefs and commitments are mirrored by those whom I take to share that identity, and of course I might be wrong about this. In itself this does not distinguish nationality from other kinds of human relationship that depend on reciprocal belief.

The second feature of nationality is that it is an identity that embodies historical continuity. Nations stretch backwards into the past, and indeed in most cases their origins are conveniently lost in the mists of time. In the course of this history various significant events have occurred, and we can identify with the actual people who acted at those moments, reappro-priating their deeds as our own. Often these events involve military victories and defeats: we imagine ourselves filling the breach at Harfleur or reading the signal hoisted at Trafalgar. Renan thinks that historical tragedies matter more than historical glories. I am inclined to see in this an understandable French bias, but the point he connects to it is a good one: 'sorrows have greater value than victories; for they impose duties and demand common effort'.[9] The historic national community is a community of obligation. Because our forebears have toiled and spilt their blood to build and defend the nation, we who are born into it inherit an obligation to continue their work, which we discharge partly towards our contemporaries and partly towards our descendants. The historical community stretches forward into the future too. This then means that when we speak of the nation as an ethical community, we have in mind not merely the kind of community that exists between a group of contemporaries who practise mutual aid among themselves and which would dissolve at the point at which that practice ceased; but a community which, because it stretches back and forward across the generations, is not one that the present generation can renounce. Here we begin to see something of the depth of national communities which may not be shared by other more immediate forms of association.

The third distinguishing aspect of national identity is that it is an active identity. Nations are communities that do things together, take decisions, achieve results and so forth. Of course this cannot be literally so: we rely on proxies who are seen as embodying the national will: statesmen, soldiers, sportsmen, etc. But this means that the link between past and future that I noted a moment ago is not merely a causal link. The nation becomes what it does by the decisions that it takes – some of which we may now regard as thoroughly bad, a cause of national shame. Whether this active identity is a valuable aspect of nationality, or whether as some critics would allege merely a damaging fantasy, it clearly does mark out nations from other kinds of grouping, for instance churches or religious sects whose identity is essentially a passive one in so far as the church is seen as responding to the promptings of God. The group's purpose is not to do or decide things, but to interpret as best it can the messages and commands of an external source.

The fourth aspect of a national identity is that it connects a group of people to a particular geographical place, and here again there is a clear contrast with most other group identities that people affirm, such as ethnic or religious identities. These often have sacred sites or places of origin, but it is not an essential part of having the identity that you should permanently occupy that place. If you are a good Muslim you should make a pilgrimage to Mecca at least once, but you need not set up house there. A nation, in contrast, must have a homeland. This may of course be a source of great difficulties, a point I shall return to when considering objections to the idea of nationality, but it also helps to explain why a national community must be (in aspiration if not yet in fact) a political community. We have seen already that nations are groups that act; we see now that their actions must include that of controlling a chunk of the earth's surface. It is this territorial element that makes nations uniquely suited to serve as the basis of states, since a state by definition must exercise its authority over a geographical area.

Finally it is essential to national identity that the people who compose the nation are believed to share certain traits that mark them off from other peoples. It is incompatible with nationality to think of the members of the nation as people who merely happen to have been thrown together in one place and forced to share a common fate, in the way that the occupants of a lifeboat, say, have been accidentally thrown together. National divisions must be natural ones; they must correspond to real differences between peoples. This need not, fortunately, imply racism or the idea that the group is constituted by biological descent. The common traits can be cultural in character: they can consist in shared values, shared tastes or sensibilities. So immigration need not pose problems, provided only that the immigrants take on the essential elements of national character. Indeed it has proved possible in some instances to regard immigration as itself a formative experience, calling forth qualities of resourcefulness and mutual aid that then define the national character – I am thinking of the settler cultures of the New World such as the American and the Australian. As everyone knows, there is nothing more illustrious for an Australian today than to have an ancestor who was carried over in chains by the First Fleet.

When I say that national differences must be natural ones, I mean that the people who compose a nation must believe that there is something distinctive about themselves that marks them off from other nations, over and above the fact of sharing common institutions. This need not be one specific trait or quality, but can be a range of characteristics which are generally shared by the members of nation A and serve to differentiate them from outsiders. In popular belief these differences may be exaggerated. Hume remarked that the vulgar think that everyone who belongs to a nation displays its distinctive traits, whereas 'men of sense' allow for exceptions; nevertheless aggregate differences undoubtedly exist.[10] This is surely correct. It is also worth noting that people may be hard pressed to say explicitly what the national character of their people consists in, and yet have an intuitive sense when confronted with foreigners of where the differences lie.[11] National identities can remain unarticulated, and yet still exercise a pervasive influence on people's behaviour.

These five elements together – a community constituted by mutual belief, extended in history, active in character, connected to a particular territory, and thought to be marked off from other communities by its members' distinct traits – serve to distinguish nationality from other collective sources of personal identity. I shall come in a moment to some reasons why such identities may be thought to be particularly valuable, worth protecting and fostering, but first I should emphasize what has so far merely been implicit, namely the mythical aspects of national identity. Nations almost unavoidably depend on beliefs about themselves that do not stand up well to impartial scrutiny. Renan once again hit the nail on the head when he said that 'to forget and – I will venture to say – to get one's history wrong, are essential factors in the making of a nation'.[12] One main reason for this is that the contingencies of power politics have always played a large part in the formation of national units. States have been created by force, and, over time, their subject peoples have come to think of themselves as co-nationals. But no one wants to think of himself as roped together to a set of people merely because the territorial ambitions of some dynastic lord in the thirteenth century ran thus far and no further. Nor indeed is this the right way to think about the matter, because the effect of the ruler's conquests may have been, over time, to have produced a people with real cultural unity. But because of the historical dimension of the nation, together with the idea that each nation has its own distinct character, it is uncomfortable to be reminded of the forced nature of one's national genesis. Hence various stories have been concocted about the primeval tribe from which the modern nation sprang. The problem is, of course, particularly acute in the case of states created relatively recently as a result of colonial withdrawal, where it is only too obviously the case that the boundaries that have been drawn reflect the vagaries of imperial competition. It is easy for academic critics to mock the attempts made by the leaders of these states to instil a sense of common nationhood in their people. I myself recall, when teaching in Nigeria in the mid-1970s, reading with some amusement earnest newspaper articles on the question whether the country did or did not need a national ideology – it seeming obvious that a national ideology was not something you could just decide to adopt.

Nationality defended

The real question, however, is not whether national identities embody elements of myth, but whether they perform such valuable functions that our attitude, as philosophers, should be one of acquiescence if not positive endorsement. And here I want to argue that nationality answers one of the most pressing needs of the modern world, namely how to maintain solidarity among the populations of states that are large and anonymous, such that their citizens cannot possibly enjoy the kind of community that relies on kinship or face-to-face interaction.[13] That we need such solidarity is something that I intend to take for granted here.[14] I assume that in societies in which economic markets play a central role, there is a strong tendency towards social atomization, where each person looks out for the interests of herself and her immediate social network. As a result it is potentially difficult to mobilize people to provide collective goods, it is difficult to get them to agree to practices of redistribution from which they are not likely personally to benefit, and so forth. These problems can be avoided only where there exists large-scale solidarity, such that people feel themselves to be members of an overarching community, and to have social duties to act for the common good of that community, to help out other members when they are in need, etc.

Nationality is *de facto* the main source of such solidarity. In view of the broadly Humean approach that I am adopting, where our moral and political philosophy bends to accommodate pre-existing sentiments, this in itself would be enough to commend it. But I should like to say something more positive about nationality before coming to the difficulties. It is precisely because of the mythical or imaginary elements in national identity that it can be reshaped to meet new challenges and new needs. We have seen that the story a nation tells itself about its past is a selective one. Depending on the character of contemporary politics, the story may gradually alter, and with it our understanding of the substance of national identity. This need not take the crude form of the rewriting of history as practised in the late Soviet Union and elsewhere (airbrushing pictures of Trotsky out of the Bolshevik central committee and so on). It may instead be a matter of looking at established facts in a new way. Consider, as just one example, the very different interpretation of British imperialism now current to that which prevailed at the time of my father's birth in Edwardian Britain. The tone has changed from one of triumphalism to one of equivocation or even mild apology. And this goes naturally along with a new interpretation of British identity in which it is no longer part of that identity to shoulder the white man's burden and carry enlightenment to the heathen.

From a political standpoint, this imaginary aspect of nationality may be a source of strength. It allows people of different political persuasions to share a political loyalty, defining themselves against a common background whose outlines are not precise, and which therefore lends itself to competing interpretations. It also shows us why nationality is not a conservative idea. A moment's glance at the historical record shows that nationalist ideas have as often been associated with liberal and socialist programmes as with programmes of the right. In their first appearance, they were often associated with liberal demands for representative government put forward in opposition to established ruling elites. Linda Colley's studies of the emergence of British nationalism in the late eighteenth and early nineteenth centuries show that nationalist ideas were developed by middle-class and popular movements seeking to win a place in the public realm, and resisted by the state and the landowning class that supported it.[15] This picture was repeated in its essentials throughout Europe.[16] It is easy to see why a conservative may resist nationalism.[17] Nationality invokes the activist idea of a people collectively determining its own destiny, and this is anathema to the conservative view of politics as a limited activity best left in the hands of an elite who have been educated to rule. Two of the most swingeing of recent attacks on nationalism have come from acolytes of Michael Oakeshott, Elie Kedourie and Kenneth Minogue.[18] Minogue regards nationalism as essentially a revolutionary theory and 'therefore a direct enemy of conservative politics'. He offers a reductive psychological explanation of its appeal: 'Nationalist theories may thus be understood as distortions of reality which allow men to cope with situations which they might otherwise find unbearable.'[19]

Nationality, then, is associated with no particular social programme: the flexible content of national identity allows parties of different colours to present their programmes as the true continuation of the national tradition and the true reflection of national character.[20] At the same time it binds these parties together and makes space for the idea of loyal opposition, an individual or faction who resist prevailing policy but who can legitimately claim to speak for the same community as the government of the day. But its activist idea of politics as the expression of national will does set it against conservatism of the Oakeshott–Kedourie–Minogue variety.

The liberal objection

I have referred to the liberal origins of the idea of nationality, but the first objection that I want to consider amounts essentially to a liberal critique of nationality. This holds that nationality is detrimental to the cultural pluralism that liberals hold dear; it is incompatible with the idea of a society in which different cultural traditions are accorded equal respect, and whose vitality springs from competition and exchange between these traditions. The classic statement of this critique can be found in Lord Acton's essay on 'Nationality' in which he argues in favour of a multinational state in which no one nation holds a dominant place.[21] Such a state, he claims, provides the best guarantee of liberties, 'the fullest security for the preservation of local customs' and the best incentive to intellectual progress.

This argument derives from the assumption that national identities are exclusive in their nature; that where a state embodies a single nationality, the culture that makes up that nationality must drive out everything else. There is no reason to hold this assumption. Nationality is not of its nature an all-embracing identity. It need not extend to all the cultural attributes that a person might display. So one can avow a national identity and also have attachments to several more specific cultural groups: to ethnic groups, religious groups, work-based associations and so forth. A line can be drawn between the beliefs and qualities that make up nationality, and those that fall outside its scope. The place where the line is drawn will be specific to a particular nationality at a particular time, and it will be a subject for debate whether its present position is appropriate or not. For instance one may argue in a liberal direction that a person's religion, say, should be irrelevant to their membership of this nation, or argue in a nationalist direction that language is not irrelevant, that each member should at least be fluent in the national tongue. The Acton argument supposes that no such line can be drawn. It supposes, contrary to all evidence, that one cannot have a pluralist society in which many ethnic, religious etc. groups co-exist but with an overarching national identity in common.

Indeed one can turn Acton's argument around, as J.S. Mill did by anticipation in his chapter on 'Nationality' in *Representative Government*. Unless the several groups that compose a society have the mutual sympathy and trust that stems from a common nationality, it will be virtually impossible to have free institutions. There will, for instance, be no common interest in stemming the excesses of government; politics becomes a zero-sum game in which each group can hope to gain by the exploitation of the others.

This was Mill's argument, and there is plenty of subsequent evidence to back it up. But I want now to consider a more subtle variation on the theme that nationality and liberalism are at odds. This concedes that national identity and group identity can be kept separate, but points to the fact that national identities are always in practice biased in favour of the dominant cultural group, the group that historically has dominated the politics of the state. The state may be liberal in the sense that it does not suppress minority groups, but it does not accord equal respect and equal treatment to cultural minorities. Practical examples of this would include what is prescribed in the curricula in state-run schools, the content of what is broadcast through the national media, and so forth. The national identity includes elements drawn from the dominant culture, this is reproduced politically through the state, and minority groups are put at a disadvantage both in various practical respects and in the less tangible sense that their cultures are devalued by public neglect.

Concrete versions of this critique will be familiar to most readers. I want to reply to it first by conceding that it is descriptively true in many historical cases – national identities have very often been formed by taking over elements from the group culture that happens to be dominant in a particular state – but then adding that it is not integral to national identities that they should be loaded in this way. I have stressed the malleability of nationality already, and one thing we may be doing in the course of redefining what it means to be British, French, etc. is to purge these identities of elements that necessarily entail the exclusion of minority groups. Here there is one particular aspect of nationality that needs underlining. Although in standard cases a national identity is something one is born into – and I have argued that this factor of historical continuity is a source of strength – there is no reason why others should not acquire it by adoption. In this respect it contrasts with ethnic identities which generally speaking can only be acquired by birth. Although *a priori* a nation might define itself tightly by descent, in practice nations extend membership more or less freely to those who are resident and show willingness to exhibit those traits that make up national character. So although this does impose certain constraints on them, minority groups, particularly those migrating to the society in question, have the option of acquiring a new identity alongside their existing ones. Nationality, precisely because it aims to be an *inclusive* identity, can incorporate sub-groups in this way without demanding that they forsake everything they already hold dear.

Indeed one can take this further and say that what best meets the needs of minority groups is a clear and distinct national identity which stands over and above the specific cultural traits of all the groups in the society in question. The argument here has been well put by Tariq Modood, who has particularly in mind the position of Muslims in British society. He writes:

> As a matter of fact the greatest psychological and political need for clarity about a common framework and national symbols comes from the minorities. For clarity about what makes us willingly bound into a single country relieves the pressure on minorities, especially new minorities whose presence within the country is not fully accepted, to have to conform in all areas of social life, or in arbitrarily chosen areas, in order to rebut the charge of disloyalty. It is the absence of comprehensively respected national symbols in Britain, comparable to the constitution and the flag in America, that allows politicians unsympathetic to minorities to demand that they demonstrate loyalty by doing x or y or z, like supporting the national cricket team in Norman Tebbit's famous example.[22]

To make my position clear here, I do not suppose that the superimposition of national identity on group identity that I am arguing for can be

wholly painless on either side. While national identities are thinned down
to make them more acceptable to minority groups, these groups themselves must abandon values and ways of behaving that are in stark
conflict with those of the community as a whole. National identity cannot
be wholly symbolic; it must embody substantive norms. This will be
readily apparent if a formal constitution occupies a central place in such
an identity, as I believe it should. Forms of belief and behaviour inconsistent with those laid down in the constitution will be ruled out. So, as I
have argued elsewhere,[23] one cannot aspire to unlimited tolerance in this
area. But the view I am defending does appear consistent with the kind of
politically sensitive liberalism exhibited by J.S. Mill.

The Balkan objection

This, I hope, sufficiently addresses the liberal objection to nationality.
Now I want to come to a second objection which might be termed the
Balkan objection. This claims that the principle of nationality cannot in
practice be realized, but meanwhile the belief that it can leads to endless
political instability and bloodshed. This is because would-be nationalities
are so entangled with one another that there is no way of drawing state
boundaries that can possibly satisfy all claims. Minority group B secedes
from state A in search of national self-determination, but this only
provokes group C *within* B to attempt secession in its turn and so on *ad
infinitum*. I call this the Balkan objection because of a view one frequently
hears expressed nowadays that so long as the peoples of that region were
governed from afar by the Austro-Hungarian and Turkish empires different ethnic groups lived and worked happily side-by-side, but once those
empires were weakened and the idea of national self-determination was
let loose, impossible conflicts were generated.[24] Recent events in Yugoslavia seem to confirm the view, and any day now I expect to hear
President Tito's reputation being salvaged on the same terms as that of
Emperor Franz Josef.

   The principle of nationality as formulated earlier holds that people
who form a national community in a particular territory have a good
claim to political self-determination. This principle should not be con-
fused with a certain liberal view of the state which makes individual
consent a necessary and sufficient condition of a state's authority. If
each person must consent to the existence of the state, it follows that
the borders of states should be drawn wherever people want them to be
drawn. The practical implication is that any sub-community in any state
has the right to secede from that state provided that it is in turn willing to
allow any sub-sub-community the equivalent right and so on indefi-

nitely.[25] This view confronts the Balkan problem in its most acute form: where populations are intermingled, consistent application of the consent principle points directly towards an anarchic outcome in which no stable frontiers can be established.

The principle of nationality is quite different from this. Central to the idea of nationality is not individual *will*, but individual *identity*, even though some formulations confuse these two – Renan's idea of the nation as 'a daily plebiscite' which I cited earlier is *in this respect* misleading. When we encounter a group or community dissatisfied with current political arrangements the question to ask is not 'Does this group now want to secede from the existing state?' but 'Does the group have a collective identity which is or has become incompatible with the national identity of the majority in the state?' There are broadly three answers that might be given to this question. First, it may turn out that the dissatisfied group is an ethnic group which feels that materially speaking it is not getting a fair deal from the existing set-up and/or that its group identity is not being properly respected in national life. Black Americans would exemplify this: what is needed in such cases is domestic political reform, perhaps of a quite radical and painful kind, not dreams of secession. Second, the group may have a national identity, but one that is not radically incompatible with the identity of the majority community, there being common elements as well as elements of difference. The dissenting group thinks of itself as sharing a common historical identity with the majority, but also as having its own distinct national character which is currently not recognized.[26] This may (I say this with some trepidation) represent the position of the Scots and Welsh in Britain, or the Bretons in France, and the appropriate outcome is again not outright secession (which violates the shared identity) but a constitutional arrangement which gives the sub-community rights of self-determination in those areas of decision which are especially central to its own sense of nationhood.

Finally there are cases where the state as presently constituted contains two or more nations with radically incompatible identities. The reason for this might be that one community takes as constitutive of its identity some feature such as language or race not shared with the others, or that its historical self-understanding includes military conquest of the territory now occupied by the second community, or some other such factor. In these cases there is no realistic possibility of formulating a shared identity, and the minority group has a *prima facie* case for secession. But to make the case a conclusive one, further conditions must be met.[27] First, there has to be some way of redrawing the borders such that two viable states are created and this in itself may pose insoluble problems. Second, the territory claimed by the seceding community should not contain minorities whose own identity is radically incompatible with the new majority's, so that rather than creating a genuine nation-state, the secession would simply reproduce a multi-national arrangement on a smaller scale. Third, some consideration must be given to small groups who may be left behind in the rump state; it may be that the effect of secession is to destroy a political balance and leave these groups in a very weak position. It is, for instance, a strong argument against the secession of Quebec from the Canadian federation that it would effectively destroy the double-sided identity that Canada has laboured to achieve, and leave French-speaking communities in other provinces isolated and politically helpless.

What I am trying to stress is that the principle of nationality does not generate an unlimited right of secession. What it says is that national self-determination is a good thing, and that states and their constitutions should be arranged so that each nation is as far as possible able to secure its common future. Since homogeneous nation-states are not everywhere feasible, often this will require second-best solutions, where each nationality gets partial self-determination, not full rights of sovereignty. Equally, there may be cases where communities are intertwined in such a way that no form of national self-determination is realistically possible, and the best that can be hoped for is a modus vivendi between the communities, perhaps with a constitutional settlement guaranteed by external powers.

Justice and sentiment

That, somewhat elliptically, is my answer to the Balkan objection. The final objection I want to consider arises from the second aspect of the idea of nationality, the claim that nations are ethical communities. It runs as follows. You say that nations are ethically significant, that the duties we owe to fellow-members are greater in scope than those we owe to outsiders. Yet you base this on a shared sense of identity which is based not upon concrete practices but upon sentimental ties, on historical understandings which you have conceded to be imaginary in part. But how can duties of justice, especially, depend in this way on our feelings about others? Does this not make justice an entirely subjective idea, and abandon its role as a critical notion which serves to correct both our beliefs and our behaviour?

Observe to begin with that our sense of national identity serves to mark out the universe of persons to whom special duties are owed; it may do this without at the same time determining the content of those duties. In particular my recognition of X as a co-national to whom I have obligations may depend upon a sense of nationality with sentimental content, but it does not follow that my duties to X depend on my feelings about X as a person. An analogy with the family makes this clear. A family does not exist as such unless its members have certain feelings towards one another, yet obligations within the family are not governed by sentiment. I may feel more sympathy for one child than another, yet in allocating the family's resources I ought to consider their needs impartially.

It appears nonetheless that obligations in this account are being derived from the existence of a certain kind of community, while in the national case the community is sentiment-based. It would follow that if nation A embodies a strong sense of fellow-feeling whereas nation B embodies a relatively weak sense, then obligations within A are more extensive than those within B, and this seems paradoxical. What this overlooks, however, is the role played by political culture within national identity. It is not merely that I feel bound to a group of people defined in national terms; I feel bound to them as sharing in a certain way of life, expressed in the public culture. The content of my obligations stems immediately from that culture. Various interpretations of the public culture are possible, but some of these will be closer to getting it right than others, and this also shows to what extent debates about social justice are resolvable. It follows that what social justice consists in will vary from place to place, but not directly in line with sentiments or feelings. A Swede will acknowledge more extensive obligations to provide welfare for fellow-Swedes than an American will for fellow-Americans; but this is because the public culture of Sweden, defining in part what it means to be Swedish, is solidaristic, whereas the public culture of the US is individualistic. It is not part of the story that Swedes must have more sympathetic feelings for other individual Swedes than Americans do for other Americans.

This may still sound an uncomfortably relativistic view to some. What I have argued is that nationalists are not committed to the kind of crude subjectivism which says that your communal obligations are whatever you feel them to be. Membership of a national community involves identifying with a public culture that is external to each of us taken individually; and although we may argue with one another about how the culture should be understood, and what practical obligations stem from it, this is still a question to which better or worse answers can be given.

Conclusion

Philosophers may find it restricting that they have to conduct their arguments about justice with reference to national identities at all. My claim is that unless they do they will lose contact entirely with the beliefs of the people they seek to address; they must try to incorporate some of Hume's gross earthy mixture, the unreflective beliefs of everyday life. Nonetheless there is a tension here. We should return to Kenneth Grahame's Rat who on his first appearance seems to stand for unlimited acquiescence in the everyday world of the river bank. As the story draws towards its conclusion, however, a more troubled Rat emerges. Disturbed first by the departure of the swallows to Southern climes, he then encounters a seafaring rat who regales him with tales of the colourful and vibrant world beyond the river bank. The Rat is mesmerized. His eyes, normally 'clear and dark and brown', turn to 'a streaked and shifting grey'. He is about to set out for the South with stick and satchel in hand, and has to be physically restrained by the Mole, who gradually leads his thoughts back to the everyday world, and finally leaves him writing poetry as a kind of sublimation of his wandering instincts.

The Rat's earlier refusal to contemplate the Wide World, it emerges, was a wilful repression of a part of himself that it was dangerous to acknowledge. Something of the same dilemma confronts the philosophical nationalist. He feels the pull of national loyalties, and he senses that without these loyalties we would be cast adrift in a region of great moral uncertainty. Yet he is also alive to the limitations and absurdities of his and other national identities. He recognizes that we owe something to other human beings merely as such, and so he strains towards a more rationally defensible foundation for ethics and politics. There is no solution here but to strive for some kind of equilibrium between the everyday and the philosophical, between common belief and rational belief, between the river bank and the Wide World. But, as the cases both of the Rat and of David Hume in their different ways demonstrate, this is far easier said than done.

3

Citizenship and Pluralism

The problem of citizenship and pluralism is easy to state but very difficult to solve. Its premise is the cultural fragmentation of modern states. Members of these states are in the process of adopting an ever more disparate set of personal identities, as evidenced by their ethnic affiliations, their religious allegiances, their views of personal morality, their ideas about what is valuable in life, their tastes in art, music and so forth. In all these areas there is less convergence or agreement than there once was. Yet at the same time the individuals and groups having these fragmented identities need to live together politically, and this means finding some common basis or reference point from which their claims on the state can be judged. Citizenship is supposed to provide this reference point. Our personal lives and commitments may be very different, but we are all equally citizens, and it is as citizens that we advance claims in the public realm and assess the claims made by others. Yet if fragmentation is as far-reaching as the premise implies, how is it possible for us to share a common identity as citizens? We may share a common legal status, a formally-defined set of rights and obligations, but how can we agree about what it means to be a citizen, what rights and obligations *ought* to be included in the legal status, and beyond that how we ought to behave when occupying the role of citizen? The very state of affairs that makes common citizenship so important to us seems at the same time to expose it as a pipe-dream.

This view of citizenship as a unifying force in a divided world has appealed recently to political thinkers both of the centre-right and of the centre-left, although the underlying motivation has been somewhat different in the two cases. The new-found enthusiasm of conservatives for the idea of citizenship arises from a belated recognition that the individualism associated with the free market is not a sufficient basis on which to hold a society together. If the role of the state is cut back, and each person encouraged to behave as a self-sufficient individual, two problems may arise. One is that people cease to take an interest in the welfare of those around them in the local community, so that those not able to stand on their own feet in the marketplace will have no means of assistance when state support is withdrawn. The other is that individualism may take the form of criminal activity, whether common-or-garden crime of the kind revealed in the steadily rising figures for burglaries, car thefts and so forth, or the more sophisticated activities of insider dealing on the stock market, corporate raiding and the like. What is needed in both cases, conservatives will argue, is a reassertion of moral values and social responsibility, and the citizen is portrayed as a person who sticks to the rules of the economic game while at the same time performing acts of public service such as charitable work in his or her local community.[1]

For the centre-left, by contrast, the rediscovery of citizenship has coincided with the gradual dissolution of the working class as a potential majority basis for social-democratic politics. If it is no longer possible to appeal to the interests of a unified working class to defend redistributive economic policies, or the provision of social welfare, then some other basis is needed. Citizenship is the obvious candidate: economically our positions may be increasingly divergent, but we are all citizens, and as such we are entitled to provision by the state of a minimum income, health care and so forth. Moreover an appeal to citizenship is needed to weld together the array of social groups that are now looked to in order to secure the election of a social-democratic government – the residual working class, welfare claimants, ethnic minorities, radicalized women, etc. It is not possible to create a political platform simply by appealing to the special interests of each group. There have to be some general principles which can both incorporate and harmonize the demands of these constituencies. The idea of citizenship, it is hoped, will provide just such a set of principles.[2]

This coincidence of interest between right and left has created a climate of enthusiasm for citizenship as a political concept, which in the British case peaked in the late 1980s: this led to the establishment of a cross-party Commission on Citizenship which came up with a set of recommendations for, as its report was entitled, *Encouraging Citizenship* (London, HMSO, 1990). Among these were proposals for citizenship education in schools, and proposals to encourage and co-ordinate volunteer activity on a nation-wide basis. But as a number of commentators at the time pointed out, agreement that citizenship was a Good Thing may have been bought at the cost of ineradicable vagueness about what precisely the idea was supposed to mean. If the brief diagnosis offered above is correct, quite disparate conceptions of citizenship were invoked in the course of party-political debate. So we are left with two major problems: one is to see whether there is indeed a single core idea of citizenship that is being invoked by the various camps, or whether we should instead think in terms of different conceptions of citizenship; the other is to see whether *any* of the available conceptions can cope with the problem of pluralism – whether they can provide an understanding of citizenship that can accommodate the kind of radical cultural disagreement I gestured towards at the beginning of the chapter.

Before beginning to tackle these problems, it is worth noticing that uncertainty over the meaning of citizenship is not confined to members of the political elite. There is some interesting research by Conover, Crewe and Searing on how members of the public in the US and Great Britain think about their rights, duties and identities as citizens.[3] I shall not attempt a full summary of their findings, but the following points are worth noting here. First, although understandings of citizenship in both countries were shaped by the existing legal status of citizens in each, people did not on the whole think of citizenship as defined entirely by their legal rights and obligations – they recognized an ethical element in citizenship as well, an idea of what it *should* imply for social and political practice. Second, there was substantial disagreement about what citizenship amounted to – some understanding it primarily in terms of a liberal notion of civic rights, others having a more communitarian understanding of citizenship as entailing responsibilities to promote the common good through active participation in the community's life. This suggests that, although citizenship may not be a word on everybody's lips from day to day, it has a certain political resonance – when asked to say what it means (in this case in the context of an open-ended group discussion) people are able to give fairly elaborate accounts. It also suggests, as we might have anticipated, that theoretical disagreement about the meaning of citizenship is reflected in popular understandings of the idea.

The liberal conception of citizenship

In order to tackle this disagreement, I am going to distinguish three conceptions of citizenship, which I shall label liberal, libertarian and republican.[4] These are not the only possible ways of understanding citizenship,[5] but what unites them for present purposes, as I shall try to show, is that each can claim with some plausibility to accommodate pluralism of the kind described at the beginning of the paper. I begin with the liberal view because it seems to me the dominant understanding, both in the literature of political theory and in public opinion as revealed by the study cited above. However it runs into difficulties when faced with the challenge of pluralism, and this paradoxically may lead one towards either the libertarian or the republican view. The main lines of the liberal conception can be seen in the classic statement by T.H. Marshall.[6] Citizenship should be understood as a set of rights enjoyed equally by every member of the society in question. In Marshall's analysis these are classified as civil rights, political rights and social rights. When fully developed it embodies an idea of social justice: everyone is to enjoy entitlements which stand apart from and to some extent conflict with the outcomes of a market economy driven by considerations of efficiency. Citizenship carries potentially redistributive implications: citizens are entitled to benefits such as free health care and free schooling for their children which they might not be able to afford out of their market earnings. (Marshall stresses, however, that there is a definite limit to the equalizing tendency of citizenship.) It is not seen as involving any particular pattern of activity. Although citizens enjoy equal political rights, nothing is said about how zealously they are supposed to exercise them. Marshall presupposes that the bundle of rights constituting citizenship is, or at least has become, a matter of common agreement. Writing in the relatively homogeneous Britain of 1950, he is preoccupied with the relationship between citizenship and class inequalities, and can assert confidently that 'Citizenship requires a bond of a different kind, a direct sense of community membership based on loyalty to a civilisation which is a common possession.'[7] This common civilization would set the standard for, in particular, the social rights of citizenship; it would define a minimum level of education, income, housing and so forth that citizens must have as part of their common heritage.

Marshall's view runs into difficulties, however, once the idea of a common civilization is challenged by the emergence of radical cultural pluralism.[8] If there is no longer a shared 'common heritage' or 'way of life' by reference to which citizens' rights can be defined, how are we to arrive at the conception of social justice that defines citizenship? It is from this perspective that I am going to consider the work of John Rawls, whose recent writing in particular can be seen as an attempt to develop a conception of citizenship in response to what he calls 'the fact of pluralism' – the fact that 'the diversity of comprehensive religious, philosophical and moral doctrines found in modern democratic societies is not a mere historical condition that may soon pass away; it is a permanent feature of the public culture of democracy'.[9] In the light of this fact, Rawls aims to delineate a political conception of justice which will 'specify a point of view from which all citizens can examine before one another whether or not their political institutions are just.... Questions of political justice can be discussed on the same basis by all citizens, whatever their social position, or more particular aims and interests, or their religious, philosophical or moral views.'[10]

It may not be clear in what sense Rawls's theory of justice represents a conception of citizenship. In his earlier presentations of the theory, most especially *A Theory of Justice*, justice is identified as the set of principles that rational individuals could endorse to fix the terms of social co-operation. Although the principles include rights of citizenship, it seems that the parties who make the hypothetical contract are simply human agents advancing their individual conceptions of the good life. In later presentations, however, Rawls signals that the principles of justice are developed for people who are already citizens of a liberal-democratic state: they are supposed to think of themselves as citizens, and Rawls aims to show them what they are more concretely committed to when they adopt this perspective. One sign of this shift of approach is that Rawls in his later writings always uses the language of citizenship: whereas in *A Theory of Justice* the subjects of his theory are 'persons', 'men' or 'parties', now (as in the above quotation) they are always 'citizens'. More substantially, the theory of justice is no longer regarded as being a *complete* account of what people can justly demand of one another in their social life, but as a specifically *political* conception of justice, where this implies not only that its subject matter is a society's political arrangements (as opposed to its social or domestic arrange-ments) but also that it is addressed to people who have taken up the role of citizen. The arguments that Rawls advances for the theory pre-suppose that this perspective has already been adopted.

To put this another way, Rawls now sees the members of liberal democracies as having a double identity.[11] In their personal or private capacity they are seen as holding a conception of the good, a view about what a valuable life consists in, which may include, for instance, their personal tastes or their religious beliefs. This conception is pursued in day-to-day life and forms the basis of the many voluntary associations that flourish in a liberal society. Rawls assumes that these conceptions of the good are radically divergent, and there is no prospect of people coming to agree about what is of ultimate value to them. In their capacity as citizens, by contrast, people are capable of reaching agreement on principles of justice which will then govern their political arrangements – the constitution and so forth. Moreover, Rawls claims, citizen identities should take precedence over personal identities in the sense that people will agree to confine the pursuit of their conceptions of the good within the bounds prescribed by the principles of justice. Thus my religion may demand that, say, no commercial activity should take place on the Sab-bath. My co-religionists and I will respect this norm ourselves, but we will not attempt to pass legislation making it mandatory for those who do not share our beliefs. We think of ourselves as citizens first, and as citizens we implement only measures which we can justify to others who do not share our personal conceptions of the good.

Clearly Rawls's task is to explain why it is reasonable for all of us to give citizenship this sort of priority. Before examining his account more closely, I should explain why I regard it as the paradigm of a liberal theory of citizenship developed in response to the challenge of pluralism. What, for Rawls, does it mean to be a citizen? It is first of all to adopt a certain perspective on the world, and then to govern one's behaviour in accordance with principles derived from this perspective. The perspective is to see oneself as one among many free and equal individuals and to acknowledge that the political society to which these individuals belong must be governed by principles that all can potentially accept. In other words, I acknowledge that each other person (a) has his or her own conception of the good life and (b) is as capable as I am of reasoning about principles of justice, and I then ask what principles we could all accede to. Having arrived at the principles – if Rawls is right, the famous two principles of justice – I then comply with them in my day-to-day life, respecting others' rights to free speech, for example, or according them equal opportunities in the assignment of jobs.

It may strike us straight away that this is a particularly cerebral view of citizenship. A citizen is just someone who subscribes to a certain set of principles. Rawls appears to assume that citizens are always citizens of some national society – this is what determines membership – but this assumption is kept well hidden in the background, presumably for fear that if it were to be brought out into the open, it might cause trouble for the distinction between justice and conceptions of the good. Equally a citizen is not conceived as being an active participant in politics: although political rights are included as part of the first principle of justice, so by definition a citizen is someone who has the right to participate, all that is actually required of him or her is acknowledgement of the principles of justice. So long as one can adopt the citizen perspective in thought, one may live an entirely private existence. Rawls makes this clear when he argues against a strong version of civic humanism which holds that we are political beings 'whose essential nature is most fully realized in a democratic society in which there is widespread and vigorous participation in political life', and defends the division between politically active citizens and the rest as good for society 'in the same way as it is generally beneficial that people develop their different and complementary talents and skills, and engage in mutually advantageous co-operation'.[12] Participation is required only insofar as it is necessary to protect people's basic rights and liberties.

Liberal citizenship and pluralism

How successfully can this liberal conception of citizenship deal with pluralism? Let us begin by observing that the citizen identity to which Rawls wishes to attach priority is an unencumbered identity in the following sense: it is part of that identity that people should regard their private aims and attachments as contingent and open to revision. This is made clear when Rawls states that citizenship embodies a conception of the person as having the moral power not only to pursue but also to revise their ideas of the good life. 'As free persons, citizens claim the right to view their persons as independent from and as not identified with any particular conception of the good, or scheme of private ends.'[13] But he also concedes that people's private identities may be encumbered ones. 'They may regard it as simply unthinkable to view themselves apart from certain religious, philosophical, and moral convictions, or from certain enduring attachments and loyalties.'[14] In other words people who, say, belong to a certain church or are members of an ethnic community may not see these memberships and the value-commitments that go with them as even potentially open to revision – they are definitive, for these people, of their personal identity. The problem is to see why people whose identities are encumbered in this way should give priority to an unencumbered citizen identity which, as we saw, entails restricting the pursuit of their private goals within the bounds set by the principles of justice. Why shouldn't the principles of justice themselves be made responsive to the demands of an (encumbered) personal identity?

We can look at the problem in the following way. In a liberal society there are likely to be many people whose personal identities are themselves unencumbered: they regard themselves as freely choosing a plan of life according to their own tastes and preferences without being inhibited by their ascriptive characteristics or other unrevisable attachments. For these people adopting the citizenship perspective costs nothing, because the view of the person they are required to take up is more or less the one they already hold (as Rawls would put it, their 'comprehensive' doctrine of the good life already supports the political conception of justice). But there will also be people whose personal identities are encumbered, who see themselves as tied to a particular ethnic group, for instance, and here to adopt the citizen perspective is already to concede a good deal, because it means bracketing off all *political* claims that cannot be expressed using the language of liberal citizenship. You cannot, for instance, advance arguments that rely on the truth of a certain religious belief, even though your personal identity depends precisely on that belief's being true.

Has Rawls any response to this problem? He invokes the ideal of a society which is based on free public reason, where we live under a set of institutions that each of us can justify to the rest, using forms of argument that the others will find acceptable. But to make this the basis of his argument is either to make an empirical claim about what is overwhelmingly important to people – in which case it is surely dubious – or else it is simply to restate the liberal position. Once you adopt the liberal conception of citizenship, as Rawls understands it, then you are committed to a certain way of justifying social and political institutions, but our problem was to see why people whose personal identities did not support the liberal view spontaneously could be induced to give it priority. Faced with someone belonging, say, to a fundamentalist church who argues that religious moral standards should be inscribed in law (that homosexuality should be criminalized, for instance), the liberal may say: as a citizen first and foremost you must see that the law must be based on principles that every citizen can accept. But the reply is equally obvious: why should I see myself as a citizen first and foremost? My first duty is to God, and my political activities must fit in with that primary commitment.

The failure of Rawls's argument here appears to leave a liberal with only two alternatives. The first is to retreat to a pragmatic defence of liberal institutions. Given the deep-seated nature of the cultural pluralism that formed our starting point, there is never going to be universal or even perhaps majority consensus on any comprehensive doctrine of the good life. In order to avoid open conflict between groups, the only option is to adopt liberal institutions which, while emasculating many groups politically, at least gives them the security of knowing that their personal identities are protected from invasion by other groups. Since we cannot get the whole loaf, each of us must settle for half, which in this case means a set of rights and liberties that gives each group at least some chance to pursue its own conception of the good life. Rawls calls this a *modus vivendi*. It is plainly a less satisfactory defence of liberal citizenship than the one that he aims for, appealing as it does to political prudence. Moreover, as Will Kymlicka has argued, it is not clear that this defence will necessarily lead to liberal institutions: it might instead point towards a segmented society in which each group is given the authority to regulate the affairs of its own members within a general framework of law.[15] Kymlicka cites as an example the millet system under the Ottoman empire, which was pluralist and stable, but illiberal insofar as the various communities that co-existed under the system were allowed to impose severe restrictions on the freedom of their members, in matters of religious belief especially.

The second alternative is to go on to the offensive, admit that liberalism is a distinct and morally contestable way of life, but declare that it is valuable and worth defending politically. This strategy abandons any pretence of neutrality. Everyone is to be treated as a liberal citizen, and political claims and demands which do not conform to the liberal model are simply ruled out as inadmissible. Moreover it is legitimate to attempt by non-coercive means to channel people's identities in a liberal direction – so for instance the liberal may insist on everyone's participating in a liberal form of education which lays emphasis on choice and autonomy. In this way, it is hoped, pluralism of the sort which initially posed problems for the liberal view of citizenship can be converted into a benign form of pluralism in which everyone agrees to treat their conception of the good life as a merely private matter, to be pursued by non-political means.[16]

Militant liberalism of this type has the virtue of honesty, but its solution to the problem of pluralism amounts in effect to declaring war on those groups who are not prepared to accommodate themselves to the liberal understanding of citizenship, since it no longer tries to give reasons for liberal institutions which these groups might accept. Members of such groups will inevitably feel alienated from the political realm; their citizenship remains simply a formal status. Moreover liberals underestimate the difficulty of 'liberalizing' non-liberal identities; they cannot see how much has to be given up if people are going to see their conceptions of the good life as freely chosen and revisable. Communities whose identities are encumbered will fiercely resist liberalization and, as the American example shows, this resistance can be successful over several generations even in the context of a society permeated with liberal values.

The libertarian conception of citizenship

For these reasons the liberal conception of citizenship does not constitute a fully adequate response to pluralism, and we should explore the alternative conceptions to see whether either of them provides a better solution. What I shall call the libertarian conception has not to my knowledge been articulated in the definitive way that Marshall and Rawls have articulated the liberal conception, but its outlines will I think turn out to be reasonably familiar to anyone who has followed recent political debates. I believe, that is, that something like the libertarian conception of citizenship lies behind various proposals emanating from the New Right which aim to alter the relationship between the individual and the state so that it becomes explicitly contractual. This will become clearer as I proceed.

The easiest way to introduce the libertarian conception is to ask why, from this perspective, citizenship is needed at all. People seek to satisfy their preferences and values through private activity, market exchange and voluntary association with like-minded individuals. The need for a common framework arises only because there are generally desired goods that cannot be obtained in these ways. Citizenship is not valued for its own sake; we are citizens only because we demand goods that require public provision. The citizen, to put it briefly, is a rational consumer of public goods. As far as possible his activities as a citizen should be modelled on his behaviour in the economic market, taken to be a paradigm of rationality. In its most extreme version, this means that the state itself should be regarded as a giant enterprise and the citizens as its (voluntary) customers. This view is expressed in Robert Nozick's *Anarchy, State and Utopia*, where the state is seen as originating in the competition of protective associations to provide their customers with rights-enforcement services. More commonly, however, it is recognized that the state must have a monopoly in the enforcement of basic personal and property rights, and the citizens are seen as parties to a universal contract which gives it that authority. The picture is quite different, however, with all the other goods and services that the state may provide. Here consumer sovereignty can be implemented by two means: contract, so that the citizen who feels that she is not getting the service she is entitled to can take legal action to oblige the agency in question to provide it, and choice, so that the dissatisfied citizen can turn to some alternative provider, thereby creating a quasi-market in the service in question. And this allows the libertarian to respond to pluralism. If citizens differ in their conceptions of value, through contract and choice each can gain access to his or her preferred bundle of public goods. Provided the state responds efficiently to the demands of its customers, the citizens, there is no need to reach agreement *in principle* about what the rights of citizens, beyond the minimum set, ought to be.

But this formulation begs a number of important questions. One has to do with deciding what the demands of citizens actually are. Clearly if the state provides everyone with an amenity such as a free health service or a road system, it is possible to deduce from the use made of the amenity that it is of *some* value to citizens. But we cannot say on this basis alone *how much* value is being provided, either to one particular person or to the collectivity of citizens; we cannot tell, for example, whether they would like more of the budget to be spent on health care or more on roads. Again, introducing choice into the system may provide evidence about particular features of the service being provided that are liked or disliked, but it fails to resolve the issue of overall value. If female patients when given a choice of doctors overwhelmingly prefer to be treated by women, this gives state officials good reason to encourage more women to train in medicine, but it tells us nothing about the general level at which medical services ought to be provided.

In the case of goods and services which are not public in the technical sense – goods that are excludable like schooling or health care, or goods like roads whose users can with technical ingenuity be identified – one solution is to charge their consumers a fee which covers at least a part of the cost of providing them. As soon as someone's use of a good or service can be quantified, a market or quasi-market can be introduced to provide it, with successful suppliers being rewarded with fee income. Either the state can hand over provision of the good to private firms, or public agencies can be set up in competition with one another with their budgets being made dependent on their success in attracting customers.

But let us note the limitations of this solution. If the consumers of public goods are to be made into genuine customers, this implies that access to such goods will depend upon market-determined incomes.[17] In other words, the redistributive character of citizenship is entirely lost: no longer do free citizen entitlements serve partially to offset the inequalities of the market, as they do under the Marshallian conception. Now a hard-bitten libertarian may well argue that this is no criticism, since the kind of rights which would lead to redistribution under Marshall's scheme – social rights, rights to housing, education, health care and so forth – have no standing on libertarian principles. Even someone who stuck in this way to a strict Nozickian definition of rights might however be moved by the observation that people generally have an altruistic desire that their fellow citizens should enjoy living conditions that meet certain minimum standards; they should not have to live rough on the streets, for instance. If that desire is to be respected, access to public goods cannot be made to depend entirely on market income.[18]

The other equally obvious limitation of the citizen-as-customer approach is that it cannot apply to cases where citizens want goods that really are non-excludable. Many cultural goods are of this character. People want their society's way of life to have a certain character: they want it to be non-violent, or to respect religious beliefs, or to validate collective identities. As we saw when considering the liberal conception of citizenship, to say that such values can be pursued in private or through voluntary association is not an adequate response: it will not satisfy someone who thinks that pornography is harmful to women to tell them that the decision to use pornography is a private choice, nor can an animal rights activist be assuaged by the observation that everyone can choose to be a vegetarian. The demand in this case is for a good which is necessarily public: the society must be pornography-free or respectful of animals' rights. I am not here endorsing such demands, which may eventually turn out to be impossible to satisfy, but simply underlining

the point that there are certain goods which necessarily cannot be provided if we install the libertarian conception of citizenship.

Faced with these problems libertarians may look to a second way of
ensuring that citizens have access to the public goods they want, an
alternative to the fee-paying approach. This is to suggest that the society
should encourage the formation of *enclaves* within which people are
supplied with a package of goods and services and pay a local tax to
cover the cost.[19] The idea here is that people should exercise choice by
moving to the enclave whose package best answers to their preferences.
Thus someone who wants to live in a community where moral or religious standards are enforced can choose to do so; someone who prefers
moral laissez-faire can live elsewhere. One area might have high taxes and
a high level of environmental protection and amenity; another might
reverse these features; and so on. Citizens here would exercise consumer
choice by moving from enclave to enclave, and they could thereby express
preferences even for non-excludable public goods insofar as their provision could be limited more or less to particular geographic areas.

We can readily recognize tendencies in contemporary liberal societies
which point to something like this conception of citizenship. But it faces
some obvious difficulties. There is first of all a simple question of feasibility. Most people do not have the option of upping sticks and moving to
a new neighbourhood because they find the public goods package on
offer there more attractive. They are tied by job and by family connections more or less to one particular locality. Furthermore, mobility
chances are generally much greater for more affluent citizens. One illustration of this is the much-remarked flight of the middle classes from the
inner cities to suburbs and leafy villages. This certainly reveals the value
people attach to the essentially public good of living in a safe and
attractive physical environment; but the price of obtaining this can only
be paid by a minority of the population.

More serious than these practical issues is the question whether a
society in which citizenship meant nothing more than the right to choose
a local enclave whose package of goods and services suited you best could
possibly be stable. Citizens cannot in the end confine their demands to the
local package. For one thing there are certain to be spillover effects. The
vegetarians in enclave A, where meat-eating is banned, cannot be indif-
ferent to the fact that when the wind is in the West, the fumes from the
abattoir in enclave B blow over their territory. Other concerns extend by
definition to all the members of a particular society (or even beyond this),
such as the concern that they should not read books which blaspheme
against your religion. Moreover, even if we think that some public goods
problems can be solved by allowing citizens to express their preferences
by physical mobility, this must depend upon a common framework of

entitlements covering such things as rights to education and social security. Without such a framework people who cannot supply themselves with such basic goods by market exchange will converge on enclaves with relatively generous schemes of provision, creating a classic problem of adverse selection. (This problem was illustrated by the Elizabethan Poor Laws, where in order to prevent parishes offering more adequate levels of poor relief from being overwhelmed by vagrants, it was necessary to pass laws confining paupers to the parish of their birth.)

The strength of the libertarian position is that it takes pluralism seriously. It assumes that people have radically different conceptions of the good life, and argues that the way to cope with this is to depoliticize citizenship, to convert the public realm into an ersatz version of the market. People should exercise consumer choice either through individual contract with public agencies, or through voting with their feet, moving to the place which gives them the best kind of collective life. It founders on the fact that citizenship at its core concerns common rights and goods enjoyed in common. If we try to privatize or localize the provision of goods that are not in the core, in other words to pare down the rights of citizenship to the minimum, the effect may be to weaken people's sense of citizen identity, and to erode the core itself. If I can avoid the problems of inner-city crime by moving to the suburbs, why continue to pay for the extra levels of policing necessary to protect the rights of those left behind? The libertarian view in the form I have presented it is finally unstable: either it embarks on the kind of utopian fantasy that you find in the last chapter of Nozick's *Anarchy, State and Utopia*, where nothing remains to citizenship but the right to contract into the community of your choice, or else it pulls back to something like the centre-right position identified at the beginning of the chapter, which tries to compensate for the paring down of rights of citizenship by morally exhorting people to be 'good citizens' through volunteer activity and the like.

The republican conception of citizenship

The republican conception of citizenship conceives the citizen as someone who plays an active role in shaping the future direction of his or her society through political debate and decision-making.[20] It takes the liberal conception of citizenship as a set of rights, and adds to it the idea that a citizen must be someone who thinks and behaves in a certain way. A citizen identifies with the political community to which he or she belongs, and is committed to promoting its common good through active participation in its political life. Now it might seem that this conception is simply obsolete in the face of contemporary pluralism. Whereas both liberal and libertarian views can be seen as originating in the fact of disagreement about questions of ultimate value – liberalism springs, as has often been argued, from the ideal of religious toleration which emerged in the aftermath of the European wars of religion, and libertarianism simply takes this ideal to its furthest point – republicanism conjures up the image of a small homogeneous society with common traditions, a shared civil religion and so forth – fourth-century Athens or fifteenth-century Florence as mirrored through Rousseau's *Social Contract*. Insofar as the republican conception appeals to something akin to the notion of a general will – the idea that citizens through debate and discussion can come to an agreement about what ought to be done politically – it appears to be defeated by pluralism of the kind I have been considering. Pluralism excludes genuinely voluntary agreement of this kind: the appearance of agreement can be obtained only through force or manipulation whereby some groups are induced to limit their claims within bounds established by the stronger groups in the polity.

This is certainly the charge laid by critics such as I.M. Young against the republican view. Young argues that, like liberals, republicans are committed to an ideal of impartiality which acts to the disadvantage of those groups in society she identifies as oppressed, including women and ethnic minorities. She claims that the ideal of the civic public

> excludes women and other groups defined as different, because its rational and universal status derives only from its opposition to affectivity, particularity and the body. Republican theorists insisted on the unity of the civic public: insofar as he is a citizen every man leaves behind his particularity and difference, to adopt a universal standpoint identical for all citizens, the standpoint of the common good or general will. In practice republican politicians enforced homogeneity by excluding from citizenship all those defined as different and associated with the body, desire or need influences that might veer citizens away from the standpoint of pure reason.[21]

Young concedes that contemporary republicans (she cites Benjamin Barber and Jürgen Habermas) no longer wish formally to exclude such groups from the public sphere. She claims, nevertheless, that participation in that sphere is governed by an idea of reason that will exclude claims based on the particular needs and desires of women and other groups.

The issue we must address, therefore, is what conception of reason or rationality lies behind the republican idea of a general will. Republicans claim that a citizen body can, through open discussion, reach a substantial degree of consensus on issues of common concern. To justify this claim is it necessary to appeal to a strong ideal of impartiality such that a citizen, upon assuming that role, sets aside all his or her particular aims and preferences and reasons from a completely universal standpoint, as Young alleges?[22]

Whatever the views of particular republicans, such as Rousseau, on this question, the answer seems to be negative. All that is necessary in order to embark on political dialogue is a willingness to find reasons that can persuade those who initially disagree with us, and one cannot say *a priori* how abstract those reasons will have to be. Suppose a group comes into a political arena bearing a proposal that springs from the particular circumstances and needs of that group – say women demanding a change in the terms and conditions of maternity leave. The first requirement of deliberation is simply that the reasons behind the proposal must be elaborated, which might simply mean explaining why the existing rules were burdensome to women and the proposed ones less so. Beyond that it would be necessary to connect the reasons given to more general reasons that others were likely to accept, but this requirement again might not be a very arduous one. Suppose, for instance, that the maximum period of maternity leave had already been agreed, and the proposal was to introduce greater flexibility into its timing. Supporters could argue that the new proposal would be likely to place no greater financial burden on employers or the state than the old – appealing by implication to the premise that the existing arrangement was fair, and that the new one would not change this materially.

Of course few political arguments are as simple as this. In most cases engaging in political dialogue involves both moderating the claim that you might initially wish to make and shifting somewhat the ground on which you make it.[23] Consider the case of a pacifist engaging in a debate on nuclear weapons. Her 'maximalist' position would presumably be the complete abandonment of all weapons of destruction, and she would argue for this on the ground that no one might legitimately engage in acts of violence towards another person. Seeing, however, that this position commanded little support, she might limit her claim in the present context to nuclear disarmament, and argue for this on the grounds, for instance, of the undiscriminating nature of the damage inflicted by nuclear weapons – a reason which might appeal to many. Young does not deny that initial claims may have to be moderated in this way in political contexts. She distinguishes between demands stemming from self-interest and those stemming from justice and says that 'the test of whether a claim upon the public is just or merely an expression of self-interest is best made when those making it must confront the opinion of others who have explicitly different, though not necessarily conflicting, experiences, priorities and needs'.[24] Indeed it would be absurd not to make some such concession. Since no group can hope to win in political argument all of the time, unless it is willing to moderate its demands in search of agreement, and to appeal to reasons which are generally accepted in the political community, it cannot expect other groups to reciprocate. In this way a weaker kind of impartiality emerges spontaneously from the search for agreement itself.[25]

Is there any reason to think that impartiality of this kind disadvantages groups whose claims depend upon particularity, i.e. groups whose claims arise from and refer to features that are specific to them, such as women's claims to maternity leave? Very broadly we can separate two kinds of claim that may be advanced in political debate. On the one hand there are claims that appeal at base to an interest common to all the citizens of a particular country, such as an interest in security from attack. On the other hand there are claims that reflect the interest of a particular group and whose satisfaction would typically impose some costs on other groups. In the second case but not the first, in order to reach agreement an appeal has to be made to a norm of justice, such as a principle of equal treatment. However this does not necessarily mean that claims in the second category are more difficult to advance than claims in the first. The norm itself may be relatively uncontroversial: the problem may be to convince hearers that the group in question really does have a case under the norm, which may be a matter of drawing attention to facts that have hitherto gone unnoticed. In both cases the degree of difficulty will depend on how extreme (relative to others in your political community) your views are: as I suggested earlier, if you are a pacifist you may have to shift your ground quite radically in order to persuade your fellow-citizens even where there is no disagreement about the ultimate end – a conflict-free world. Equally if you are a radical feminist who believes that every act of heterosexual intercourse is equivalent to rape, you won't be able to rely on that premise in a debate about criminalizing rape within marriage – but again that reflects the extreme nature of your views, not the fact that the issue concerns the body.

It is fair to say that republican citizenship cannot accommodate everything that passes under the name of 'the politics of identity'. If the public sphere is regarded as essentially a means whereby various group identities are given legitimacy through public recognition, then at a certain point this will inevitably collide with the ideal of decision-making through open debate sketched above.[26] Group identities are recognized in the sense that all groups are given access to decision-making forums, and there are no barriers to the claims and demands they may make. If presence and the making of demands are sufficient for recognition, the republican view can provide it.[27] But there can be no guarantee that any particular demand will win acceptance, no matter how strongly the group making it feels that the demand is integral to its identity. Everything will depend on whether the demand can be linked to principles that are generally accepted among the citizen body, such as principles of equal treatment. So, for example, in a context in which the state already supports Christian and Jewish schools, Muslims arguing for similar support for Islamic schools may validly claim that the status quo unfairly privileges some religious identities at the expense of others, and demeans Muslims. But on the other hand, if existing policy were to be based on the principle that all formal education must be secular in character, the claim that Islamic schools were essential to Muslim identity would have to be assessed on its own merits, and might well be rejected in a democratic forum. For a group to insist that only the full recognition of its demands can respect its identity is to reject the very essence of republican citizenship.

The republican conception of citizenship, then, places no limits on what sort of demand may be put forward in the political forum. It does not discriminate between demands stemming from personal conviction – say demands for animal rights – and demands stemming from group identity – say demands for religious schooling. In all cases the success of any particular demand will depend upon how far it can be expressed in terms that are close to, or distant from, the general political ethos of the community. It requires of citizens a willingness to give reasons for what they are claiming, but not that they should divest themselves of everything that is particular to them before setting foot in the arenas of politics.

A second claim made by Young is that the republican ideal relies on a public/private distinction which again serves to discriminate against those whose concerns have traditionally been seen as private matters. What are we to make of this?

There seem to be two places at which a public/private distinction emerges within the republican conception. First of all there is certainly a distinction between a person acting in his or her private capacity and as a citizen, as evidenced by the different arguments that may be used in the two contexts. A person trying to persuade his fellow church-members to engage in some charitable work will typically reason in different ways from the same person trying in a public forum to persuade his fellow citizens to increase welfare expenditures. I have argued already that there is no *a priori* way of drawing the boundary here; nevertheless there will typically be arguments that can legitimately be deployed in the first context but not in the second. Secondly, a public/private distinction will emerge *from* public deliberation, in the sense that there will be matters that it is agreed should be confined to the private sphere. This may be done for reasons of principle – for instance, it may be felt that there are areas of each citizen's private life in which it is illegitimate for the state to intervene – or simply on the grounds that substantive political agreement on some issue is impossible to achieve, so the fairest course is to let citizens pursue their own preferences by voluntary means (thus if we cannot agree about which kinds of state support for the arts are justifiable, we may decide to leave arts funding entirely to the market). No doubt wherever the line between public and private is drawn there will be some groups who would like it drawn in a different place, but there is no reason to think that the groups identified by Young as oppressed will automatically be the losers.

Might it be argued that the republican ideal of citizenship rests upon a conception of the human good which may conflict with the private conceptions held by individual citizens? There is not much doubt that the republican tradition has held up the active and virtuous citizen as a model, valuing the life of public participation above the various forms of private life that citizens might engage in. Once again, however, we need to distinguish what (some) classical republicans have said from what the republican view of citizenship actually requires. What it requires is something weaker: that it should be part of each person's good to be engaged *at some level* in political debate, so that the laws and policies of the state do not appear to him or her simply as alien impositions but as the outcome of a reasonable agreement to which he or she has been party. This is consistent either with regarding political activity as intrinsically fulfilling or with regarding it as a necessary precondition for other activities which do have intrinsic value, just as gourmets may regard eating as intrinsically worthwhile, whereas the rest of us may regard it merely as providing the sustenance which enables one to engage in other pursuits. This difference will be reflected in the structure of republican politics: some people may be engaged in it on a full-time basis, while others may listen to the arguments being presented but only become actively involved from time to time, when major issues are being decided. One need not, then, regard political activity as the *summum bonum* in order to adopt the republican view, but can hold the more modest position that although politics is indeed a necessary part of the good life, different people can be expected to give it a different weight according to their own personal values.

Where does this leave people whose conceptions of the good categorically exclude political participation, for instance religious believers who hold that trafficking with the secular world compromises their faith? Clearly from a republican perspective such people cannot be regarded as full citizens, even though there will usually be sufficient grounds to extend to them the formal rights of citizenship (one good reason is that we cannot predict how the thinking of such groups may develop, or what their individual members may choose to do). So does the republican view alienate some groups from citizenship in much the same way as the liberal view? The relevant difference is this. On the liberal view to be a citizen just *is* to accept a certain set of principles, and to regulate your private conduct within the boundaries set by those principles. This means that the liberal has nothing to say to someone whose own conception of the good is non-liberal except that he must set that conception aside for political purposes. Groups who wish to influence the parameters of politics, but attempt to do so by appeal to conceptions of the good that are not already tailored to liberal requirements, are *personae non gratae* in this perspective. Thus fundamentalists whose political arguments appeal to the truth of certain religious doctrines are excluded *a priori* from citizenship on the liberal conception. The republican view makes no such prior demand; the only demand it makes is that each citizen should try to persuade the others of the rightness of her cause, and not, say, resort to violence to impose it. There is no set limit on the kind of argument that can be advanced. Each person will in practice be forced to shift to a more impartial standpoint, but this comes about precisely because of the need to reach agreement. So here the only groups who are excluded from citizenship are those groups who voluntarily exclude themselves because their beliefs prohibit them from taking part in affairs of state (anarchists, for instance, or religious groups such as the ultra-orthodox Jews who live in Jerusalem but do not recognize the state of Israel as legitimate). And although from a republican perspective this may be regrettable (and republicans may want to take steps to discourage the formation of such groups), it is difficult to see that the excluded groups themselves have any grounds for complaint. Unlike groups who wish to be politically active but are deterred from participating under the terms and conditions of liberal citizenship, these anti-political groups cannot regard their exclusion as diminishing their dignity or self-esteem.

Although liberal and republican conceptions of citizenship diverge at the level of principle, in a society which exhibits a high degree of pluralism, they are likely to converge substantially in practice. For the reasons given earlier, what will emerge from public discussion, in a plural society, will be a liberal constitution, and broadly liberal policies on what we might call the enforcement of specific conceptions of the good. There are, moreover, reasons internal to the republican conception of politics for having a formal constitution that places some limits on what decision-making majorities can do. I am thinking here of the idea that a constitution represents a desirable form of self-binding which is likely to enhance the quality of democratic decision-making in the long run.[28] Thus it is not true that republican citizenship gives minorities no assurance that their rights will be protected in the face of majority will. The contrast between republicanism and liberalism is not that the liberal recognizes the value of entrenched rights whereas the republican does not, but that the liberal regards these rights as having a pre-political justification while the republican grounds them in public discussion. One institutional corollary is that liberals will seek to make the judiciary the supreme arbiters of constitutional rights – in effect the interpretation of liberal citizenship is entrusted to them – while the republican gives this role to the citizen body as a whole. Thus the constitution will have a different status in a republican regime. It will constrain everyday politics, but will itself be open to amendment if the rights and liberties it protects are judged, following public discussion in which all have opportunities to participate, to stand in need of revision. There will be constitutional politics and not merely, as the liberal would want, constitutional interpretation by judges.

Contrary to what one might suppose, then, the republican view has resources to deal with the question of pluralism. I do not wish to claim that citizenship in this mode can cope with radical disagreement about the very existence of the state of the kind which gives rise to separatist movements. Faced with such disagreement, it is very unlikely that the conflicting groups will be sufficiently motivated to search for political agreement on the basis of reasons that all can accept. For this reason, as I have argued elsewhere, a common sense of nationality is an essential background to politics of this kind.[29] The pluralism which forms the starting point of this chapter is not of the sort which puts the continued existence of the state in question: it is pluralism in personal identities and conceptions of value of the kind that is endemic in liberal societies even where problems of nationality are not at stake.

Conclusion

The liberal view of citizenship set out by Marshall and Rawls is presently the dominant view, but it is also recognized to be under stress. We have seen that it embodies a conception of justice whose underpinnings may be unacceptable to some groups, and to these groups no reasons (other than pragmatic ones) can be given for accommodating themselves to liberalism. In the face of disagreement, the libertarian alternative is to fragment citizenship so that, over and above the minimal core, each person is to choose his or her own package of 'citizen rights'. This we saw to be a recipe for social disintegration, albeit one to which liberal societies seem increasingly drawn in practice. The republican solution involves, paradoxically, the search for a higher level of agreement between individuals and social groups, but it aims to achieve this in a more pragmatic way, through the give and take of politics. It does not require participants to subscribe to any fixed principles other than those implicit in political dialogue itself – a willingness to argue and to listen to reasons given by others, abstention from violence and coercion, and so forth. If a plural society is to be held together and legitimated by a common understanding of citizenship, this third conception is the best place from which to start our thinking.

4

Group Identities, National Identities and Democratic Politics

One of the most distinctive features of the politics of our time is the demand by various cultural groups for the political recognition and affirmation of their distinct identities. This 'politics of recognition' or 'identity politics'[1] has perhaps reached its fullest development in the United States, but similar tendencies can be observed in all the other liberal democracies, including Britain. The groups making this demand have primarily been defined by their ethnicity, their religion, their gender or their sexual orientation: Hispanics, Muslims, women or gays, for instance. The demand is that the democratic political system should open itself up to these groups, should abandon procedures or policies that damage or ignore them, and should strive to give them equal recognition alongside the bearers of mainstream cultural identities. Although politics in the narrow sense is not the only arena in which this demand is made – as readers will know, there has been much debate within educational institutions about whether and how to give equal recognition to group identities in curriculum design and so forth – it is the arena I want to consider in this chapter.

I want to ask what the demand for recognition amounts to, how it has arisen, whether it is justified in its own terms, and whether meeting it would be compatible with preserving the conditions for successful democratic politics. As my title indicates, I am particularly concerned with the relationship between group identities of the sort indicated above and the more encompassing national identities which, in the view of many people, myself included, create the solidarity among citizens that democratic politics requires.

The politics of recognition

The politics of recognition goes beyond toleration as it has come to be understood in liberal societies. A policy of toleration involves leaving groups free to assert their identity and express their cultural values in private or through associations of their members. The state's role here is primarily negative: it should not force minority groups to conform to the dominant culture, nor should it erect artificial barriers that make it harder for minority cultures to thrive. Some liberals would argue that, in addition, the state has a positive responsibility to protect minority cultures when they find themselves in an unequal competition with the mainstream.[2] For advocates of the politics of recognition this is inadequate, because it relegates groups to the private sphere, and fails to give public endorsement to their distinct identities. The public sphere is then governed by norms which appear to be universal and culturally neutral, but which in fact reflect the cultural values of the dominant social categories – middle-class white males, for instance. As Young has argued:

> The standpoint of the privileged, their particular experience and standards, is constructed as normal and neutral. If some groups' experience differs from this neutral experience, or they do not measure up to those standards, their difference is constructed as deviance and inferiority. Not only are the experience and the values of the oppressed thereby ignored and silenced, but they become disadvantaged by their situated identities.[3]

On this view, then, the level playing field for different groups, which liberals hope to create through policies of toleration and cultural support, cannot be created by such means. Instead what is needed is a transformation of the political sphere itself. This has three main aspects:

1   The political sphere must be purged of procedures, symbols and norms which embody the values of the groups that have hitherto dominated it. For instance, politics should not be conducted exclusively in the language of the majority group in a bilingual society. Public life should not be geared to the needs and preferences of male heads of households, for instance in the timetables followed by parliamentary institutions. No particular religion should be given a privileged place in the ceremonies which mark important moments in political life, such as Presidential inaugurations; and so forth.

2   Groups should participate in the political realm on an equal basis, and should be encouraged to affirm their distinct identities and

perspectives in the course of doing so. On the one hand, this requires that members of each group should actually be present in political forums such as legislatures in sufficient numbers to make their presence signific-ant.[4] On the other hand, they should participate not on terms set by those groups that are already ensconced, but in whatever way their particular experience demands. This entails that groups should organize themselves separately. 'Separate organization is probably necessary in order for these groups to discover and reinforce the positivity of their specific experience, to collapse and eliminate double consciousness. In discussions within autonomous organizations, group members can determine their specific needs and interests.'[5] Group consciousness thus formed is to be carried into political arenas and presented to other groups who have arrived at their own standpoints in a similar way.

3   The policies that emerge from decision-making forums should be sensitive to group differences. This rules out in particular any straightfor-ward majoritarian procedures for making decisions. Groups are entitled to insist that certain policy outcomes are essential to their self-respect and well-being, and this may justify giving them a veto in these policy areas: for instance women may properly insist on self-determination in relation to their reproductive capacities (a right to abortion etc.). 'Equal treat-ment' will not be enough in circumstances where different groups are very unequally affected by the policies that are chosen.

Young sums up the 'politics of difference' that she advocates as fol-lows:

> A democratic public should provide mechanisms for the effective recogni-tion and representation of the distinct voices and perspectives of those of its constituent groups that are oppressed or disadvantaged. Such group repres-entation implies institutional mechanisms and public resources supporting (1) self-organization of group members so that they achieve collective empowerment and a reflective understanding of their collective experience and interests in the context of the society; (2) group analysis and group generation of policy proposals in institutionalized contexts where decision-makers are obliged to show that their deliberations have taken group perspectives into consideration; and (3) group veto power regarding specific policies that affect a group directly, such as reproductive rights policy for women, or land use policy for Indian reservations.[6]

We can illuminate the politics of recognition further by contrasting it with two other familiar models of democratic politics. One is interest group pluralism, which sees the democratic state as an arena in which different interest groups negotiate and bargain with one another, so that what finally emerges as public policy represents a fair compromise between the demands of each group. The politics of recognition goes beyond this in two ways. First, although interest group pluralism is alive to the problems caused by the fact that different groups have unequal amounts of resources at their disposal, and therefore do not enjoy real equality of access to the political sphere, it assumes that political institutions themselves are neutral as between groups: once access has been achieved, each group's success depends on its bargaining strength, its ability to form coalitions, etc. The politics of recognition, in contrast, sees the existing public sphere as embodying norms which designate certain groups as legitimate and acceptable, others as deviant. So the problem for incoming groups that fall into the deviant category – gays, for instance – is not just one of gaining access, but of having the group identity recognized as legitimate, which involves challenging the prevailing norms concerning who counts as a good citizen and so forth. Second, interest group pluralism envisages groups bargaining with one another over their demands, and a policy emerging which reflects a fair compromise between their interests. The politics of recognition, on the other hand, looks for a redistributive tilt in favour of those groups it designates as disadvantaged or oppressed. Each group is to present an interpretation of its needs, and these needs are to carry moral weight with members of other groups. In other words, political debate on this model is to be governed by norms of justice which will favour groups, such as blacks or the disabled, at the expense of already advantaged groups, such as businessmen or professionals.

The second model of democratic politics that stands opposed to the politics of recognition is the republican model. On this model, people acting in political forums should adopt an inclusive identity as citizens which transcends their sectional identities as women, members of ethnic minorities, etc. It is important for democratic politics that all perspectives should be represented in the political arena, but in reaching policy decisions, citizens should set aside their personal commitments and affiliations and try to assess competing proposals in terms of shared standards of justice and common interest. (This aspect of the model found its most extreme expression in Rousseau's demand that all factions must be banned from public assemblies if a general will was to emerge.) The politics of recognition claims that the universality appealed to by republicans is spurious. The norms that are supposed to guide public debate will in fact be the norms that have been sponsored by existing powerful groups.[7] There is no good reason for group members to set aside their specific identities when participating in political forums. To do so would be to capitulate before an artificially homogenized citizen identity. In contrast to the republican model, Young argues, the politics of difference invokes a conception of the public that 'does not imply homogeneity or the adoption of some general or universal standpoint. . . . To promote a politics of inclusion, then, participatory democrats must promote the ideal of a heterogeneous public, in which persons stand forth with their differences acknowledged and respected, though perhaps not completely understood, by others.'[8]

The identity politics I am describing has both a symbolic and a material aspect. On the one hand, it involves the public recognition of group identities, the winning of legitimacy for ethnic, religious or sexual identities that, according to its advocates, have traditionally been regarded as inferior to the dominant identity – that of the male WASP, for instance. On the other hand, it involves the redistribution of resources to these groups, in the form of affirmative action programmes, minority cultural programmes and so forth. It would be a caricature, therefore, to say that the conception of politics implied by the politics of identity is a purely expressive or symbolic one. Nevertheless it is the symbolic aspect that I am going to concentrate on, for it is this aspect that is simultaneously the most distinctive and the most puzzling feature of this form of politics. It is not hard to understand why blacks should press for affirmative action programmes of which they will be the beneficiaries, or Welsh speakers for Welsh-language education and television. But the search for recognition through politics – the idea that group identity is not secure unless it is given political endorsement – is a phenomenon that requires further investigation.

Group identities and political recognition

It is plainly not a universal truth that social groups with distinct identities must seek political recognition *as* bearers of those identities. Generalizing broadly, we can say that, historically, the first demand of minority groups has been to be left alone by the state, to be given the space to develop their own social and cultural institutions. The first priority is not to be persecuted and not to be forcibly converted to the dominant religion or culture. If one takes groups such as the Jews in medieval Europe or the Amish today, it would be absurd to represent them as demanding political recognition. This is not merely because at earlier times it was only too evident that no such recognition would be forthcoming; it is also because these groups attach no particular value to political recognition by outsiders. Each member gains respect from his or her standing within the group. The opinion of outsiders does not matter unless this is expressed in acts that seek to degrade or thwart the group. Insofar as each group regards outsiders as alien to its way of life, it neither expects nor seeks recognition from them.

The second stage can be characterized as the quest for inclusion. At a certain point in the development of the modern state, the idea of common citizenship appears – the idea that each member of the political community should have a status as citizen over and above his or her particular position in the occupational structure, as member of this or that religious confession, and so on. Originally the image of the citizen favours certain members at the expense of others – for instance the view that to be a full citizen one must be a property owner, or able to bear arms to defend the community – but these images are challenged as new groups press for inclusion on equal terms. Often this is associated with changing ideas of national identity, of what it means to be a loyal and contributing member of the nation in question. Thus we can examine the process whereby Catholics were admitted to full citizenship in Protestant cultures such as Britain, or women's fight to establish themselves as equal contributors with men to social well-being, and therefore as entitled to equal rights of citizenship. The essential logic of the argument here is that a group with distinguishing characteristic C seeks to show that the possession or non-possession of C is irrelevant to a person's claim to enjoy equal rights of citizenship – either because C is simply irrelevant to citizenship (as a Catholic might claim that religious belief is a private matter having no bearing on one's public role as citizen) or because having C makes one neither worse nor better from the point of view of citizenship than having −C (as a woman in the nineteenth century might have claimed that female virtues, though different from male virtues, provided an equally good foundation for life as a citizen). Whatever the precise form of the argument, the claim is that one is entitled to be treated as an equal citizen regardless of group differences. Admission to the public realm should not depend on the particular characteristics, culture or beliefs one has as a member of group C.

The quest for inclusion is partly a quest for the tangible benefits that come with the new citizenship rights – access to public office and the lifting of restrictions on landholding in the case of the Catholics, for instance – but it is also a quest for recognition. Members of the excluded groups want the dominant groups to recognize them as equal citizens. This implies that they now to some extent share a common identity which makes recognition by outsiders important. It is no longer enough to be awarded respect by fellow-members of one's group. On the other hand, the recognition sought is recognition *qua* citizen, not recognition *qua* group member, and this is what distinguishes the quest for inclusion from the politics of identity that I have been discussing. The claim is, roughly, 'I may be a Catholic, a woman, a homosexual, etc. but I'm also a (British) citizen, and as loyal and valuable a citizen as you are.' So here, then, we have groups who bear two identities – a particular group identity, and a national identity that they share with others – which they want to express in different ways. In some contexts – in their dealings with fellow-members, for instance – they want their group identity to be recognized and respected. In other contexts – public contexts, especially – they want their group identity to be treated as irrelevant, and their over-arching identity as fellow-nationals to be respected.

What can explain the recent shift, on the part of some groups (or at least their most vociferous spokesmen), from the politics of inclusion to the politics of recognition? Why has it become important to participate in politics not merely as equal citizens but as public bearers of a sectional identity? Two answers can be given to this question. The answer favoured by those sympathetic to the politics of recognition is that the politics of inclusion could never succeed on its own terms. Ultimately it was imposs-ible for women, blacks or gays to be treated as equal citizens merely by asking that their group characteristics should be treated as irrelevant for political purposes. The public realm was biased against them because it embodied norms with which it was harder for members of these groups to comply. The bias may have been less overt by comparison with earlier conceptions of citizenship, but it existed none the less. Young, for instance, claims that

> the traditional public realm of universal citizenship has operated to exclude persons associated with the body and feeling – especially women, Blacks, American Indians, and Jews. Many contemporary theorists of participatory democracy retain the ideal of a civic public in which citizens leave behind their particularity and differences. Because such a universalist ideal con-tinues to threaten the exclusion of some, the meaning of 'public' should be transformed to exhibit the positivity of group differences, passion, and play.[9]

I have argued elsewhere that such claims about the inherent biases of the public realm do not stand up to close scrutiny. In particular, there is no reason to think that a republican conception of citizenship, which sees the citizen as someone who plays an active role in shaping the future direction of his or her society through political debate and decision-making, places groups such as women or ethnic minorities at a disadvant-age.[10] I should therefore like to explore a second answer to our question about the politics of identity. This proposes that the public recognition of group identities becomes important to groups when these identities them-selves become insecure and threaten to dissolve for reasons having noth-ing directly to do with the political exclusion of the groups in question. Political recognition is required to consolidate and legitimize collective identities that sociological factors would otherwise cause to decline in importance. Since ethnic identities are the most commonly cited instances of group identities that, in cases where the group in question is subordinated or oppressed, demand special recognition, I shall focus on these. It is obviously open to discussion how easily the ethnic model can be extended to other collective identities such as those arising from gender differences.[11]

When we think about an ethnic group, we often begin by thinking of a closed and compact community whose members all recognize one another and are identified by outsiders as belonging to that community. There is a shared culture, a high rate of intermarriage, an ethnic quarter in the main cities and so on. We think of the Jews in nineteenth-century Russia, or the Italians arriving by sea in New York. As part of this picture, people are assigned their ethnicity by birth, and group identity does not depend on choices made by individual members. Although in certain cases ethnic membership may approximate to this picture, in many others it is seriously misleading. At the other extreme, we could regard ethnicity as a matter of choices made either by groups or by individuals. Groups can choose whether to identify themselves in this way or that, whether more or less inclusively, etc.; equally individuals frequently have a range of ethnic options to choose between, and it is up to them which they use in the course of self-identification.

Let me give a couple of examples to illustrate this idea of ethnicity as a chosen identity. How should people of Bangladeshi origin in contemporary Britain identify themselves? Should they think of themselves specifically as people whose native language and culture is Bengali? Or, taking into account their commonalities with other groups from the Indian subcontinent, should they think of themselves more broadly as Asians? Alternatively, since their religious background is Islamic, should they identify themselves as Muslims, in both British and international contexts? Yet again, when considering the prejudice and discrimination they experience at the hands of the white majority, should they emphasize what they have in common with other dark-skinned immigrant groups and think of themselves as blacks? Over and above all this, should they think of themselves as British (or British Asian or British Bengali) or should they stick to an ethnic identification as, for example, a Bengali-who-happens-to-be-living-in-Britain? Each of these identities is available to members of the group in question, and on the available evidence different individual members have made different choices.[12] Moreover the whole group's centre of gravity may shift over time, as its internal culture and external circumstances change. In the case in question, an exclusively Bengali identity may become less easily available as language use declines, whereas a Muslim or (for some young Bangladeshis) a black identity may become more attractive as a way of marking out the group's distinctive position within English society.

My second example is taken from a study of ethnic identities among white middle-class Americans.[13] This highlights the extent to which individuals are able to select which aspects of their ethnic genealogy to highlight, in circumstances where almost everyone has a mixed ancestry. Thus someone whose ancestors include Irish, French and German immigrants may decide to think of himself simply as Irish; or a woman of Polish, German and English ancestry may present herself as ethnically German in family contexts and ethnically Polish to outsiders.[14] In these circumstances, most people choose not to forgo an ethnic identity in favour of a uniform identity as Americans, but select a single or hybrid identity according to their personal cultural preferences and also according to the relative social attractiveness of different ethnicities.[15] This is 'symbolic ethnicity' in its full-blown form.[16] People benefit from their sense of belonging to an identifiable community, while at the same time the choice they have made imposes no real costs on them in terms of personal lifestyle or career options.

It would clearly be a very serious mistake to regard symbolic ethnicity of this kind as the standard version of ethnicity in contemporary liberal societies. For groups such as blacks or Hispanics in America, the position is very different: to a large extent, their ethnic identity is conferred externally upon them by the wider society. Nevertheless symbolic ethnicity represents the opposite pole of the ethnic spectrum from our initial picture of a closed and stable ethnic community, and moreover (I suggest) it is the pole towards which group identities in contemporary liberal societies are slowly but steadily moving. Social mobility, cultural mixing and intermarriage mean that for increasing numbers of people, their self-ascribed ethnicity depends on choosing which of several possible lines of descent to highlight.[17] To say this is not to say that it *feels* like a matter of choice to the individual concerned. The search for one's roots appears from the inside to be a search for who one really is. Nor is it to say that a person's ethnicity is less important to them than it once was: as physically identifiable communities, such as local communities, become weaker, it may be more important to find a symbolic community with which to identify.

If my suggestion is correct, and in general we find ourselves in a situation in which ethnic identities are in flux (in the sense that people can move more freely between them, and many choose to adopt hybrid or composite identities), then we can offer a different interpretation of the politics of recognition. The political recognition of group identities may be important because it fixes and consolidates identities which in the free play of civil society would otherwise become amorphous. If a group succeeds in winning political recognition, then, on the one hand, it establishes one among many possible lines of social cleavage as the relevant line; on the other hand, it is able to define publicly what it means to belong to the group. Suppose, for instance, that in contemporary Britain Muslims were to win political recognition for themselves as a group, in the sense that candidates stood for parliament as Muslims (perhaps as members of a separate party), offices were reserved for Muslims, Muslims were given veto rights over certain legislative issues and so forth. This would immediately establish that the most important line of division for people in this ethnic region lay between Muslims and non-Muslims rather than between whites and blacks or between Pakistanis and Bangladeshis. It would also provide a public statement of what it means to be a Muslim – for instance which issues touch in an essential way on the well-being of Muslims and which do not. The position of those such as the Bangladeshis I discussed earlier becomes quite different: they now have a clear and publicly defined identity which they may either accept or reject. Not everyone will welcome this clarification, but many will, and this, I am suggesting, provides the impetus behind the politics of recognition that we are seeking to understand.

I asked earlier whether the conclusions we might reach about ethnicity could be extended to other forms of group identity, such as those based on gender or sexual orientation. One might think that, whereas ethnic identity increasingly becomes a matter of choice for the reasons I have given, if one is a woman or gay there is no choice in the matter. Although in one sense this may be true, it is also clear that having a particular female or gay *identity* is to a large extent within the control of the individual. There are many different versions of femininity, from the traditional role of subordination within the patriarchal family at one extreme to, say, radical lesbianism at the other. There is also the much debated issue of how one's identity as a woman is to be related to one's identity as, say, black or working-class: should one regard oneself as a woman first and a black person second, or vice versa? Roughly the same questions can be asked about a gay identity. Once more a politics of recognition, if it were successful, would fix the answers to these questions. It would generate a distinct sense of what it means to be a woman, what women's basic demands are, and so forth. What is now fluid and uncertain would become clearly specified for all those who chose to accept the politically-defined identity.[18]

Group identities and democracy

In the last section I asked what might propel groups beyond demanding toleration or inclusion as equal citizens towards the politics of recognition. My suggestion is that the politics of recognition emerges not so much from the failure of the politics of inclusion as from a condition in which group identities, although still important to their bearers, become increasingly fluid and subject to individual choice. My next question is whether a politics of this kind is viable: whether a democratic state can provide the conditions under which groups are given equal recognition and have their identities validated in political settings.

One problem that arises directly from the analysis I have given is that of identifying the groups who would qualify for political recognition. Writers such as Young lay down as one criterion that a qualifying group must be 'oppressed or disadvantaged', but aside from the difficulties involved in applying this criterion to a heterogeneous group such as women, this still leaves in play a very wide range of possibilities. Consider just three possible dimensions of disadvantage: gender, class and race. One possible way of constituting groups would be to take each dimension separately: women, workers and blacks would each qualify for political recognition. Another way would be to combine two dimensions, so that women workers, black women and black workers would count as separate groups. Then again, it would be possible to use all three dimensions, so that white women workers, black women workers, white middle-class women and so forth would each count as distinct categories. Which way is the right way?

Young's answer, in general, is that the more separately identifiable groups people want to have, the more there should be. She appeals to the idea of the affinity group.

> My 'affinity group' in a given social situation comprises those people with whom I feel the most comfortable, who are more familiar. Affinity names the manner of sharing assumptions, affective bonding, and networking that recognizably differentiates groups from one another, but not according to some common nature. The salience of a particular person's group affinities may shift according to the social situation or according to changes in her or his life. . . . Group identity is constructed from a flowing process in which individuals identify themselves and others in terms of groups, and thus group identity itself flows and shifts with changes in social process.[19]

This account fits in well with the analysis of ethnic and other group identities offered in the last section, where I was at pains to stress that such identities should be regarded not as fixed and primordial, but as fluid and open, both at the level of the group and at the level of individual members. But it poses severe difficulties for the idea of group representation and the other practical components of the politics of recognition. For what such a politics inevitably does is to fix and privilege certain group identities at the expense of others. If women are selected as one of the groups to enjoy special rights of representation, policy vetoes and so forth, then a subset of women – lesbian women, for instance – cannot also enjoy such rights. Suppose an affinity group of lesbians is formed and applies for group recognition. Would this involve retrenching on the political rights already granted to women in general, or creating new rights (and if the latter, what happens to the idea that groups should enjoy a veto over certain policy issues)?

This might seem at first glance to be merely a question of practical detail. But in fact it demonstrates the incoherence involved in defending identity politics in tandem with the claim that group identities are not pre-given and fixed but continually remade according to the affinities felt by different individuals. For identity politics cannot be infinitely flexible. It must designate certain groups for political recognition, fix their membership and determine what rights they are going to enjoy. In practice it relies on taking some characteristic such as gender or race that can be readily identified in the great majority of cases and using this as the basis for group classification. This may or may not work politically – I shall have more to say about this later – but in so far as it works it does so by fixing and privileging certain identities at the expense of others. It is simply not compatible with the claim that each person must be able continually to shift their preferred group identity on the basis of feelings of affinity.

A second problem concerns what it means for a group identity to be recognized politically. So far I have been deliberately vague about this, because it is not easy to explain the politics of recognition without resorting to vagueness. But now we must begin to be more explicit. What is being claimed, in respect of some group G, is first of all that those who are not members of G must understand what it means to be part of G, what the perspective of those who belong to G actually is. But second, this identity must be recognized as a valuable identity, indeed as an identity that is of equal value to the identities of groups outside G (a Muslim identity is of equal value to a Christian identity, a Jewish identity, etc.). Finally, this valuation must be expressed practically in policies that respect the demands of the group, for instance in policies that extend the privileges of non-G members to members of G (since a homosexual lifestyle is of equal value to a heterosexual lifestyle, gay men and lesbians should enjoy the same rights to sexual freedom, to marry, etc., as heterosexuals). Let us call these three elements of recognition comprehension, valuation and practical endorsement.

The first element, comprehension, presents no particular difficulties. Indeed it seems to me a powerful argument in favour of having group members present in political arenas in sufficient numbers to make their voices heard that this helps non-members to understand what really matters to members of G, to make sense of claims and demands that might at first sight seem trivial or irrelevant. Presence does not guarantee comprehension, but it comes close to being a necessary condition for it. And comprehension is surely essential to any view of politics which embodies the democratic principle that each person's voice should count equally. If we do not understand what members of G want and why they want it, we cannot even begin to weigh their demands equally against others.

Valuation and practical endorsement are, however, more problematic. For sometimes there will be a conflict between attaching value to the identity proclaimed by G and upholding your own values, whether these are group-specific or more general social values. Consider someone who believes in the values represented by the conventional two-parent family confronting a radical feminist group who argue that male–female conjugal relations are always exploitative, so that good personal relationships are only possible in same-sex couples.[20] Or consider a Christian facing an Islamic group who declare that their goal is to make Britain into an Islamic state.[21] In these cases valuing the identity espoused by the group facing you commits you to denying values you already hold: if you are a Christian, then you must believe that the Christian life is a valuable life, and therefore you cannot value the project of eradicating Christianity in the name of Islam.

To avoid misunderstanding, I do not mean to suggest that we can never find value in the lives of those who live by different standards than our own. If we take, not militant Islam of the kind referred to in the last paragraph, but Islamic religious identity of the more usual kind, it is perfectly possible for a Christian to value this identity while holding to Christian values. There is likely to be sufficient overlap in the virtues embodied in the two ways of life for the Christian to endorse the Muslim identity, even while recognizing that this is not an identity he or she would wish to embrace. The point I am making is that such valuation cannot be guaranteed in advance of knowing what particular identities we will be called on to endorse. To value something is to judge that it meets certain standards, and since our standards, even if they are broad, are not infinitely flexible, to seek unconditional ratification of group identities is not a reasonable demand.[22]

The same must apply to the third element, practical endorsement. To endorse the demands made by a group whose identity we do not find positively valuable would be to support what we find less valuable at the expense of what we find more valuable, and this cannot be reasonable. And even where the identity in question *is* regarded as a valuable one, there may still be conflicts over the distribution of freedom or over resource allocation. This means that not everything that the group demands can be accepted by outsiders. We may, for instance, find value in a feminist identity, and come to believe it important that children should be educated to understand the obstacles facing women, as well as the opportunities open to them. But how much curriculum time should be devoted to this in competition with, say, religious education? We cannot require that whatever feminist groups think is the right answer in this area must commend itself to all other groups, for they will have competing priorities which they can rightfully pursue.

I shall return shortly to the question of how such conflicts are to be resolved. What I wish to emphasize here is the dangerous and possibly counterproductive way in which the politics of recognition raises the stakes in relations between groups. Toleration requires groups to leave one another free to pursue their own values (within certain limits). The politics of inclusion requires that citizens deal with one another as equals, regardless of group identity. Neither requires groups actively to value one another's way of life or practices. The politics of recognition looks for such a positive valuation, but carries with it the risk that such valuation will be refused. And it also carries with it the near-certainty that some of the policies that particular groups cherish will not be enacted when political compromises are found. Radical feminists will be dismayed when it turns out that women are not given an absolute right of free choice over abortion; fundamentalist Christian groups will be equally dismayed when the sanctity of life is not fully respected in the case of the foetus. If these groups experience these defeats as failures of recognition, as devaluations of their identity as distinct social groups, a politics of equal respect is clearly going to be an impossibility.

Group identities and nationality

I have so far made two critical observations on the politics of recognition. The first is that there appears to be a severe tension, perhaps even contradiction, between recognizing the openness and fluidity of group identities in contemporary liberal societies and seeking to ensconce certain groups in the political system, giving them rights of access and policy vetoes which by definition are denied to other groups. The second is that political recognition – where this includes the positive valuation and practical endorsement of group identities and not merely their comprehension – cannot be universally guaranteed in advance. It may simply be impossible for some groups to recognize and endorse certain other groups in the way that is required without violating their own identities. Toleration may be possible, but recognition is not. The politics of recognition is liable to backfire by exposing groups to outright rejections and rebuffs which they would not experience under a less politically charged regime of toleration.

But now I want to move on to a third and final issue which requires us to consider the relationship between ethnic and other such group identities and the more encompassing identities that people may have as members of national communities.[23] Here I should like to begin by stressing that the politics of recognition makes sense only if we assume that these more encompassing identities already exist. For why should it matter to me, as a member of group G, that my identity is endorsed by the members of groups A–F and H–Z? It matters only if these other people are 'significant others' – that is, people whose estimation of my practices and way of life affects my own sense of worth. We don't demand recognition from people who are complete strangers to us: all we demand is that our basic rights are respected, and in particular that we are left to get on with our lives in our own way. As I argued earlier, self-contained groups living in close proximity, such as the religious communities in medieval Europe, did not demand recognition (in our sense) from one another, but simple toleration. We ask for recognition from those with whom we already identify as members of a larger community such as a nation; and equally, we are only disposed to *grant* recognition to those with whom we already have this identifying bond.

This point is worth stressing because advocates of the politics of recognition often seek to disparage these larger identities as artefacts of the dominant groups which members of oppressed and disadvantaged groups should repudiate. Young argues that the idea of the unified nation is associated with the idea of a homogeneous public which excludes deviant groups, especially groups such as women and gays whose identities are conceived of in bodily terms (in contrast to the rationality of the bourgeois heterosexual male).[24] It follows that a 'just polity' should be radically heterogeneous:

> Group differences of gender, age, and sexuality should not be ignored, but publicly acknowledged and accepted. Even more so should group differences of nation or ethnicity be accepted. In the twentieth century the ideal state is composed of a plurality of nations or cultural groups, with a degree of self-determination and autonomy compatible with federated equal rights and obligations of citizenship.[25]

Young reaches this conclusion partly because she equates the ideal of national unity with the idea that minority groups should be forced to abandon their native cultures in order to assimilate to a single national culture. For instance, in the case of language policy, she interprets the policy of making English the official language of the United States as involving the forcible assimilation of other language groups and indeed as requiring 'self-annihilation' on the part of cultural minorities.[26] But in fact it is quite possible to treat English as the public language of the state, and to require everyone to acquire competence in the language as a prerequisite of citizenship, while at the same time recognizing and indeed encouraging the transmission of other languages as the first languages of particular ethnic groups.[27] This illustrates the general fallacy in regarding common nationality as implying cultural homogeneity: there can be a shared public culture which defines the national identity (including in most cases a national language) alongside a plurality of private cultures which help define people's identities as members of sectional groups (including perhaps minority languages). Although there will be points of tension between the two sets of cultural values, nothing has been said by Young or other supporters of the politics of difference to show why such co-existence is impossible.

Minority groups do not currently seek to promote their own identities at the expense of shared national identities; on the contrary, they are often especially eager to affirm their commitment to the nation in order to pre-empt the accusation that their cultural differences must make them dis-loyal citizens, and for other reasons.[28] But suppose, following the logic of the politics of difference, that groups were to abandon their national allegiances, identifying themselves exclusively in terms of their group membership. What would politics be like in a state composed of such groups? It would inevitably take the form of bargaining in which each group used the resources available to it in order to promote its material and cultural interests. No group has any particular reason to accede to the demands of any other, unless it can gain some advantage from doing so. Appeals to the common good or to obligations of justice would fall on deaf ears in these circumstances, since in the absence of a common identity or sense of belonging, each group would interpret such appeals as mere masks for the interests and perspectives of the group making them. In short this would, at best, be interest group politics with the gloves off.[29]

This is not at all the kind of politics that advocates of the politics of recognition envisage. They seek a form of politics in which groups, having worked up a genuine set of demands through dialogue within the group, can appeal to standards of justice accepted by other groups in order to get those demands accepted. As Young puts it, 'In a humanist emancipatory politics, if a group is subject to injustice, then all those interested in a just society should unite to combat the powers that perpetuate that injustice. If many groups are subject to injustice, more-over, then they should unite to work for a just society.'[30] And she explicitly contrasts a politics of this sort with interest group pluralism, under which:

> Each interest group promotes its own specific interest as thoroughly and forcefully as it can, and need not consider the other interests competing in the political marketplace except strategically, as potential allies or adversaries in its own pursuit. The rules of interest-group pluralism do not require justifying one's interest as right, or compatible with social justice. A heterogeneous public, however, is a *public*, where participants discuss together the issues before them and come to a decision according to principles of justice.[31]

The question, therefore, is under what conditions this picture of a heterogeneous public reaching decisions according to principles of justice becomes possible. As far as principles of justice are concerned, it has two aspects, one cognitive, the other motivational: under what circumstances will people come to sufficient agreement about principles of social justice for these principles to guide them in reaching collective decisions? And, under what circumstances will people be motivated to deal with one another's demands on the basis of principles of justice rather than on the basis of interest-bargaining (or indeed some more violent method of conflict resolution)?

It seems clear to me that an adequate answer to both questions must involve the idea of a community with a shared way of life which serves both as a source of ethical standards and as a framework within which people will want to justify their decisions to one another by reference to criteria of justice. I have argued this in several other places and do not want to repeat the argument here.[32] If our concern is with the politics of the state, the community in question must be the nation. Thus a common nationality provides the only feasible background against which diverse groups can resolve their differences by appeal to even partially shared standards of justice. If we want to encourage group diversity while at the same time favouring a democratic politics that aims at social justice, then rather than trying to dissipate national identities we should be aiming to consolidate them.

Young believes that a concern for justice will spring from the requirement that groups must justify their policy preferences to other groups with different experiences. This will expose the hypocrisy that now allows group interests to be passed off as common interests. It is certainly true that ensuring the presence of hitherto excluded groups in the political realm may have this desirable effect. But the crucial condition, once again, is the desire to reach agreement in terms of justice.[33] If this desire is lacking, then a group which has its hypocrisy unmasked will not be troubled by that fact; it will simply engage more openly in the politics of interest bargaining. At certain points Young appears to rely on the idea of a majority Rainbow Coalition of disadvantaged groups acting together to win concessions from the rich and powerful, but again this relies on the emergence of shared commitments and shared standards of justice to bind the coalition together, and as we know empirically this is not very likely to occur (think of the sharp differences between white and black manual workers over the justice of affirmative action, for example). Confronting other groups with different perspectives and different demands does not entail seeing the justice of those demands; it may simply have the effect of alienating groups from each other. If citizens lack a sense of common identity that transcends the particularity of their group identities, the prospects of achieving social justice are very remote.

Conclusion

This chapter has been critical of the politics of recognition, which I have sought to present as an understandable yet misguided response to the unsettling and breaking up of personal identities in contemporary liberal societies. In essence identity politics is self-defeating, for it looks to politics to provide a confirmation of identities that the political sphere by its very nature cannot provide; and in encouraging groups to affirm their singular identities at the expense of shared national identities, it undermines the very conditions in which minority groups, especially disadvantaged groups, can hope to achieve some measure of justice for their demands.[34]

To say this is not to say that groups and group identities should be regarded as politically irrelevant. There has recently been a good deal of discussion of the circumstances in which groups may be justified in claiming special rights as groups, in the light of the disadvantages suffered by their members simply by virtue of belonging to the group.[35] I do not wish to pre-empt the outcome of this debate, but simply to observe that the argument in favour of group rights can be made by appeal to standards of justice that are widely shared and not specific to any groups in particular. Thus a republican form of politics, in which group members enter the political arena as citizens and present their claims not in terms of group identity but in terms of principles and precedents that are already embedded in the practice of the political community, is consistent with groups being granted special rights. Indeed it is essential to republican politics that every significant political standpoint is represented in the political arena, so that the decisions that emerge represent either a consensus or at least a fair compromise between the range of views held in the community; this entails that whatever system of representation is chosen should ensure as far as possible that members of each group are present in legislative assemblies and other political forums.[36] This also entails a return to the politics of inclusion, and a continuation of the battle to free the public sphere of symbols, practices and unstated assumptions that prevent the members of some groups from participating as equal citizens. I do not mean that the public sphere should become culturally neutral: it expresses the shared national identity of the citizens, and this must have some determinate content that varies from place to place. But national identities have always been in a state of flux, and the challenge now is to remake them in a way that is more hospitable to women, ethnic minorities and other groups without emptying them of content and destroying the underpinnings of democratic politics.

5
Bounded Citizenship

In this chapter I shall argue that the practice of citizenship must, for as far ahead as we can reasonably envisage, be confined within the boundaries of national political communities. I shall argue, in other words, that those who aspire to create transnational or global forms of citizenship have failed to understand the conditions under which genuine citizenship is possible. Either their aims are simply utopian, or else what they aspire to is not properly described as citizenship. So I shall begin by saying something about what citizenship actually means, what is involved in someone being a citizen, and then go on to address the question where (if anywhere) the boundaries of citizenship must lie.

Let me enter two caveats straight away so that the scope of my argument isn't misunderstood. First I am not in the business of defending what in the international relations literature is called 'realism': the idea that neither political communities nor their individual members have moral obligations to outsiders, that morality stops at the borders of the nation-state. What I have to say is consistent with the view that there are international obligations of justice, for instance. What these obligations might be is the subject of another paper.[1] All I am doing in this chapter is denying that the way to discharge those obligations is through strengthening or creating transnational practices of citizenship.

Second, the position I am defending could be attacked from precisely the opposite direction. My target is those who want to push the bounds of citizenship beyond nation-states with their present extent, which as we know can encompass hundreds of millions of people. It would be quite possible to argue that genuine citizenship is anyway not feasible in states of that size, but belongs rather within city-states on the scale of ancient Athens or Renaissance Florence. For what it is worth, I think that this argument has greater force than the claim that citizenship should become transnational or global. But I shall not pursue this point at length, except for some remarks about Rousseau, who I believe admirably articulates this small-is-necessary perspective on citizenship.

The meaning of citizenship

If we are going to talk about the boundaries of citizenship, we first need to get clear about what citizenship means. Unfortunately, like most concepts in political theory, this one is contested, in the sense that there are rival interpretations of its meaning which carry with them different normative implications. Citizenship is a valuable practice – we think that it is desirable for people to function effectively as citizens – but there is disagreement about what it entails. For present purposes I want simply to nail my colours to the mast and say that I shall be using a republican conception of citizenship. As I far as I can see, this is also the conception that inspires those who advocate transnational or global forms of citizenship, so I do not think that my premise begs any questions in this particular debate. My argument will be, however, that advocates of cosmopolitan forms of citizenship draw upon the republican conception without reflecting sufficiently on its preconditions – on the circumstances in which republican citizenship can be made to work.

The main rival to the republican conception of citizenship is the liberal conception according to which citizenship should be understood as a set of rights and corresponding obligations enjoyed equally by everyone who is a citizen of the political community in question.[2] To be a citizen is to enjoy rights to personal security, to freedom of speech, to vote and so forth; correspondingly one has an obligation to keep the law, and generally not to interfere with others' enjoyment of their rights. Central to the liberal view is the idea of a fair balance of rights and obligations: we can find this expressed in the now-classic exposition by T.H. Marshall and more recently in the work of Rawls.[3] By contrast, the republican conception, while not denying the importance of citizen rights, places more weight on the idea of the active citizen who takes part along with others in shaping the future direction of his or her society through political debate. Citizenship here is less a legal status (though it must of course be that too) than a role which the citizen assumes as a full member of his or her community. To be a citizen one must think and behave in a certain way: one must have a sufficient measure of what the older republican tradition called public virtue.[4]

To spell this out more fully, one can think of republican citizenship as having four main components, the first two of which it shares with the liberal conception, while the second two are distinctively republican. First, the republican citizen securely enjoys a set of equal rights, which are necessary both in order to carry out private aims and purposes and in order to play her public role. Many rights have this dual aspect: rights to property and free speech, for instance, can be seen both as enabling people to pursue their individual plans of life and personal ideals, and as preconditions for active citizenship; without a certain degree of economic independence and without the right to speak one's mind freely, one cannot be an effective participant in public discussion. Second, corresponding to these rights are a set of obligations: to respect the law (which does not mean being obliged to obey it on occasions when it seems radically unjust), to pay taxes in the interests of social justice, to serve on juries when called on to do so, and so on. The rationale for these is straightforward and need not be spelt out here.

Rights and obligations are important, but on the republican view citizenship involves more than these. It involves, third, being willing to take active steps to defend the rights of other members of the political community, and more generally to promote its common interests. The citizen is someone who goes to the aid of a fellow-citizen who collapses in the street, or who intervenes when he is able to prevent a criminal act being committed. In Britain we are likely to think of Philip Lawrence, the headmaster stabbed to death outside his school, as a good citizen, because he did more than he was legally or morally obliged to do. He felt a responsibility for the safety of his pupils in public space outside of the school gate, and in trying to protect them he gave an exemplary demonstration of what citizenship in this aspect may involve. For another example, consider the civil servant who blows the whistle on some corrupt act of government at the possible cost of her career. Finally under this heading, the citizen is someone who is ready to volunteer for public service when the need arises. The older republican tradition placed especial emphasis on military service here, with the idea that republics must depend upon a citizen militia rather than a mercenary or conscript army, but arguably technological changes in warfare have rendered this idea obsolete (unless you are Israeli or Swiss?). Public service now is more likely to take place within civil society, in revamping the village hall so that it can be used for a kids' playgroup, in volunteer work restoring damaged wildlife habitats, and so forth. What makes this part of citizenship is that it is done with an eye to the community's good; it is public-spirited work.

Fourth and last, the republican citizen plays an active role in both the formal and informal arenas of politics. Political participation is not undertaken simply in order to check the excesses of government – voting out a corrupt administration – or in order to promote sectional interests – lobbying for the producer group that you belong to – but as a way of expressing your commitment to the community. Because the citizen identifies with it, he or she wants to have a say in what it does. And he or she also wants as far as possible to reach an agreement with other citizens so that what is done is done in the name of all of them. Of course this is an ideal condition: in reality no decision is ever going to be unanimous. But if political debate is conducted with agreement as a regulative ideal, this means searching for policies that everyone can potentially endorse; or, to put it the other way round, not advocating policies that you know other people have principled objections to when there are feasible alternatives.

Republican citizenship as I have described it is an ideal that most of us fall far short of in practice. The question to ask about it is not whether we can envisage a society every member of which behaves as a perfect citizen – the answer to that is obvious enough – but whether political life in modern democracies can be guided by the republican ideal, in the sense that it can form a benchmark that we appeal to when assessing how well our institutions and practices are functioning. Here it is relevant to examine whether people do actually understand what it means to be a citizen in terms that correspond to the republican ideal. Some research has been done on this, and it reveals that ordinary members of the public are somewhat divided as between the liberal and republican conceptions as I have sketched them – some people thinking of citizenship mainly in terms of rights and duties, others thinking of it as involving community membership and a responsibility to promote the community's welfare actively.[5] Interestingly the status of citizen is rarely seen as marginal or remote: on the contrary, for the great majority of people it forms a core part of their identity.[6] The issue is not whether people feel themselves to be citizens, but the extent to which they act on that understanding in their everyday lives. Even here, however, recent studies suggest that fears about the decline of citizenship in liberal democracies have been exaggerated, and that people are as active now in their role as citizens as they ever have been; the changes that have taken place are not in the extent to which people behave as active citizens, but in their mode of political participation (essentially there has been a shift away from party politics towards non-institutional forms of participation, such as demonstrations and other forms of direct action).[7]

I don't want to dwell here on citizenship as it is currently practised. The point I do want to emphasize is just how demanding republican citizenship is. It is demanding in two respects. First it requires citizens to be sufficiently motivated to carry out the tasks – political and sub-political – that citizenship involves. These impose costs on a person's time, and may often not be experienced as pleasant (Jane Mansbridge's study of New England town meetings showed how some inhabitants preferred not to attend because they disliked having to disagree and argue in public with their neighbours).[8] The goods that are created through active citizenship are public benefits, whether in the tangible form of the restored village hall, or in the less tangible form of having laws and policies that reflect the majority's wishes and are to that extent seen as legitimate. Whether these public benefits are created or not does not depend on my participation, except in very unusual cases. The hall will be available for my children's use whether or not I personally take part in refurbishing it; what is decided by a vote or a referendum will not be affected by my own individual participation or abstention. Nor are there effective social mechanisms giving people an incentive to act as citizens: whereas in a small community such as a kibbutz, it quickly becomes obvious whether someone is pulling his weight or not, and carrots and sticks can be applied, in a city (let alone an extended nation) public reputation cannot motivate citizenship. No one suffers if they fail to vote or to attend public meetings, and although honours may be conferred for outstanding acts of public service, these are not really incentives so much as expressions of the citizenship ideal; morally important, certainly, but hardly effective in overcoming the collective action problems that citizenship imposes.

The other respect in which republican citizenship is demanding is that it requires citizens to act responsibly. They have not merely to get involved in public decision-making, but they have to try to promote the common good. This involves, for instance, taking a long-term view of the community's interests rather than a short-term one. It involves recognizing when trade-offs have to be made between different objectives and trying to achieve a consistent balance so that, for instance, you do not find yourself simultaneously voting for tax cuts and for an expanded public health service. Above all, it involves being willing to set aside personal interests and personal ideals in the interests of achieving a democratic consensus. So, for instance, you may have strong religious convictions about the sanctity of the Sabbath day, but rather than trying to enforce these in a multicultural society – even if you find yourself in a majority – you try to find a way of accommodating the convictions of each group in a fair compromise. As Rousseau would have put it, you ask not 'What is my particular or group will on this matter?' but 'What is the general will on this matter?' which may require a very considerable effort of self-discipline.

Unfortunately these two conditions of citizenship – motivation and responsibility – may work against each other. The person who is willing to take up a public role regardless of personal cost may also be the person who is single-mindedly committed to a particular ideal or interest and is therefore not responsible in my sense. Convinced of the rightness of his or her cause, such a person may not be willing to listen to the arguments of those who do not share the same assumptions, and therefore not be moved to look for a basis for agreement. Those who are most active on Green issues – opposing the building of new roads, for instance – may hold 'deep ecology' views which rule out any compromise with more conventional defenders of economic growth. The idealism which makes you willing to camp out in the depths of winter to block the bulldozers may also make it hard for you to see that ecological concerns have to be set against jobs, goods and services when policies are made. I do not mean to categorize the anti-road campaigners as irresponsible in their actions. There is a good case that given the weight of interests behind the road-building programme, single-minded opposition is necessary in order to achieve any sort of compromise. But if these issues were to be decided in the more open and democratic way that republican citizenship demands, Green activists would need to learn a different kind of responsibility; the responsibility that involves recognizing that your concerns have to be taken alongside the equally legitimate concerns of others whose priorities are different.

Responsibility involves a collective action problem too: there is an obvious temptation to free ride on others' willingness to moderate their demands in the course of public deliberation. Jon Elster tells the story of two boys coming across a cake that they would both like to eat. 'I want the whole cake' says the first boy; 'Let's be fair and divide it half each' says the second; an adult intervenes to avoid a fight: 'You should *compromise*. Give him three-quarters and take the last quarter yourself.'[9] The story shows that trying to achieve fairness only makes sense when most other people are doing the same; if others are simply pushing their interests it may actually lead to a fairer outcome if you do likewise. So to act as a responsible citizen, you must have reasonable assurance that a large majority of your fellow-citizens are going to do the same.

This is, of course, why the republican tradition placed so much emphasis on cultivating public virtue, and on taking steps to ward off corruption, which amounted to placing private interests before public responsibilities. The general assumption was that this required strong patriotic loyalty which was best achieved in a fairly small city-state. In *The Social Contract* Rousseau cites 'the waning of patriotism, the pursuit of private interests, the vastness of states' as complementary factors leading men to abandon active citizenship.[10] When the 'social bond is broken in every heart', he says, 'the general will becomes mute: everyone, guided by secret motives, expresses opinions no more like those of a citizen than if the state had never existed, and iniquitous decrees which have no other end than the private interest, are falsely passed under the name of laws'.[11] He gives the converse argument in the *Discourse on Political Economy*: 'Do we want peoples to be virtuous? If so, let us begin by making them love their homeland. But how will they come to love it, if their homeland means nothing more to them than it does to foreigners, and if it grants to them only what it cannot refuse to anyone?'[12] When confronted with the question of how to design a constitution for an extensive state – Poland – Rousseau offers an elaborate menu of suggestions – compulsory wearing of the national costume, special sporting events and festivals, and so forth – to instil an exclusive national consciousness in the would-be citizens. He lays special emphasis on the system of education.

> It is education that must give souls a national formation, and direct their opinions and tastes in such a way that they will be patriotic by inclination, by passion, by necessity. When he first opens his eyes, an infant ought to see the fatherland, and up to the day of his death he ought never to see anything else. Every true republican has drunk in love of country, that is to say love of law and liberty, along with his mother's milk. This love is his whole existence; he sees nothing but the fatherland; he lives for it alone; . . . [13]

Some commentators have seen Rousseau's *Government of Poland* as marking a point of transition between the city-state republicanism of *The Social Contract* and later nationalist doctrines.[14] In any case I want to argue that nationality has served as at least a partial replacement for the patriotic loyalty of the city-state as a foundation for republican citizenship. The nation as a focus of identity and allegiance appeared on the scene when increasing mobility and more effective means of communication, especially the printed word, made it possible for large aggregates of people to conceive of themselves as members of communities with a specific cultural character that set them apart from their neighbours. Rousseau's citizens were supposed to gather face to face under the shade of an oak to make laws. If modern social conditions make this impossible, something else must generate the trust and loyalty that citizenship requires. Common nationality has served this purpose in the advanced societies.[15] In arguing in this way I do not mean to imply that national identities were simply conjured up for reasons of political convenience. To begin with, they arose out of pre-existing ethnic identities, usually the ethnic identity of the dominant group in the relevant state. Moreover different social groups sought to mould national consciousness in different directions. Ruling elites wanted to create loyal subjects who would be willing, for instance, to fight on behalf of the state. But other groups – first the middle classes, then the working class and afterwards women – advanced understandings of nationality (and indeed of citizenship) that justified their own claims for admission to the political realm. In the course of the French Revolution, for instance, we find numerous invocations of the nation as the source of political legitimacy, and politically-charged definitions of membership: for instance Sieyès' claim that the caste of nobles cannot be assigned any place in the nation.[16]

What I am suggesting is that national identities in their developed form emerged as a by-product of the interplay between different groups competing for power, but once established they enabled large masses of people to work together as citizens. One test of this argument is to see whether we can find states whose members lack such common identities but are none the less democratic. The search will, I confidently predict, be in vain. Genuinely multinational states have either been held together by force, as was the old Soviet Union, or else have been empires which allowed a substantial degree of self-determination to their constituent parts. Neither of these possibilities makes for flourishing citizenship on the republican model. In its later stages the Habsburg empire allowed its subjects a good deal of personal liberty and cultural tolerance, but no one would hold it up as a good example of citizens actively exercising their democratic rights.

All our experience of citizenship, then, has so far been of bounded citizenship: initially citizenship within the walls of the city-state, later citizenship within the cultural limits of the nation-state. These boundaries have been actively policed. Admission to citizenship has always come with strings attached. It is common in this field to contrast the German model of citizenship with the French.[17] The German model gives citizenship a strongly ethnic basis: to become a German citizen you must be of German descent. This means on the one hand that immigrants are excluded, and even those born in Germany to non-citizens do not qualify; on the other hand people outside the state of correct descent – ethnic Germans from Eastern Europe, for instance – have been immediately granted citizenship rights on entering Germany. The French model, by contrast, works on the principle that every inhabitant of the territory of France should be eligible for citizenship, but alongside this have gone strong policies to ensure that each citizen should absorb sufficient doses of French national culture, through the education system in particular. The German model extends citizenship to all and only those it sees as German nationals by ethnic criteria; the French model works hard to make immigrants into Frenchmen, as earlier it worked hard to make peasants into Frenchmen, to quote the title of Eugene Weber's well-known book.[18]

I happen to favour the French version of citizenship, but the point here is not to adjudicate between them. The point rather is that citizenship is, and has been seen to be, a valuable status, and states therefore naturally wish to restrict its possession to those who identify themselves with the nation and are carriers of the right cultural identity. In the light of my earlier argument this is understandable: to give citizenship rights freely to all-comers is to risk undermining the conditions of mutual trust and assurance that make responsible citizenship possible. Of course citizenship in practice falls much closer to the liberal model than to the republican model, even in countries like France which have a strong republican tradition to call upon. But even liberal citizenship depends on a certain level of reciprocity: people must vote responsibly, must carry out whatever public duties are required of them, and so forth. Anyone who is unable or unwilling to do these things is free-riding on those who comply, and no social practice based on reciprocity will survive once free-riding exceeds a certain minimum point. So either active steps must be taken to instil the ethos of citizenship in everyone who is formally admitted to that status, which is the French approach, or a separate class of non-citizens is created, who are not expected to assume the responsibilities of citizenship, but who in return are not accorded full rights of citizenship either, which until recently has been the German practice.

There are of course circumstances in which it is impossible to appeal to a shared national identity as a basis for citizenship. This would be true of states whose members saw themselves as belonging to rival nationalities or which contained minority groups some of whom identified themselves with groups in neighbouring states. One solution to this may be to redraw state boundaries,[19] but if this cannot be done then a political structure has to be created that will allow the different communities to live together in comparative harmony – for instance a form of consociational democracy. The point I want to make is that this may be unavoidable, but it has to be regarded as a second best by anyone who aspires to republican citizenship. The idea of a purely political citizenship, unsupported by a shared public culture, is unfeasible for the reasons I have already given.[20]

Against cosmopolitan citizenship

Up to this point I have sketched in a normative model of republican citizenship, and argued that in the modern world citizenship of this kind has necessarily been confined within national boundaries. But now I want to move on to consider arguments for expanding or even perhaps obliterating those borders. The core of the argument is that the self-contained and self-determining nation-state has become an anachronism in the late twentieth century, so a version of citizenship that remains tied to that institution is equally outmoded.

In fact advocates of cosmopolitan citizenship tend to run two different arguments in parallel. One is empirical and concerns the extent to which the policy options open to contemporary states are constrained by the twin forces of the global economic market and the actions of other states. This argument has become so familiar that there is no need to spell it out at any length.[21] But essentially it says that on the one hand the international mobility of capital is now so great that any state wanting to participate in the global market finds that its hands are tied economically: for instance, if it tries to give enhanced protection to workers' rights, let alone something more ambitious like the Swedish Meidner plan for giving workers' organizations a stake in the ownership of enterprises, it will simply provoke international corporations into moving their operations elsewhere. On the other hand, each state finds itself at the mercy of other states in fields such as environmental protection and conservation. The British government cannot, acting alone, effectively introduce a plan to conserve the fish stocks around British coasts, because if it does so Spanish trawlers will simply come in and snap up the fish. An effective conservation plan depends on agreement between states working together. Since citizenship is supposed to be an instrument of self-determination, it follows that it must now be exercised at levels higher than the nation-state: at regional or even global level, depending on the issue that is at stake. That is the empirical argument for transnational citizenship.

The moral argument is also fairly familiar. There is no reason to think of people's moral obligations as confined within national or state boundaries. In particular we increasingly think in terms of universal human rights whose protection cannot be guaranteed within such boundaries. So we need to create cosmopolitan forms of citizenship in order to ensure that these rights are protected, and perhaps more generally to discharge our duties to people outside the borders of our state.

Notice that the empirical argument and the moral argument are independent from one another, even though they are frequently run together in practice. Sometimes it is said that it is the fact of our increasing economic and political independence that creates the obligations appealed to by the second argument. Charles Beitz once attempted to make such a link.[22] Picking up the Rawlsian idea that principles of justice apply only among people who are co-operating for their mutual advantage, he argued that it was the fact of international economic interdependence that now made it appropriate to apply Rawlsian principles on a global scale. But this argument does not work: it has never appealed to Rawls himself, and Beitz himself later withdrew it.[23] Any links between the empirical argument and the moral argument are of a much more mundane sort. If actions undertaken by members of one state have an increasing impact on the lives of members of another state, and if there is an independently derived set of rights and obligations that apply to those actions, then the empirical change triggers the obligations. For instance, people have an obligation not to damage one another's environment by polluting it. With the development of new forms of power generation, new kinds of pollution – acid rain, nuclear fall-out – become possible which were not possible before. So Britons now have concrete obligations to the Scandinavians which are triggered by the fact that westerly winds carry sulphur dioxide from British power stations to Norwegian lakes. But the basis for the obligations was there all along. Perhaps the empirical development makes us more actively aware of our obligation not to damage other people's environment, but it does not create it.

I am insisting on keeping separate the empirical argument and the moral argument for transnational citizenship because they lead in quite different directions. The empirical argument says that effective self-determination can only be achieved through creating transnational institutions of citizenship; the moral argument says that we have international obligations which we can only discharge through such institutions. These are quite distinct claims, and nothing is gained by running them together. Both, I shall now try to show, are vulnerable to the charge that they fail to take seriously the preconditions for citizenship.

What, more precisely, is proposed by those who advocate cosmopolitan citizenship? Precision is a commodity in short supply in this area, but drawing upon recent writings by David Held and Richard Falk, we can detect the outlines of three main ideas.[24] One is the idea of what Held calls a cosmopolitan democratic law, a legal framework which would serve both to regulate conflict between states and to give recourse to individual citizens whose rights had been violated by their own states. In other words, state sovereignty should be constrained by international law enforced by international courts, of which the European Court of Justice (ECJ) is often taken to be the prototype. Next, there is the idea that democratic citizenship needs to be exercised at many different territorial levels depending on the issues that are at stake; in other words, there should be concentric circles of citizenship in which either direct or representative democracy should be practised. Held says, for instance, that his model of cosmopolitan democracy 'anticipates the possibility of general referenda cutting across nations and nation-states in the case of contested priorities concerning the implementation of democratic law and the balance of public expenditure, with constituencies defined according to the nature and scope of disputed problems'.[25] Finally it is argued that people should also act as citizens within a global civil society (that is to say, as members of transnational groupings with a particular concern or interest): for instance environmental groups, or groups of lawyers concerned about the international protection of human rights.

Falk refers to the members of such groups as 'citizen pilgrims', and describes them in the following terms: 'They are committed more or less consciously to the construction of a compassionate global polity in the decades ahead, having already transferred their loyalties to the invisible political community of their hopes and dreams, one which could exist in future time but is nowhere currently embodied in the life-world of the planet.'[26]

Let me consider each of these three ideas in turn. First, there is the idea of cosmopolitan democratic law. On closer inspection this turns out to have two distinct components. One is that states should settle their disputes not by the time-honoured methods of force and economic pressure, but by appeal to a commonly agreed set of principles which are recognized as having the status of law and which, presumably, would be applied by an international body such as a reformed UN. This is plainly desirable, nor does it seem a wholly unrealistic objective as far as the democratic states are concerned. Equally there are serious difficulties in envisaging what would bring existing non-democratic states under the aegis of this cosmopolitan law: what incentive there would be for these states to subject themselves to such external regulation, or what incentive the liberal democracies have to make cosmopolitan law apply effectively to non-democratic states. It may be that we have already passed the high point of UN willingness to intervene to resolve conflicts involving such states.[27] However the main point I want to make is a different one. Whatever the chances are that we can create a more effective piece of machinery for conflict resolution, this still has to do with relations between states and nothing directly to do with citizenship. One does not become a cosmopolitan citizen because the state one belongs to is subject to a body of international law any more than one becomes a 'corporate citizen', say, because the firm one works for is subject to industrial law. The part of the cosmopolitan citizenship package which is most feasible to aim for turns out to have nothing to do with citizenship itself.

On the other hand, the idea that individual people should be able to invoke international law against their own states does bring us closer to a recognizable ideal of citizenship. About this I want to make two points. First, the kind of citizenship that is at issue here is at most a thin version of liberal citizenship. The citizen is not a law-maker except perhaps in the very indirect sense that she has at some point ratified the agreement whereby her state recognizes the authority of the court to which she takes her case. Apart from this, her role as citizen consists in asserting her rights against the state, and appealing to a higher court to make good her claim that her state has violated those rights. This involves no reciprocal recognition of obligations and no public activity; it is essentially the action of a private person. Let me make it clear that I am not denigrating such an action. If the state has acted unjustly, and it is possible to put the injustice right by invoking transnational or international law, that is all to the good. But only a minimal kind of citizenship is involved when this occurs.

My second point is to ask why the international enforcement of citizens' rights should be preferred to domestic enforcement. Instead of setting up international courts of human rights, why not ensure that each state has in place an effective constitutional mechanism for protecting the rights of its own citizens? In the world of the present, international courts are important for two main reasons. First, in the case of liberal-democratic states like Britain that have only weak mechanisms for protecting basic rights, they may serve as an effective check on government in certain cases. Following a ruling of such a court, the government may feel obliged to alter legislation or policy as the British government has in response to decisions by the ECJ.[28] Second, in the case of non-democratic states, international agreements and court decisions can be used as moral ammunition, putting pressure on these states to adopt better human rights policies. In these cases, nobody expects the ruling of an international court to be implemented directly by the government of, say, Burma or the People's Republic of China, but it can none the less be a useful propaganda weapon in dealing with such states.

This second function is likely to remain important for as far ahead as we can see. As far as the first function is concerned – rights protection within states that are already democratic   the issue is whether this is not better performed by a domestic constitutional court. It may be held that such a court will lack the guaranteed independence of an international court. Against this I would press the following question: apart from a core of basic human rights which should be recognized globally, are democratic states not entitled to define the rights of their citizens in different ways, depending on the political culture of a particular national community? In the field of social provision, for instance, should rights not reflect different understandings of social justice and individual need? If the citizens of one state decide to opt for an entirely public system of education, while their neighbours prefer a mixture of public and private provision, why should a transnational court adjudicate on citizens' rights (discovering, say, a right to private education and applying it to both states)? I am arguing, in other words, that where domestic protection of citizens' rights is feasible, as it is in all liberal democracies, citizenship is better served by constitutional reform within those states, than by the creation of transnational bodies, whose likely effect is to dilute the quality of citizenship by applying uniform criteria in fields where uniformity is neither necessary nor appropriate. In states with dilapidated constitutions, such as Britain, courts such as the ECJ and the European Court of Human Rights may have a valuable role to play in the short term, but a far better solution in the long term is to have an effective internal mechanism for protecting rights (for instance a powerful and independent constitutional court).

I am therefore sceptical of cosmopolitan law as a vehicle of *citizenship*, whatever other virtues it may have. Let me now return to the other ideas on the agenda of cosmopolitan citizenship. The second of these ideas is an expanded version of democracy, where instead of there being a single arena of citizenship – the nation-state – people would act as citizens in many such arenas, sub-national as well as transnational, with (as Held puts it) 'constituencies defined according to the nature and scope of disputed problems'. Here, I am afraid, my scepticism is even more severe. To begin with, unless politics as we know it is to vanish from the face of the earth, the problem of defining the relevant constituency to resolve a particular issue immediately becomes crucial. This can be illustrated by the familiar case of secession. If we say that the question whether a particular community should be permitted to secede from an existing state and constitute one of its own should be decided by a democratic referendum, then the scope of the constituency within which the refer-endum is to be held at once becomes the key issue. Should the future of Northern Ireland be decided by a vote of the Irish people as a whole, or by the inhabitants of Ulster? The point is a very obvious one, and can be extended to other issues, such as environmental questions, where the question who has a relevant interest in the environmental policy pursued by a particular political community may be hotly contested. Now this is not to say that there can never be agreement about the appropriate site for taking political decisions. But as far as I can see, the only possibility here is to have a proper constitution which specifies in advance which policy areas are to be assigned to which levels of decision-making: for instance something like the Spanish constitution which reserves to the regional governments authority over issues such as social welfare and language policy. Part of the reason that this can work is that it may not be clear in advance who will be winners and losers from any particular assignment of authority; the constitution is intended to be a relatively permanent fixture, and the precise issues that may arise under its aegis are unpre-dictable. To try to resolve the question issue by issue, on the other hand, would be fairly hopeless for the reason I have suggested: all the political manoeuvring would be directed towards defining the constituency within which the decision would be taken.

This is a fairly grave practical defect of Held's idea, in the absence of an international authority able to define in advance the proper constituen-cies for decisions of different sorts. From the perspective of citizenship, a second problem emerges. Suppose that it proves possible to define the relevant constituency to decide, say, an environmental issue, perhaps by referendum as Held envisages. Why should any member of that constituency behave as a responsible citizen, rather than voting merely according to personal or sectional interest? The constituency is created as an artificial body to decide this particular issue. Its members have no reason to expect that they will be called upon to decide things together in future. They are not involved in relations of reciprocity, whereby I may agree to promote your interest on this occasion on the understanding that you will support mine sometime in the future. Nor are they held together by communal ties or relationships of mutual trust. What creates the constituency is merely the physical fact that its members are so placed that their actions impact on one another: that there is, for instance, a pollution problem that arises from the physical proximity of the communities which make up the decision-making constituency. That fact does not make the members of the constituency into responsible citizens.

Of course it is possible that, notwithstanding the complete absence of the preconditions for responsible citizenship in the constituency I am envisaging, many people will behave and vote responsibly, trying to achieve a fair balance between the competing interests and priorities at stake. But if this happened it would be because the ideal of citizenship had become thoroughly ingrained in them, and they carried it over from their local or national community (where the preconditions for citizenship do exist) to the new level of decision. Even here, I think, there has to be some anticipation that others will behave responsibly too. But the main point is that such possibilities for transnational citizenship as may exist depend upon first strengthening citizenship and inculcating civic virtue within national boundaries, and then hoping that these qualities may carry across to wider constituencies.

We come finally to the global civil society argument, and in particular to Falk's idea of the 'citizen pilgrim' committed to the as-yet-unseen global polity of the future. It is worth pausing for a moment to reflect on 'citizen pilgrim', which is certainly an oxymoron, though it is less clear whether Falk recognizes it to be such. The etymology of the terms is interesting: 'citizen' originally referred to a town-dweller, and later more specifically to someone enjoying the rights and privileges of a burgess. It suggests someone firmly rooted in the life of a particular community, which also exerts a civilizing effect upon him.[29] 'Pilgrim', in complete contrast, originally meant a stranger or foreigner, a wandering person who might dwell for a time within the city but had no attachment to it. To this was then added the idea of someone journeying to a sacred place on a religious quest. The only city of which the pilgrim could be a citizen was the Heavenly Jerusalem.

In Falk's usage the pilgrim is a person devoted to a cause which she pursues with like-minded others regardless of conventional boundaries: a Greenpeace activist, for instance. Characteristically such a person will be driven by adherence to a particular conception of the good, to use Rawlsian language, which is also what makes the pilgrim metaphor somewhat apt. She is likely to try to convert others to the cause, but one thing she is not is a citizen as I have understood the term here. There is no determinate community with which she identifies politically, and no one, except perhaps other members of her group, with whom she stands in relations of reciprocity. So there is no group of fellow-citizens with whom she is committed to seeking grounds of agreement. If confronted by individuals who do not share her commitment to the cause, she must either convert them or oppose them by whatever means she has at her disposal. To say this is, once again, not to condemn her. If the cause is a good one, and she pursues it in a way that respects the rights of others (non-violently, for instance), she may act heroically and well – many of us, I am sure, will feel this about the Greenpeace campaigns on nuclear testing and whaling. But this is not citizenship in any but the most empty and inflated sense. The only quality that the pilgrim shares with the republican citizen is political motivation, and, as I argued earlier, this may conflict with the other condition of citizenship, which is responsibility.

Conclusion

It might be felt that the argument I have developed against cosmopolitan citizenship is merely a verbal one: if you mean by a citizen someone rooted in a bounded political community, then these other forms of political activity won't count as citizenship, but so what? I do not accept this reading. I take citizenship, especially in its republican form, to be an achievement of immense value. It represents the best way in which people of diverse beliefs and styles of life can live together under laws and institutions which they can endorse as legitimate. It is a social practice that needs bolstering by institutional change and civic education in the liberal democracies. But it has clear empirical preconditions; it cannot simply be conjured up *ex nihilo*. These preconditions are not as severe as Rousseau believed, but they exist none the less. International peace, international justice and global environmental protection are very important objectives, and we must hope that republican citizens will choose to promote them externally. But this cannot be achieved by inventing in theory cosmopolitan forms of citizenship which undercut the basis of citizenship proper.

6

Communitarianism: Left, Right and Centre

My title is meant to suggest two things about communitarianism. The first is that there is a lot of it around. I am not sure which political philosopher was the first to say 'I am a communitarian' in the way that Pierre-Joseph Proudhon founded the (self-conscious) anarchist tradition when he wrote, in 1840, 'I am an anarchist', but what is certain is that by the mid-1980s it was becoming common to speak of communitarianism as an ideological rival to liberalism;[1] soon after that, indeed, with the political collapse of socialism, and the passage of most conservatives into the libertarian New Right, as the main or only ideological rival. In political philosophy we learnt to talk of a liberal-communitarian debate – an idea that I shall be looking at critically in a moment. Not long after, there appeared a political movement of communitarians. There was the Communitarian Network founded by Etzioni, with threads stretching outwards from Washington to connect to chapters in European and other liberal democracies.[2] Politicians of the centre-left – Clinton and Blair, for instance – began regularly to invoke community in their speeches. And this seemed to catch the spirit of the age, which was preoccupied with issues such as crime and social order, drug abuse and homelessness – problems for which 'more community' in some sense seemed to offer a solution.

Yet communitarianism considered as a political programme was and remains strangely amorphous. Does it really provide a new perspective on politics, or is it merely a rhetorical device by which fairly standard liberal (in the American sense) or social-democratic (in the European sense) policies can be sold to the electorate? It is one thing to invoke community as a moral ideal, to encourage us all to be good neighbours, to keep our lawns neatly mown and try to ensure that children can walk safely to school along our streets. It is another thing to say that the state can legitimately enforce communal values, using the coercive apparatus at its disposal to oblige us to behave as good citizens. In avoiding the charge that they are moral totalitarians, communitarians seem to leave themselves open to the equally damaging charge, levelled by critics such as Stephen Holmes, that their attacks on liberalism are all hot air. 'Nebulousness about nonliberal politics', Holmes says, 'is not an incidental feature of communitarianism; it is an essential one.'[3] The charge is that communitarianism cannot deliver an alternative political programme; it is made up merely of a series of rhetorical attacks on the alleged premises of liberal theory.

At this point I want to draw out the second idea contained in my title. Communitarianism as political theory comes in sharply different versions. There is a communitarianism of the left, an egalitarian communitarianism defended by many socialists and social democrats. There is also a communitarianism of the right, an authoritarian communitarianism less popular today than it was in the past, but still embraced by some conservatives. And finally – this suggestion may be a bit less familiar – there is a liberal version of communitarianism. I shall try to bring out as clearly as I can the crucial features that differentiate these three forms of communitarianism, and I shall also try to show that each taken by itself has fairly definite political implications. In other words, even if communitarianism as an umbrella term is politically amorphous, the three doctrines sheltering under that umbrella that I shall identify are not.

I draw the distinction between left, right and centre not just for the sake of intellectual clarity, but because I want to defend a form of left communitarianism. One unfortunate effect of the liberal v. communitarian framework is that people are put under some pressure to declare which team they support, to use Charles Taylor's metaphor. It is of some interest here that among the political philosophers who are usually nominated for the communitarian team, none has shown himself enthusiastic about wearing the team colours. Taylor and Michael Walzer have both offered subtle diagnoses of why there has been the appearance of a liberal–communitarian debate, avoiding in doing so the need to declare for either side.[4] MacIntyre roundly declares that he has strongly dissociated himself from contemporary communitarians whenever he has had the opportunity to do so.[5] Michael Sandel did self-apply the communitarian label in his introduction to *Liberalism and its Critics* – the book which probably did most to inspire the two teams model – but in his more recent work chooses instead to describe himself as a republican.[6] If my claim that communitarianism comes in radically different versions is correct, this reluctance is hardly surprising: no one wants to sign up to something which is liable to place them in the same camp as others whose political views they heartily despise – Michael Walzer with Roger Scruton, for instance. Once the relevant distinctions are drawn, however, each can unashamedly espouse and defend his or her favoured version of communitarianism without fear of confusion or misunderstanding.

The liberal–communitarian debate

Let me now say briefly why it was misleading to speak of a debate between communitarians and liberals. Any political theory, I want to suggest, contains two analytically separable elements: on the one hand a philosophical anthropology, a general account of the human person, of the conditions of moral agency, of the nature of human relationships, and so forth. (This account may be implicit or explicit, but it is always there.) On the other hand, the theory will contain a set of prescriptive principles, principles specifying how social relationships are to be ordered, how the state is to be constituted and so on. The relationship between the philosophical anthropology and the prescriptive principles is one of support rather than entailment; the picture of human personhood helps to make plausible a certain political doctrine, but much additional legwork, often of a broadly empirical kind – claims about how different institutions are likely to function, for instance – needs to be done to back the doctrine up fully.[7]

If we apply this distinction between philosophical anthropology and prescriptive political doctrine to the case of communitarianism, we can see that what brings together those political thinkers who are called communitarians is primarily a convergence at the level of philosophical anthropology. As I shall argue in a minute, their political doctrines may be highly disparate. So what is the core element in a communitarian philosophical anthropology? It is a thesis about the social constitution of the self: the self cannot be understood apart from the social relations in which it is embedded. Putting this in different terms, the thesis is that we cannot understand human beings except against the background of social institutions, practices, forms of life which give them concrete identities. The contrast here is with individualism. For those who accept an individualist anthropology, the basic elements in the social world are individual human beings, each with the capacity to form their own beliefs, preferences and goals. The social world is made up of the practices and institutions that these individuals have created in order to pursue their aims in collaboration with one another. From a communitarian perspective, the individualist picture of the human condition is an incoherent one. It cannot make sense of the fact that we have identities that are not

STRANMILLIS
UNIVERSITY COLLEGi
BELFAST

reducible to contingent matters of preference and belief: in other words that when I ask the question 'Who am I?', the answer I give does not merely list features of myself that I could change tomorrow, like my job or my taste in music, but unchosen characteristics deriving from the social setting in which I was formed – my ancestry, my gender, my ethnicity.[8] Equally, communitarians claim, an individualist anthropology cannot make sense of our ethical experience: our capacity to judge things, including our own tastes, right or wrong in some objective sense.[9] The claim is that this capacity can only be understood against the background of a community which provides us with a language of shared evaluation. (Or, in the variant of this claim associated especially with Alasdair MacIntyre, it is that the relevant community has largely disappeared – only fragments are left – so moral evaluation collapses into subjective preference.)[10]

So here then we have two broad philosophical anthropologies: the individualist picture which sees people as independent, freely choosing agents, and the communitarian picture which sees them as essentially embedded in communal relations. It is a difficult task to say exactly what is the nature of the disagreement between the two pictures – how far the disagreement is strictly philosophical, and how far it might be amenable to resolution by appeal to empirical evidence, for instance – but fortunately for my present purposes there is no need to pursue this question any further. What I do want to argue is that when we use 'communitarianism' as an umbrella term embracing a range of social theorists whose political outlooks are often sharply at variance with one another, the proper contrast to draw is with individualism and not with liberalism. Communitarianism in this sense is a philosophical anthropology rather than a political doctrine.

So why did we start talking about a liberal–communitarian debate? The answer, I believe, is that a certain widely held form of liberalism, which for the sake of convenience rather than historical accuracy I shall call standard or mainstream liberalism, does have a natural affinity with individualist anthropology. People who are liberals of this sort characteristically defend their political positions by invoking an individualist view of the self. Mainstream liberalism typically involves such doctrines as the priority of rights (rights as trumps), the notion that the principles of a just social order should be established by reference to a hypothetical social contract, and the idea that the state should preserve its neutrality as between conceptions of the good life. These doctrines are very often defended by appealing to the picture of the individual as a freely choosing agent, and society as a set of arrangements designed or evolved to permit such individuals to pursue their ends. We can fairly easily point to examples of political philosophies which move in this way from individualist premises to mainstream liberal conclusions: Nozick's theory of rights, for instance, Rawls's theory of justice (particularly in its original version when the contractarian element was highlighted), Dworkin's theory of liberal equality.[11] Those critics who get classified as communitarians take exception to this pattern of argument; they claim that the argumentative assumptions – for instance Rawls's picture of individuals, each with his or her own conception of the good, choosing principles of justice from behind a veil of ignorance – fail to recognize the social preconditions for individual agency. But they object much more to the pattern of argument than to the conclusions reached. In that sense they are not critics of liberalism unless we misleadingly enlarge the meaning of liberalism so that it includes not only a set of political doctrines but also a philosophical anthropology.

That, then, is my diagnosis of the so-called liberal–communitarian debate. Insofar as we can describe the miscellaneous set of political philosophers who are labelled communitarians as a group, what unites them are their anti-individualist philosophical anthropologies. They appear to be critics of liberalism only because there is some affinity between individualism and standard liberalism. (This affinity, by the way, is just that: an affinity, not a logical connection. Holding an individualist anthropology is neither a necessary nor a sufficient condition for adopting liberal political doctrines: to see that it isn't a sufficient condition, think of the case of Hobbes, who moved from individualist premises to authoritarian political conclusions.)

Three forms of communitarianism

But if communitarians are not rightly understood as critics of liberalism, how are we to make sense of their political doctrines? If we begin from a communitarian anthropology, one that emphasizes the social constitution of the self and the embeddedness of the individual in social relations, what follows about the shape of our social and political institutions?

On the basis of what has been said so far about communitarian anthropology, the answer seems to be: nothing of very much substance. There are two paths along which we might try to move from the anthropological premise to some sort of political conclusion. On the one hand, we might argue that, because our identities are socially constituted, and therefore shared with others, it is both legitimate and desirable for these identities to be reflected in the way that our institutions are constructed and our policies are designed. The public sphere should express those aspects of the self that we hold in common with others. If that common identity involves adherence to a particular religion, for example, then our political institutions should be guided by the principles and symbolism of that religion. On the other hand, the claim may be that our communal identities cannot survive without political support; that we are in danger of becoming deracinated unless public policy is directed towards strengthening and reproducing these identities, for instance through the education system. As they stand, however, these claims are remarkably unspecific; they do not go very far in specifying how the public sphere should be constituted. It looks as though Holmes' charge that communitarianism as a political doctrine is essentially nebulous has been vindicated.

What I should like to suggest, however, is that it takes on much more definite shape when we distinguish left, right and centre variants. I want now to provide brief sketches of each, though I should say right away that the three versions are not exhaustive of communitarian political theory. There are communitarianisms of the far right and the far left that I shall not consider: I am identifying forms of communitarianism that have at least some prospect of taking hold as the public philosophy of one of the technologically advanced liberal democracies. I'll start in the centre, with liberal communitarianism.

Liberal communitarians, among whom Jo Raz and Will Kymlicka are distinguished representatives in recent political philosophy, hold two central convictions that are characteristically liberal.[12] One concerns the irreducible plurality of individual values or 'conceptions of the good': there are many valuable ways of life which people may choose to pursue, and these cannot be derived from any single model or more fundamental principle. The other concerns the importance of autonomous choice: whichever way of life a person follows, it is important that he or she should have chosen to follow it after reflection on alternatives, rather than simply having been inducted into it, through a Jesuitical upbringing, for instance. These, as I said, are fairly standard liberal convictions. The communitarian twist occurs when it is argued that both the availability of a spectrum of ways of life and the capacity for autonomy depend upon a communal background. People can't engage in practices such as family life, religious observance or musical performance unless there are groups of people in their society who engage in such practices; moreover the capacity for autonomous choice – the capacity to stand back from and reflect critically upon any particular way of life – is not something that people are natively endowed with, but a capacity that is nurtured by autonomy-supporting practices and institutions whose existence cannot be taken for granted.

The key idea in the liberal communitarian vision of things is that a political society should be made up of a plurality of communities which ought as far as possible to have the character of voluntary associations. That is, they are communities which individuals are free to leave, and which they therefore remain within by voluntary consent. The liberal communitarian does not deny that, as a matter of fact, individuals are born into some of these communities, and acquire their memberships not by choice but as a matter of brute historical fact. But ideally each person should reflect upon, and freely reaffirm, his or her membership of each of the communities with which he or she is associated. This is made possible by the fact that typically each person belongs to several such communities – say family, ethnic or religious group, work association, neighbourhood – and can criticize the norms and values of one group from the perspective of the others. Thus pluralism becomes a condition of autonomy, and recognition of the role of communities is squared with the liberal emphasis on autonomous choice.

How does this translate into liberal politics? On the one hand, standard liberal commitments – to individual rights, freedom of movement and association, the rule of law – can be defended as providing the conditions under which communities can flourish, while at the same time ensuring that as far as possible they take on the character of voluntary associations. On the other hand, the liberal communitarian is prepared to depart from what I earlier called standard liberalism in certain areas in order to recognize or foster community. One lively area of controversy here is the role of the state in relation to cultural groups of various kinds. How far is it justified to offer additional resources or special protections to such groups in order to support them against erosion by influences stemming from the wider society? On the other hand, how far should the state go in insisting that groups must adopt liberal norms such as freedom of expression internally?[13] These debates are familiar ones, but they are inevitable given the liberal communitarian assumptions (1) that group membership provides members with valuable forms of life and the resources to become autonomous; but (2) that autonomy cannot be fully achieved unless members are able to reflect critically upon the assumptions and ethos of any particular group to which they belong.

This, then, is the liberal form of communitarianism. Let me turn now to communitarianism of the right, which can be introduced most easily by seeing what its advocates would see as the deficiencies of liberal communitarianism. As a representative of this position I shall take the conservative philosopher Roger Scruton.[14] What, according to Scruton and those who think like him, is wrong with liberal forms of communitarianism? The first deficiency of liberalism is that it fails to address the problem of social unity: what ties together all the various associations and subgroups into a cohesive whole? The liberal looks to the state itself to perform this unifying function: we are held together by our mutual subscription to the authority of the state and its laws, but on the conservative view this is a shallow answer. Political legitimacy depends upon a pre-political sense of common membership. We have to feel that we belong together in a common society before we can address the question of the political institutions that will govern us.

So the first distinguishing mark of right communitarianism is that it looks to inclusive community as a source of social union. The second point is that it sees community as a source of authority. In identifying with a community, I subject myself to the customs and conventions that it embraces. Whereas the liberal sees communities as facilitating choice, on the conservative view, the point of communal identification is precisely to foreclose choice and provide people with a substantive way of life to adopt. And communities have to have a certain character if they are to do this. 'The real price of community', Scruton says, 'is sanctity, intolerance, exclusion, and a sense that life's meaning depends upon obedience, and also on vigilance against the enemy.'[15] Clearly if communities are like that they cannot be voluntary associations. They should be authoritatively structured, hard to leave and preferably hereditary in character. Using a loose metaphor, if the liberal ideal of community is something like a Quaker meeting, the conservative idea is something like the Roman Catholic Church.

If the two keynotes of right communitarianism are unity and authority, it is fairly easy to see why pride of place in conservative thinking should be given to nationality as a form of community. A national community by definition unifies those within the boundaries of the nation; and its nature is such as to exercise a deep influence on the characters of the people who belong to it. Scruton lists a shared language, shared associations, a shared history and a common culture as factors typically contributing to nationality, and clearly these are features that are pervasive and virtually impossible to shed: you cannot escape the fact that you were born in a certain place, into a certain culture, speaking a certain language, and so forth. The conservative recipe thus calls for the nation-state – a state whose boundaries coincide with that of the nation – as the basis for political order. From this there follow a number of policy prescriptions which distance communitarianism of this sort from the liberal version – for instance a highly restrictive approach to immigration, which is seen as diluting the common culture which supports the authority of the state; a more directive approach to education, part of whose function is to transmit the established cultural identity to the new generation; and so forth.

Let me turn by way of contrast to communitarianism of the left. Again we can most easily grasp this by seeing first of all how it is distinguished from the right communitarianism that I have just outlined. The two identifying features of the left communitarianism that I want to capture are that the community it seeks to preserve or create should be one formed on the basis of equality, and that the community should be actively self-determining rather than subject to the authority of tradition. Let me elaborate a little on these features. First, left communitarians look for communities in which each member enjoys equality of status. What does this mean? It means that although members may enjoy unequal standing in certain particular respects – one is regarded as more expert than another at solving engineering problems, one is seen as more capable than another at holding positions of responsibility and so forth – overall they regard and treat one another as equals. There are, in other words, no hierarchical class divisions such that one could say that, regarded simply as persons, Smith enjoys a higher status than Jones.[16] As to the second feature, although the community may have a special ethos that distinguishes it from other communities, this is not seen as sanctified by past tradition, but as open to revision when the members deliberate collectively about their aims and purposes. Thus it is essential that the community should have some mechanism to allow this deliberation to proceed – some form of democratic self-government. The anthropological assumption is that people flourish best when they associate together on the basis of equality, and have a deep interest in shaping their physical and social environment collectively.

Now the left communitarianism that I have in mind here is not the radical version, espoused by many communists and anarchists, which looks for an all-embracing form of community; which seeks to re-order society so that people are related to one another entirely through small encompassing communities – a world of friendly kibbutzim, if you like. This I take not to be a live political option in the world we live in. My interest is in the more moderate version espoused by many socialists and social democrats which recognizes that community has to compete with other forms of affiliation. It is perhaps best expressed through a doctrine of strong citizenship: this says that though people may choose to relate to one another in many different ways, their most basic form of association must be as equal citizens engaged in collective self-determination. Michael Walzer has perhaps expressed this most eloquently in the chapter of *Spheres of Justice* where he argues that equal membership of a political community is the precondition for all the more specific practices of distributive justice that citizens may engage in.[17]

I have pointed out what differentiates left communitarianism from right. What do left communitarians have to say about liberal communitarianism? Two things, mainly. First, if people define their identities through a plurality of specific communities without at the same time giving priority to an inclusive politically organized community, there is a danger that the social fabric will begin to unravel, with the different communal groups becoming increasingly alienated from and hostile to one another. This, if you like, is the left critique of multiculturalism: an exclusive emphasis on the celebration of specific cultural identities may be incompatible with preserving just that form of political community which allows such separate identities to co-exist in relative peace.[18] Second, there is no general reason to think that liberal communitarianism will be egalitarian. Communities may adopt hierarchical structures internally, which may be morally offensive in their own right – if they are sexist or racist, for instance – but even if they are not, may tend to undermine people's equal standing as citizens. Furthermore, allowing full autonomy to each community may produce inegalitarian outcomes over-all even if the various groups are democratic and egalitarian internally. Consider, for instance, a system of private schooling based on religious groups in a society where by and large the Protestants are rich and the Catholics are poor; or consider a system where ethnic groups run their own housing associations and there are big differences in the economic standing of different groups. From a left perspective, inequalities of this kind pose a grave danger to equal citizenship, and can only be combated if members of the various groups – Catholics and Protestants, blacks and whites – see themselves as belonging to the same inclusive community, which can then be organized politically to combat group inequalities in life-chances.

This completes my sketch of the three versions of communitarianism: there is a liberal communitarianism which seeks to create and support a plural society whose very pluralism, by the possibilities it offers for turn-ing your back on one group and joining another, provides the conditions for individual autonomy. There is a conservative form of communitarian-ism which argues that preserving the authority of a single inclusive community is the precondition for social cohesion and a legitimate state. And there is a left communitarianism, which also looks to an inclusive community, but wants it to be egalitarian and self-determining in a fairly strong sense.

If we reflect a bit on these three models, one thing we can see is that the anthropological idea of the social constitution of the self takes on a rather different meaning in each case. For the liberal communitarian the self is socially constituted in the sense that people acquire their conceptions of the good and their capacity for autonomy from their membership, typ-ically, of several social communities; in other words a flourishing set of cross-cutting communities provides the soil from which the autonomous self springs. For the conservative communitarian, by contrast, what mat-ters is that we should identify with, and recognize the authority of, an inherited way of life. The proper relation between self and community here is one of willing subjugation. The left communitarian has a different view again. Communities matter because each of us seeks recognition from those around him, and so the quest is for a form of community that unites us as equals, with every member being regarded as of equal standing and worth. But there is nothing sacred about the inherited culture or ethos of any particular community; this is a proper matter for collective deliberation and reform. The left communitarian, like the liberal communitarian and unlike the right communitarian, values personal autonomy, but whereas the liberal picture is of each individual choosing which way of life to adopt after encountering several possibilities, the left picture is of us choosing our way of life together, through critical reflection on the one we now have in common. Autonomy here has a political character that is missing from the liberal version. So my earlier suggestion, that communitarians converge at the level of their philosophical anthropology but then diverge at the level of prescriptive political doctrine, turns out to need qualification. There is some convergence, certainly, particularly if we juxtapose any of the positions I have just sketched with a crudely individualistic view of the self. But what emerges from my analysis is that claims such as 'community is constitutive of personal identity' which are loosely bandied about in discussions of communitarianism actually need a good deal of unpacking before it is clear what they mean; and in the course of the unpacking we discover some major ambiguities about what precise relationship between self and community is being envisaged.

Is left communitarianism feasible?

So far my argument in this chapter has mainly been diagnostic. But behind this there lies a more practical question: what are the political prospects of communitarianism, and in particular a communitarianism of the left? At the moment the debate about community tends to oscillate between the centre and the right versions. One way of putting the challenge of Holmes and other liberals sceptical of communitarianism would be as follows: either communitarianism takes an innocuous form in which it departs from standard liberalism only in minor ways, for example in arguing for policies to help support cultural groups under threat of collapse; or it becomes authoritarian and involves using the state to impose a received set of moral values on unwilling subjects. This way of putting the challenge assumes that there is no feasible communitarianism of the left. Now what is certainly true is that whereas we can readily imagine what right communitarianism might look like in practice – we can point to states like Singapore or other places in Asia which approximate to the model – and we can equally imagine how liberal communitarianism would work by extrapolating a bit from the policies of multiculturalism that are currently practised in North America and else-where, it is harder to envisage how left communitarianism might take shape in the real world. Even though I have distanced it from radical communism, it might still seem to fall below the horizon of feasibility, so that the real communitarian options are either Asian authoritarianism or multicultural America. So what are the main problems that left commun-itarianism has to face? I think that there are three, but here I can only signal very briefly the solutions that I should want to propose.

The first is whether it is plausible to suppose that people can identify strongly with an inclusive political community as left communitarianism demands. Or is it the case that the identities that really count when we ask what constitutes the person are much more localized – are they ethnic or religious identities, for instance? It is in response to this problem that I have argued elsewhere[19] that in today's world strong citizenship can only be made to work when it is supported by a shared national identity, and that the left must therefore reconsider its traditional intellectual hostility to ideas of nationhood (I say 'intellectual' here because in practice the political left has always been willing to invoke national solidarity to help win support for its policies). The problem, then, is how to recast national identities so that they can both include everyone who is a member of the political community, and yet be strong enough to bind people together in a form of citizenship that can override sectional loyalties based on class, profession, locality, ethnicity, etc.

The second issue is whether citizenship alone can support a form of equality that is sufficiently robust from a left communitarian perspective. Citizenship is expressed concretely in the form of equal rights and prin-ciples of equal treatment. In the face of the substantial economic and other material inequalities that seem to be endemic in market societies, is this sufficient to create a community whose members genuinely regard themselves as one another's equals? You will recall Marx's charge, in his early essay on the Jewish question, that citizenship as a form of commun-ity must remain illusory in face of the divisions of civil society, where in Marx's view people's real life is led.[20] So how can we bolster the formal rights of citizenship in order to secure an equal status for each member of the relevant political community? Here I believe we must draw inspira-tion from Michael Walzer's idea of complex equality, the idea, to put it very briefly, that in a society which recognizes many separate spheres of distribution, inequalities in one sphere can be offset by countervailing inequalities in other spheres to sustain an overall equality of status.[21]

The third issue springs from the requirement that the values which animate the community should be adopted or re-adopted following col-lective deliberation on the part of the members – in other words that they should not merely be accepted as a received tradition, but be subject to critical scrutiny at regular intervals. How can this be achieved in a large society where face-to-face discussion between all members is out of the question? Is it not inevitable that the values which are adopted to govern policy decisions should be the values of the political elite, or of white heterosexual males? In other words, how can we achieve democratic deliberation of the kind that the left communitarian picture requires, if it is to be genuinely distinct from the right communitarian picture of an inherited national identity imposed on outsiders? Here I believe we need to explore new forms of democracy that take us beyond representative assemblies and conventional parties – for instance local forums, citizens' juries, deliberative opinion polls, referendums and other mechanisms which can draw ordinary citizens into the political dialogue.[22]

These three problems – how to generate a strong but inclusive political community, how to defend equal citizenship in face of economic inequality, how to ensure that the self-governing community is genuinely democratic – are all hard ones. What I find so unsatisfying about contemporary communitarianism *qua* political movement is that it addresses none of them. By remaining vague about the actual locus of community, it avoids taking a stand on the issue of nationality. It has almost nothing to say about increasing material equality or more generally issues of distributive justice (Etzioni is candid about this: 'What is the communitarian economic agenda? The short answer is, there is none'),[23] and in this way it avoids the crucial issue of how community can be sustained at all in the face of market-driven economic inequalities. Finally it does not argue for changing political structures to enhance democracy, seeking instead to moralize existing representative systems by combating the corruption of legislators by special interest groups.[24] In short, then, the communitarian political movement, avoiding controversial political issues in order to appeal to as wide a range of constituents as possible, ends up as little more than a moral appeal to us all to behave better: take more responsibility for our social environment, avoid corruption, etc., etc. My argument in this chapter has been that communitarians must come off the fence: a politically relevant form of communitarianism may be a communitarianism of the left, the right or the centre, but it cannot be all of these at once.

7

Secession and the Principle of Nationality

The secession issue appears to many contemporary thinkers to reveal a fatal flaw in the idea of national self-determination. The question is whether national minorities who come to want to be politically self-determining should be allowed to separate from the parent state and form one of their own. Here the idea of national self-determination may lead us in one of two opposing directions. If the minority group in question regards itself as a separate nation, then the principle seems to support its claims: if the Québécois or the Catalans come to think of themselves as having national identities distinct from those of the Canadians or the Spanish, and to seek political independence on that basis, then if we are committed to national self-determination we should support their claims. But we then face the challenge that once national identities begin to proliferate there is no feasible way of satisfying all such claims, given elementary facts of geography and population spread. As Allen Buchanan, citing Gellner, puts the point, 'the normative nationalist principle is a recipe for limitless political fragmentation'.[1] And he rightly points out that this process may bring with it quite unacceptable moral costs, in the form, for instance, of the disruption, displacement or even annihilation of communities that turn out to be territorially in the wrong place.

On the other hand, the idea of national self-determination may be appealed to in defence of the political status quo. The Canadians and the Spanish have a claim to be self-determining too, and a claim to determine the future of the territory that has historically been identified as Canada or Spain. If the principle is used in this more conservative way, it is subject to a different critical charge: that it turns out in practice to call for self-determination for *states*, not nations, or at least for states that are territorially compact.[2] Self-determination comes to mean the claim of a state to exercise sovereignty within its established borders, not to be invaded or coerced by its neighbours, for instance. But interpreted in this way the idea loses much of its original moral appeal, which came from the vision of a body of people sharing a common identity and wishing to be associated with one another deciding on their own future. The second reading collapses the crucial distinction between nations and states by treating 'the nation' simply as the set of people who fall *de facto* within the jurisdiction of a particular state.

The charge, then, is that the issue of secession reveals the idea of national self-determination either to be a recipe for political chaos and human bloodshed or to be a conservative defence of the rights of established states. My aim here is to see whether it is possible to develop a coherent position on the issue that avoids both extremes, starting out from the principle of nationality that I have defended elsewhere.[3]

Why do we need a theory of secession?

Before we embark on matters of substance, it is worth pausing to ask what purpose we intend our theory of secession to serve. Some writers have proposed that we should be seeking to define a quasi-legal right of secession that might be inscribed in the constitution of a state, or in the charter of an international body such as the United Nations.[4] In other words, we should try to identify a set of conditions that might be formally codified, and that any group attempting to secede from an existing state might appeal to in order to justify its claim. This proposal has some obvious attractions. It holds out the promise that secessionist claims might be treated in a detached way by a constitutional or international court, rather than being fought over with words or guns. But this promise comes at a price. First, the conditions justifying secession would need to be stated in a form that a judicial body could apply, and this immediately slants the discussion in favour of certain criteria and against others. For instance there is likely to be a bias in favour of procedural criteria (is there a majority in favour of secession in the territory in question?) whose application is relatively uncontroversial, and against substantive criteria whose application may depend upon difficult and contested matters of judgement (is the existing state suppressing or eroding the distinct culture of the minority applying to secede?). Second, as Buchanan points out, we have also to think about the incentive effects of different definitions of the right of secession; we have to ask how inscribing one or other version of such a right in a constitution would alter the behaviour either of the existing state or of the would-be secessionists.[5] For instance, would the effect be to make established states less willing to devolve power to regions which might subsequently foster secessionist demands? But it seems to me a mistake to allow our thinking about the secession issue to be dominated by such considerations. We should establish the basic principles first, then ask what effect the public promulgation of these principles might have on the behaviour of different political actors.

In contrast to the legalistic approach sketched in the last paragraph, I believe that a theory of secession should be seen as a political theory, meaning one that articulates principles that should guide us when thinking about secessionist claims. 'Us' here means the would-be secessionists, non-secessionist citizens of the relevant state, and members of the international community who may be called upon to intervene on one side or the other. We are looking for guidance when we have to decide (say in a referendum) whether to vote for secession or for remaining in association with a larger state. Equally we need guidance about how to respond, as British citizens say, to demands for Scottish or Welsh independence. We likewise need to know whether to recognize and support a Slovenia that has chosen to sever its ties with the rest of the Yugoslav federation. A theory of secession should tell us in broad terms when secession is justified and when it is not.

Some critics might argue that the questions I am raising here are insubstantial. If a referendum is being held on secession, then I should vote for secession if I want it, and against if I do not. The issue is settled procedurally, by a majority or a qualified majority, or however. It is irrelevant to ask about the principles that might guide me when casting my vote. But notice that this is not how we think about democratic decision-making in general. We agree, of course, that the party which wins an election should form the government, or that when a referendum is held the result should be adopted as policy, but that does not deter us from putting forward principles which we think voters ought to follow – principles of social justice for instance. Sometimes we will say that the voters got it wrong, that they supported the party whose policies were less just, or less in their interests, than the opposition's. We can say this while still thinking that the democratic procedure should be followed. How are things different when the issue is one of secession? Even if we come to believe that such questions should be resolved procedurally, there may still be good grounds and bad grounds for secession, and it is surely not irrelevant to try to spell these out.

It is in any case implausible to think that a purely procedural theory of secession could be satisfactory. If we say, for instance, that a majority vote to secede is sufficient to justify secession, this immediately raises the question of how the constituency for the vote is to be established, and how the territory which the seceding group would take with them is to be defined. In practice we are likely to think of regions like Quebec which are already administratively defined, and where we can pick out a 'people', the Québécois, among whom a referendum might be held. Here we are tacitly invoking a background theory about the circumstances which make a referendum on secession appropriate: whether on balance we think the secessionist claim justified or unjustified in this case, we can at least recognize it as a plausible candidate. If, by contrast, someone were to propose holding an independence ballot among the Jews of Montreal, we would immediately recognize this as a not-very-serious proposal and react accordingly.

A substantial theory of secession is not likely to be simple. To break up a state and create a new one is a serious matter. It raises questions about political authority, about historic identities, about economic justice and about the rights of minorities. Any adequate theory must address all of these issues, and this means that it will have to be multi-criterial. Instead of looking for a set of necessary and sufficient conditions to justify a secessionist claim, we must accept that the different criteria may pull in opposite directions, and so to reach a verdict on any concrete case we are likely to have to balance conflicting claims. Keeping that in mind, what guidance can an appeal to nationality offer us?

The principle of nationality

The principle of nationality I defend holds, as one of its three elements, that where the inhabitants of a territory form a national community, they have a good claim to political self-determination. Although a sovereign state is not the only possible vehicle of self-determination, both now and in the past it has been the main vehicle, and so this principle grounds a claim to secession made by a territorially compact nation which is currently subject to rule by outsiders. I say 'a claim' rather than 'a right' in order to signal that the claim in question is not necessarily an overriding one, but may be defeated by other considerations that we shall come to in due course. This is not the place to set out the reasons supporting self-determination; I want instead to consider some of the ramifications of this apparently simple principle.

As has often been pointed out, territories occupied by homogeneous nations are very much the exceptions in today's world. Let me say, very briefly, what I take a nation to be: a group of people who recognize one another as belonging to the same community, who acknowledge special obligations to one another, and who aspire to political autonomy – this by virtue of characteristics that they believe they share, typically a common history, attachment to a geographical place, and a public culture that differentiates them from their neighbours.[6] If, with this definition in mind, we look inside those entities popularly described as 'nation-states' we are likely to find some combination of the following: (1) minority groups (especially immigrants) who do not see themselves as sharing in the national identity of the majority (e.g., Turkish immigrants in Germany); (2) regionally gathered minorities who see themselves as forming a separate nation and who aspire to a greater or lesser degree of autonomy (e.g., Kurds in Turkey); (3) regions with intermingled populations identifying with different adjacent nations (e.g., Rumanians and Hungarians in Transylvania); (4) regions in which a substantial part of the population bear a dual or 'nested' identity, as members of a national minority within a larger nation (e.g., Catalans in Spain).

If we want to apply the principle of nationality to cases fitting one or more of these descriptions, our question must be: what structure of political authority will best fulfil the principle for each community, given that the simple solution (homogeneous nation/unitary state) is not available in these circumstances? This involves first of all making qualitative judgements about how people conceive of their identity, and how the identity of one group relates to that of others. Compare, for instance, the position of the Kurds in Turkey with that of the Catalans in Spain. Although the Catalans regard themselves as a distinct people, there is no deep-seated hostility between them and the Spanish people as a whole. There is a considerable cultural overlap (in religious belief, for instance), living standards are somewhat higher than the Spanish average (traditionally Catalonia has been one of the more prosperous regions of Spain), Catalans are not held in low esteem elsewhere in Spain, and so on. In these circumstances, it is not problematic for Catalans to regard themselves as both Catalan and Spanish, as many of them do.[7] The Kurdish case is in many respects different: per capita income in the Kurdish region of Turkey is less than half the national average, Kurdish language and culture are vigorously repressed by the Turkish state, and there is a long history of armed conflicts and massacres between the two communities.[8] Furthermore the Turkish leadership has for many years been committed to the ideal of a unified, homogeneous Turkish nation which leaves no space for cultural pluralism. Given these differences, the Kurds have a claim for independence that is qualitatively different from that held by the Catalans. Short of a dramatic reversal in mainstream Turkish attitudes, there is no chance of the Kurds achieving cultural recognition in a Turkish state, or of Turks and Kurds working together to achieve political democracy and social justice. This is not to say that full secession would necessarily be the right solution for Turkish Kurdistan. Various practical considerations count heavily against this solution, and it seems that few Kurds themselves are actively seeking secession.[9] My point is that to apply the nationality principle to this problem, we have to begin by looking at the actual content of group identities, in order to discover whether group X has a distinct national identity whose substance places it at odds with that of group Y to whose political institutions it is presently subjected. To the extent that this is so, any claim that the group may make for political independence is strengthened – which is not to say that its claim is decisively vindicated for, as indicated above, it may eventually be defeated by countervailing factors.[10]

One such factor which we must now consider is the competing claim of group Y, the larger nation whose present territory would be broken up if the secession were to go ahead. Do they not have a claim which is at least as strong as that of the would-be secessionists? Here we need to take account of the following empirical fact: in most of the cases under discussion, there will be an asymmetry between the way the smaller group sees its relationship with the larger and the way that the larger group sees its relationship with the smaller. The larger group will play down the distinctness of the minority: rather than regarding them as a nation with a separate identity, they will tend to see them as one variation on a common theme. not as distinct Xs, but as Ys who speak a different language or have their own quaint folk culture. Thus whereas the Québécois tend to see themselves as belonging to a nation separate from the rest of Canada, Canadians at large are likely to regard the Québécois just as French-speaking Canadians, and parallels to this case can be found in many other places, for instance between the Scots and the English or the Macedonians and the Greeks.

There may be a temptation to think that in such instances, the majority has simply got it wrong – that if the Xs no longer identify themselves as Ys, then for the Ys to assert a common identity with the Xs amounts to ignorance or a refusal to face up to the facts. But the issue will very rarely be as clear-cut as this. Assuming that the Xs and the Ys share a single citizenship and have been associated politically for a substantial period of time, they do indeed have a good deal in common. And the Xs themselves are very likely to recognize this when not actively waving their nationalist banners – for instance by acknowledging the two-sidedness of their national identity, as do most Catalans and most Scots. So the issue is how best to interpret a complex state of affairs in which the minority group has both a distinct identity and a sense of belonging to the larger community. Members of the majority group are very likely to be unperceptive and to behave in ways that are insensitive to the minority, but this does not mean that they are simply in error when they invoke a shared identity in order to resist the Xs' claim to secede.

A second tempting error is to think that if the seceding group wants to break up the political union, the majority's sense of identity is irrelevant. Some authors draw a parallel with individuals divorcing: if Anne decides she no longer wants to be married to Brian, then Brian's belief that they are still a viable domestic unit is neither here nor there. The union must rest on the continuing consent of both parties.[11] This analogy cannot be sustained, however. Most obviously, nations are not individuals with a single will. They are likely to embrace a wide range of opinions about how national identity is best expressed – through union with a larger nation, through devolution, through an independent state, and so forth. This point hardly needs to be laboured: it raises issues that I return to in the following section. A bit less obviously, secession does not only involve a political separation, but also a partition of territory. Here we must address the difficult question of how best to understand the rights of peoples to the territory that they occupy.

We might think initially that what is at stake here is an aggregate of property rights: I own this plot, you own that, and so all of us together own the territory that we call Britain.[12] If that were the right way to think about the problem, then a secessionist group occupying a compact area would simply have to assert their joint property rights to establish a conclusive claim to the land they want to take with them. But, as Buchanan has argued, the relationship between a people and their territory cannot properly be understood in these terms.[13] When we say that Iceland belongs to the Icelanders (to take a simple case), we do not mean that they own it as property: we mean that they have a legitimate claim to exercise authority over Iceland, to determine what happens in that island, including what individual property rights there are going to be. (If they were to decide to leave it as common land, that would be their prerogative.) This authority is exercised in practice by the state on the people's behalf, but the Icelanders' claim to authority is not reducible to the authority of the Icelandic state, as we can see if (*per impossibile*) we were to imagine a revolutionary upheaval in that country which established an entirely new set of political institutions. The Icelanders' claim to control Iceland would survive such a political cataclysm.

How are such claims established? The people who inhabit a certain territory form a political community. Through custom and practice as well as by explicit political decision they create laws, establish individual or collective property rights, engage in public works, shape the physical appearance of the territory. Over time this takes on symbolic significance as they bury their dead in certain places, establish shrines or secular monuments, and so forth. All of these activities give them an attachment to the land that cannot be matched by any rival claimants. This in turn justifies their claim to exercise continuing political authority over that territory. It trumps the purely historical claim of a rival group who argue that their ancestors once ruled the land in question.[14]

If that is the right way to understand territorial claims, let us now return to the case of a divided community where a minority of Xs wish to secede (with the territory they occupy) from a majority of Ys. Can the Ys make a valid claim to continued control of the territory in question? The answer must depend on how the relationship between the two groups has developed historically. At one extreme we might have a case where the Xs were always the unwilling subjects of the Ys whom they regarded as an occupying force: the relationship between the native populations of the Baltic states and the Russian majority in the Soviet Union may have been close to this extreme. Here there has been no real political community between the Xs and the Ys, no freely undertaken collective projects, and it is hard to see the Ys having a legitimate claim to the territory occupied by the Xs except in so far as they have, say, invested physical capital in that territory (in which case some compensation may be due if the Xs secede).[15] At the other extreme we find the case where the Xs, although perhaps always having certain features that distinguished them from the Ys, have been free and equal partners in the building of the community. Their new-found nationalism is a result not of historic exploitation but of cultural developments that make them now want to have greater control over what happens in their particular territory (for instance their language is in danger of being eroded). Here I think the legitimate demand of the Xs does have to be set against the equally legitimate demand of the Ys not to be deprived of part of the territory which they and their ancestors have helped to shape, and which they quite naturally think of as theirs. In a non-economic sense, the Ys will be poorer if the Xs secede. If no compromise is possible the Xs' demand may finally prove the stronger, but in such a case there is a powerful reason to find a solution that gives the Xs a form of autonomy that falls short of independence. This argument applies, I believe, to groups such as the Scots and Welsh in Britain, the Catalans and Basques in Spain, and the French-speaking communities in Canada.

To conclude this part of the discussion, if we appeal to the principle of nationality to ground the case for self-determination, then we shall want to apply two criteria to any group of would-be secessionists. The first is that the group should form a nation with an identity that is clearly separate from that of the larger nation from which they wish to disengage.[16] The second is that the group should be able to validate its claim to exercise authority over the territory it wishes to occupy. These criteria can't be applied mechanically or by counting heads; their application requires judgement and a degree of historical understanding. But if both criteria are met, the group in question has a serious claim to be allowed to secede. This is still not a conclusive claim, however, for there may be other factors weighing in the opposite direction, but *prima facie* the group has a good case. Let me now turn to explore some of the other factors that may count in the final judgement.

Minorities and numbers

Up to this point I have been considering the artificially simple case of a nationally homogeneous group of Xs occupying a discrete piece of land, and attempting to secede from a state in which the Ys form a majority. In any real case that we might wish to consider, matters will not be so clear-cut. Within the territory that the Xs are claiming (a claim we are supposing to be legitimate by the criteria set out above) there are likely to be a number of Ys, and also members of other minorities who are neither Xs nor Ys. Within the borders of the remainder state, likewise, there may be found some Xs and also members of other groups. Secession does not simply mean shifting from a nationally heterogeneous community to one that is nationally homogeneous; it means replacing one heterogeneous pattern with two different (but still to some extent heterogeneous) patterns.

The assumption guiding our discussion is that there is a value to each member in being a citizen of a state that embraces your nation; to be part of a minority, although by no means always a disaster, is generally a worse option. So how should we compare the state of affairs prior to secession with that which would obtain afterwards, using this principle? One proposed criterion is that we should simply count up the numbers of people who live in a state in which they form a national majority.[17] In the case envisaged, this criterion will favour secession, on the assumption that the Xs form a majority in the territory which they are claiming. If the new state is formed, it will contain more Xs who now meet the criterion than Ys who now fail to meet it (they become a minority in the new state); the position of the Xs who remain in the Y state is unchanged; and so is that of the other minorities in both states.

But this proposal takes too little account of the political realities of secessionist movements. It assumes, in particular, that the treatment of national minorities in the new X-state will be no worse than their treatment in the original Y-state – for instance that whatever degree of autonomy was given to the Xs in the original state will be matched by the autonomy granted to the Ys in the new X-state. But in many cases this assumption is highly unrealistic. The sociologist Donald Horowitz has argued that secession nearly always intensifies conflicts between groups.[18] The Xs, in order to justify their secessionist demand, may have to exaggerate the features that differentiate them from the Ys. If they are successful, they are likely to want to purge the new state of the baneful influence of the Ys by cultural repression or, at the extreme, ethnic cleansing. Furthermore a side-effect of secession may be the stimulation of new group conflicts: Horowitz points out how, in Africa and elsewhere, new ethnic cleavages have almost always developed following the break-up of larger states. Differences that had little salience in the bigger unit may come to loom large in the smaller one, so that the vision of a culturally homogeneous political community gives way to infighting between the sub-groups.

It is also false to assume that there is no change in the position of those Xs who, as a result of living in the wrong place, find themselves citizens of the rump Y-state. Most obviously they now form a much smaller minority and will have less political influence than previously. There may no longer be any constituencies regularly electing members of X to parliament, for example. Special rights which may have been in place before, such as rights designed to protect the X-culture, may now be dismantled on the grounds that there are too few Xs left to bother about. Furthermore political leaders in the Y-state may argue that the very existence of the X-state provides ample protection for that culture. It is hard, for instance, to imagine a Canada shorn of Quebec accepting responsibility for preserving French language and culture in North America. Finally the creation of the X-state inevitably alters the political identity of those Xs who remain outside it. Although their sense of self-worth may in some ways be enhanced by its existence (as the self-esteem of many Jews has been bolstered by the creation of the state of Israel), they may also feel more estranged from the Ys, and this feeling may be reciprocated ('If you don't think you belong here, why don't you move out to X-land?'). On balance, therefore, the position of the stranded Xs is likely to worsen as a result of the secession.

For these reasons, the proposal to settle the minorities issue by counting heads seems to me seriously inadequate. Once again qualitative judgements about how the status and welfare of different groups would be altered by the creation of a new state must be made. How can the principle of nationality guide us here? Let me make it clear first of all that the principle as I understand it does not advocate the creation of states that are culturally or ethnically homogeneous through and through. To say that fellow-citizens should as far as possible share a common national identity leaves space for a rich pattern of social diversity along lines of religion, ethnicity and so forth. So alongside the principle of nationality we may – and surely should – hold other principles that protect the rights of minorities – principles of human rights, of equality and so forth. These principles must also be brought into play when judging a claim to secession. Looking at the facts of a particular case, we have to try to estimate whether minority rights are likely to be better or worse protected if the secession goes ahead.

Such estimates are clearly difficult to make. One thing we cannot do, however, is simply to take whatever reassurances the secessionists may give at face value. Political philosophers writing on this topic are prone to say, in effect, 'let the secession go ahead provided that those who form the new state undertake to respect the rights of minorities within it'.[19] But how should we apply this conditional to an actual case? How are we to judge the real worth of such an undertaking? It is important to bear in mind here that once the new state is formed and recognized, powerful norms of international non-interference come into play. As the experience of former Yugoslavia demonstrates, it is very difficult to control from the outside even massive violations of the rights of minorities. So there is a serious risk that in permitting the secession to occur, we (as third parties to the conflict, say) may be tacitly condoning maltreatment of minorities in the newly formed state, which at a later stage we will be unable to do anything about.

The principle of nationality itself may guide our thinking in one further respect. Recall that the underlying vision is of a state whose citizens share an inclusive national identity that makes room for cultural differences. How far this ideal vision can be realized in any particular case will depend on the character of the identity in question – for instance, how far it includes elements that are tied to the culture of a particular ethnic group. If the national identity of the Ys is relatively amorphous whereas the identity of the Xs contains a much stronger ethnic or religious component, say, then there is clearly a much better chance of a common identity in which the Xs (and others) can share evolving in the Y-state than there is of the reverse happening in the X-state. This criterion does not necessarily tell in favour of the status quo, but in many cases it will, especially where the existing state is long-established, and over time has developed mechanisms for coping with cultural pluralism. If we consider the case of Quebec, for instance, it is reasonable to expect that an independent Quebec would protect the private rights of its English-speaking minority at least as effectively as Canada has so far protected the rights of French speakers. On the other hand it is hard to imagine that it would evolve a national identity that was as hospitable to English-speakers in Quebec as Canadian identity has become to French-speakers throughout Canada, since the active promotion of French language and French culture would necessarily be a central component of that identity.

There will, however, be some tragic cases where the project of reconciliation is simply not feasible. These are cases where two physically inter-mingled communities cannot live together peacefully because of ingrained mutual hostility, and where there is no reason to believe that under any division of the territory the rights of the minority groups will be respected. Here I think it may be necessary to contemplate some exchange of populations so that two more or less nationally homogeneous entities can be created. Most liberals will baulk at this suggestion, because it brings to mind the horrifying spectre of forced ethnic cleansing, and indeed there is no doubt that historically most population shifts of this kind have taken place more or less under coercion. But it is at least possible to envisage an internationally supervised operation in which people are given financial incentives to exchange their homes and their land, and if the alternative to this is a continuation of events such as those we have witnessed in Bosnia, or indeed on a much smaller scale in Northern Ireland, we should be prepared to contemplate it.[20]

In tackling the minorities issue, therefore, the principle should not be to allow secession whenever a territorial majority favours it, but to judge which outcome offers the best chance of creating states with national identities which are relatively congenial to internal minorities, and which are likely to protect their cultural and other rights. Numbers should count to some extent, but in so far as they are predictable, overall consequences should count for more. Where the consequences for minorities look very bad wherever the boundaries are fixed, some people – as few as possible – may have to be encouraged to move their abode.

Distributive justice

When secession occurs, it is likely over time to alter the pattern of economic distribution both between and within the new-formed and remainder states. So ought we to judge secessionist demands by applying principles of distributive justice to them – favouring secession when it seems likely to be justice-enhancing, and disfavouring it in the opposite case? Several recent discussions of the question have followed this strategy, giving principles of justice a more or less prominent place in the theory of legitimate secession.[21] How far, then, should we modify the conclusions already reached to take account of such considerations?

As Buchanan points out, the first issue that has to be settled here is the scope of the principles in question.[22] Should we see principles of distributive justice as applying globally (though no doubt given practical application through more local institutions) or do these principles themselves have a restricted scope? Buchanan analyses this issue by drawing a contrast between 'justice as reciprocity' and 'subject-centred justice', the former holding that obligations of justice hold only between the contributors to a co-operative scheme, the latter imposing no such restriction.

I want to propose a somewhat different view. Principles of distributive justice, and especially *comparative* principles, such as principles of equality, need and desert, do indeed have a restricted scope, but the limits are not set by the bounds of a co-operative practice for mutual advantage; rather they are set by the bounds of a community whose members recognize one another as belonging to that community. This view avoids what Buchanan takes to be the major weakness of justice as reciprocity, namely that it cannot recognize obligations of justice towards those who are unable to contribute to a scheme of social co-operation, such as the seriously disabled. If instead the scope of principles of justice is determined by the boundaries of the relevant community, then these principles will embrace members of the community who for one reason or another cannot contribute to the social product; for instance principles of equality and need will apply to them. And I take it that although nations are not the only communities that will count from this perspective, they are arguably the most important.[23]

If that picture (which I state rather than defend here) is right, then how should we judge the justice of a claim to secession? We begin with a single political society whose institutions are governed more or less closely by principles of justice which citizens of that society – or perhaps some portion of them – endorse. If secession occurs, we now have two political communities within which, again, each set of members' sense of justice will be more or less closely embodied. It is impossible to say in general terms whether the cause of justice is likely to have been served by the secession. In favour of the secession, it can be argued that the discontented minority – the Xs, to return to earlier terminology – will probably have suffered injustice in the large state, either because the principles they subscribe to were not adequately reflected in the state's policies, or because principles which they share with the Ys were implemented in a discriminatory way.[24] Against the secession, it can be argued that the pooling of resources that the larger state made possible served to protect the members of both communities against hardship of various kinds. What cannot be argued, though, is that the bare fact that the Xs as a group and the Ys as a group receive different treatment from their governments and other institutions after the separation is a reason against it. This follows from the premise that comparative principles of justice apply within communities rather than between them. Just as it is no injustice that the Germans enjoy on average higher incomes or better medical care than the Spanish, so if the Basques were to separate from Spain it would be no injustice if they proceeded to enjoy a higher (or lower) living standard than their erstwhile compatriots.

In general, this means that the argument from justice will tend to reinforce, rather than offset, the original argument from national self-determination. Where a state presently contains two communities whose collective identities are radically at odds with one another, this is very likely to mean that the minority community gets treated unjustly for one or both of the reasons set out above. Contrasting national identities are likely to mean contrasting public cultures, and therefore somewhat different understandings of what justice requires. Equally where there is a good deal of hostility between the communities, political leaders in the majority community will feel strongly tempted to practise discriminatory policies in favour of their fellow-members, as Protestant leaders in Northern Ireland did for many decades. Where, on the other hand, group identities converge more closely at national level, neither the principle of nationality nor distributive justice is likely to support a secessionist cause.[25]

So are there no circumstances in which justice can be appealed to in order to contest a secessionist case that otherwise seems well-founded? I can think of two such instances. First, as several other commentators have observed, a secession might be unjust if it deprived the remainder state of some valuable resource that had been created collectively – for instance if the pre-secessionist state had made a large capital investment in a power station built in the territory to which the secessionists lay claim. In principle this problem is soluble by a transfer payment from the X-state to the remainder Y-state, though it may prove hard to agree precise terms. It is possible that a similar argument might apply when the Ys have taken decisions premised upon continued co-operation with the Xs, as Gauthier suggests.[26] If the Ys suffer as a result of the Xs' withdrawal in circumstances where they could legitimately expect the co-operation to continue, they may have some claim to compensation which tapers downwards over time. These, however, are best regarded as transitional issues of justice, and should not be conflated with the idea, rejected above, that the relative position of the two communities formed by secession can be judged by applying comparative principles such as equality across both.

Second, a secession might conceivably leave the remainder state so depleted of resources that it was unable to secure its members' basic interests, and so was forced to contract an alliance with some colonial power or other neighbouring state. This could happen if a rich secessionist region chose to cast off an impoverished fringe area – not a likely scenario, perhaps, but one that is worth contemplating briefly for the light it can shed on the general principle at stake. The principle here is that the pursuit of national self-determination and justice for the Xs should not lead to a state of affairs in which the Ys are so deprived that they cannot achieve justice among themselves, and as a result have to give up a large measure of self-determination as well. This is a bit like

Wellman's condition that both secessionist and remainder states should be 'large, wealthy, cohesive and geographically contiguous enough to form a government that effectively performs the functions necessary to create a secure political environment',[27] though I do not think we can insist that each state should measure up to some pre-formed standard of liberal legitimacy. What matters is that both the Xs and the Ys should have territory and resources from which a viable political community can be created; how this is done in practice may depend upon the differing political cultures of the two groups.[28]

Conclusion

I have tried to show that the principle of nationality provides us with a perspective on the secession issue that can avoid us having to condone a secessionist free-for-all without forcing us to defend existing state boundaries regardless. Sometimes these boundaries need changing, but we can decide whether they do by applying relevant criteria, not simply by listening to how loud the clamour for independence has become. It is far too crude to suggest that any territorial majority that wants to secede has a right to do so. Instead we need to measure the strength of its claim by looking at how far different groups have or have not evolved separate national identities, at how minorities are likely to fare under various possible regimes, and so forth. Admittedly this is demanding in terms of the level of knowledge that outsiders may be called on to acquire. But only by getting to grips with the facts of each particular case in this way can we decide whether outright secession is justified, as opposed to the many other forms of partial autonomy – consociationalism, federalism, local autonomy, etc. – that a constitutional settlement within existing state borders may provide.

8

Nationality in Divided Societies

When people like myself defend the principle of national self-determination – the principle that where a body of people form a national community, they should be allowed to control their own affairs through institutions of self-government – they run into a barrage of objections from liberals. One objection, very much in the spirit of Pope's famous couplet, 'For forms of government let fools contest. Whate'er is best administer'd is best', says that what matters is good government, not self-government. More specifically, what matters is that governments should respect the liberties and rights of their subjects and pursue enlightened policies generally; who does the governing, whether compatriot or foreigner, is of no intrinsic importance. A second objection points to the external costs of national self-determination. Political communities which are empowered through self-government to pursue the interests of their members will do so at the expense of outsiders. Their policies will be based on narrow notions of national interest, and are likely to harm the freedom and well-being of the vulnerable and destitute the world over. In place of national government we should have world government, or at least a strong international regime of some kind.

These are objections of principle to national self-determination, one stemming from classical liberalism, the other from a more modern cosmopolitan liberalism. They will not be my concern here.[1] Instead I want to try to respond to a third kind of liberal objection, which runs along the following lines. 'Considered in the abstract, the idea of national self-determination is quite appealing. It is evident that people's autonomy and well-being are promoted when they are able collectively to determine the future shape of their society. If all the world were like Iceland – a culturally homogeneous political community inhabiting a well-defined territory to which no other community has any claims – the principle of self-determination would be perfectly valid. But unfortunately the Icelandic case is quite exceptional. Almost everywhere else we find territories inhabited by a kaleidoscope of groups with competing cultural identities, stemming either from long-standing historic rivalries, or from more recent patterns of immigration. Existing states are almost without exception multicultural, and in these circumstances applying the principle of national self-determination will mean one of two things. Either it will mean allowing the dominant group in any place to impose its cultural values on dissenting minorities in the name of national self-determination. Or it will justify minority groups in their struggle for autonomy, a struggle which in the nature of things is liable to turn violent. In short, the political geography of the contemporary world more closely resembles Bosnia than it does Iceland, and in that context the only sane response to nationalist aspirations is to try to damp them down as quickly as possible.'

This objection is certainly a powerful one, drawing as it does on the very underlying values that are used to support the principle of nationality itself. So how should defenders of the principle respond to it? I am going to suggest that we must scrutinize the idea of a cultural kaleidoscope more carefully, and draw distinctions between different ways in which political communities may be culturally divided. I will not deny that there are cases in which the nationality principle runs into trouble. But I shall argue that in many others it can guide us towards political arrangements that meet the cultural demands of more than one group. The mere fact of cultural pluralism does not undermine the principle; everything depends on the character of the pluralism.

For this purpose I want to distinguish between three types of social division that may be found inside a political community: ethnic cleavages, rival nationalities and nested nationalities.[2] I present these as ideal types, recognizing that in the real world there will be many mixed or intermediate cases – cases, that is, in which either different types of division are juxtaposed in the same state, or the divisions that exist seem to fall somewhere between my pure types.[3] I believe, however, that we need to begin with a relatively simple typology, in order to see that the principle of nationality has quite different implications in the three pure cases. That is, it matters a lot, normatively speaking, whether the cultural pluralism we are looking at is generated by ethnic cleavages, rival nationalities or nested nationalities. Once we know what the principle entails in each of these simple cases, we can begin to think about the messier instances of cultural heterogeneity that we find in actual contemporary states. In the present paper I am going to focus on the case of nested nationalities, partly because I've tried to address the other two cases elsewhere,[4] but mainly because this case hasn't been much discussed in the existing literature on nationalism. The example I shall chiefly use is Scotland and England and their relationship to Britain as a whole. But first I need to explain my threefold distinction properly.

Ethnic cleavages, rival nationalities and nested nationalities

A state is ethnically divided, but not multinational, when it contains two or more distinct ethnic groups each of which is nonetheless able to participate in a common national identity. So what is an ethnic group? It is a set of people with a distinct set of cultural values and a shared language, who recognize their cultural kinship with one another, and engage in practices that set them apart from outsiders: they intermarry, form clubs and associations, attend churches, synagogues and mosques, etc. The group may often embrace the myth that they form an extended family in the biological sense, although in reality ethnic identities are usually to a greater or lesser extent a matter of choice. For present purposes there is no need to delve deeply into the difficult question of how precisely ethnicity should be understood and how far it should be seen as a freely acquired and malleable source of personal identity. What needs underlining are two features that ethnicity characteristically lacks. The first is that ethnicity is not an intrinsically political identity, meaning that ethnic groups as such do not aim or aspire to become self-governing political communities. Of course ethnic groups will want to control their own churches, social clubs, trade unions and so forth. They will also very often want political representation in the shape of elected politicians willing to promote their interests and concerns in government. And they may demand symbolic recognition in the sense that national institutions should acknowledge the group's culture in one way or another (as Muslims in Britain have been arguing that the Millennium Dome should house not only exhibits connected with Christianity but others linked to Islam). But this is very different from aiming for political autonomy as an independent unit. This is connected with the second feature, namely that ethnic identity involves no particular territorial claims. There is no territory which the group claims as its own – indeed ethnic groups tend to migrate from place to place as they rise or fall in the social scale. There may well be a homeland which the group sees as its place of origin, and members may be concerned that the ancestral homeland keeps its political integrity, but this does not and cannot translate into a demand for territorial control in the state of residence. Thus Italians in the US will care about the fate of Italy, Ukrainians in Canada about Ukraine, Jews in Britain about Israel, but this is clearly very different from aspiring to control all or part of the US or Canada or Britain itself.

It follows that in principle a society divided along ethnic lines can have a common national identity and enjoy national self-determination in a relatively straightforward manner. Although ethnic identities may give rise to political demands, they are essentially cultural identities whose field of expression is civil society, and they can be combined with overarching national identities: to use the examples I just gave, Italian-Americans will standardly think of themselves as ethnically Italian but as having American nationality, and similarly for the other two cases. Of course many practical difficulties may intervene: ethnic rivalries may make co-operation within the state difficult, the national identity may include cultural elements that some ethnic groups find unacceptable, and the nation may find itself at war, literally or metaphorically, with the home-land of one of its constituent groups – Japanese ethnics in America, for example, are still feeling the repercussions of the Second World War. But the principle remains clear, that in societies with ethnic cleavages national identity should be forged or remade in such a way that all groups can take part in a collective project of self-determination.

This reveals a fairly sharp contrast with my second case, that of states inhabited by rival national groups. Here we find groups with mutually exclusive national identities each seeking to control all or part of the territory of the state. There are various possible configurations here: the groups in question can be territorially concentrated or territorially dispersed, they may or may not identify with national groups in neighbouring states, and their conflicting claims may extend across the whole of the state's territory or be confined to specific disputed areas. To mention some examples, Jews and Palestinians in Israel are two free-standing groups who make significantly overlapping claims to the territory of that state; Serbs and Croats in Bosnia are groups identifying with adjoining nationalities with conflicting claims to control parts of Bosnian territory; Catholics and Protestants in Northern Ireland illustrate the case where the two communities are intermingled and make rival claims to the whole of the territory in question. The detailed configurations differ, but the kind of division involved makes it virtually inevitable that the relationship between the groups should be an antagonistic one. This is because rival territorial claims in the present will stem from a history of conflict in which one group has moved into territory previously held by the other, or in which patterns of political control have varied historically, at one time the As governing one tract of territory, at another time the Bs governing a different tract, and so forth. So part of what it means to belong to group A is that one defines oneself in opposition to (and typically regards with some contempt) members of B, and it is this fact, along with the dispute over territorial control, that prevents an over-arching national identity emerging across the various national groups. There is no Israeli national identity over and above a Jewish or Palestinian identity, no Bosnian national identity over and above a Serb, Croat or Muslim identity, etc.[5] (Members of the rival communities may of course recognize that *de facto* they share a common citizenship, but this is not the same as conceiving of themselves as united in one community with a shared history, similar aims and values, etc.)

These are hard cases for the principle of nationality, which is not to say that the principle has no guidance to offer. When faced with rival nation-alities within an existing state, achieving the best approximation to full national self-determination will depend on how the communities are configured. In some instances the best solution may be to permit one national community to secede, in others to redraw borders so that more people fall under the aegis of a neighbouring state, in yet others to engineer an elaborate constitutional settlement which preserves a balance of power between the rival communities for the time being, and which may with the passage of time lead to the emergence of a genuinely shared identity. But I don't want here to discuss these options at any length.[6] I am more interested in showing how the cases just described differ from those in my third category, which I call nested nationalities.

We find nested nationalities when two or more territorially-based com-munities exist within the framework of a single nation, so that members of each community typically have a split identity. They think of themselves as belonging both to the smaller community and to the larger one, and they do not experience this as schizophrenic, because their two identities fit together reasonably well.[7] Among the contemporary states that fall into this category, I will argue, are Belgium, Britain, Canada, Spain and Switzerland. These are states whose citizens mostly share an overarching national identity – as Belgians, Britons, Canadians, etc. – while also identifying with, and displaying loyalty to, sub-communities within the larger nation – Flanders and Wallonia, Scotland and Wales, Quebec, Catalonia and so forth.[8] Two points need to be made immediately about the states in question. First, we cannot say that every citizen is the bearer of two neatly nested political identities. Instead we find, typically, that some citizens identify exclusively with the larger unit, some exclusively with the smaller unit, and many more identify in varying degrees with both. Thus if we take the inhabitants of Catalonia as a putative example of a nested nationality, and ask how they identify themselves vis-à-vis Spain as a whole, we find that 'Equally Spanish and Catalan' is the most popular self-description, followed by 'More Catalan than Spanish', with smaller numbers claiming exclusively Catalan and exclusively Spanish identities.[9] The second is that we can divide states with nested nationalities into those in which one community is preponderant, and those in which two or more have roughly equal weight – Britain, Spain and Canada being examples of the first, Belgium and Switzerland of the second. In the second case, we may expect to find members of each nested community displaying a dual identity – thinking of themselves as both Walloon and Belgian, for instance. In the first case, however, we may expect to find an asymmetry. Whereas people who belong to one of the minor nationalities will typically endorse a dual identity, those belonging to the numerically dominant group are likely to identify themselves nationally only with the inclusive unit. Thus English people will typically regard themselves simply as British, Canadians outside Quebec simply as Canadians, and the Castilian-speaking majority in Spain simply as Spanish. (They may in addition have regional or provincial identities, but these are not regarded as forms of nationality in the way that Scottish, Quebecois or Catalan identities are.) As we shall see, this asymmetry creates political problems in the states in question.

In describing these political communities with nested nationalities, I have deliberately side-stepped a terminological question that usually carries with it major political ramifications: shall we call the larger community a nation and the sub-groups something else – national minorities, for instance – or shall we say that Catalonia, Wallonia and Scotland are nations, in which case what term shall we use to describe Spain, Belgium and Britain? The label matters because of the power of the idea of national self-determination. Once it is conceded that a territorial community genuinely constitutes a nation, we seem already to have shown that there is good reason for the community in question to be granted political autonomy.

But in fact neither answer is correct as it stands. Both exhibit the fallacy of thinking that nations are like natural species. Just as one can be either a cat or a dog, but not a bit of each, so, it is assumed, one has either to be a Catalan or a Spaniard as far as national identity is concerned, but not both. But this is surely a mistake.[10] One can be both Catalan and Spanish (indeed as we have seen many people in Catalonia describe themselves in precisely this way), perhaps emphasizing different aspects of the double identity in different contexts or for different purposes. In that case there is no right answer to the question 'Which is really the nation, Catalonia or Spain?' The question is badly put, and we need to find terminology that is less misleading. We could use the terminology that I favour and describe the Catalans and the Scots as nested nationalities;[11] or if this does not go far enough to appease nationalist sensibilities we could call them nations-within-a-nation. The important point is that whatever terminology we use should convey the idea that national identity can exist at more than one level.

Another error that should be avoided here is that of describing the larger political community simply as a multinational state, with the implication that its source of unity consists entirely in allegiance to a common set of political institutions. What is being suggested, in other words, is that genuine nationhood is confined to the Scots, the Catalans and the other smaller communities, whereas Britain and Spain are at best examples of a kind of civic nationalism, which does not imply a common history, language, culture, etc. but merely recognition of the authority of a constitutional or political framework. Now I do not in fact think that the idea of civic nationalism is a helpful one, except perhaps as a way of marking one end of a spectrum (with ethnic nationalism at the other end) to bring out qualitative differences between different kinds of nationalism. But whether or not there are any real cases that approximate to 'civic nationalism' (the US is probably the most likely candidate – but as I have argued elsewhere, even American national identity contains historical and cultural elements that are hard to interpret as purely civic),[12] it seems clear that examples I am discussing do not belong in this category. Belgian, British, Canadian, Spanish and Swiss nationality all come heavily freighted with cultural and historical associations; by no stretch of the imagination could these national identities be regarded as purely civic. So 'multinational state' is a misleading way of describing states whose internal divisions place them in my third category; it is much more appropriate as a description of category two, states made up of rival nationalities, where the state itself is either an instrument in the hands of one nation, as in the case of Israel, or the arena where the rival nations jostle for advantage, as for example with Yugoslavia before its break-up, or many African states today.

From a normative perspective, states with nested nationalities can be seen as falling somewhere in between my categories one and two. Because the component nationalities have most of the properties of independent nations, including a territorial homeland, their claims must be treated quite differently from the claims of ethnic groups; the Scots in Britain have a claim to self-determination which Muslims, say, in Britain do not, and this is on grounds of principle, not merely the practical obstacles to granting self-determination to the latter group. But equally their claims are significantly different from those of nations in category two (rival nationality) states, because they have to be harmonized with the claims of the larger community. So full independence or secession from the existing state are not appropriate solutions. To see why, we need to look more closely at how nested nationalities are created – about the background against which split-level national identities can emerge.

The English, the Scots and British national identity

The most obvious factor, looking at the cases I have cited, is that the nations in question have co-existed for a long period in a single political unit, while at the same time each component part has kept its distinct cultural features: in particular, language has served as the main carrier of cultural difference in each case other than Britain. In the British case, language has been less important as a dividing factor, particularly if we are thinking about the English and the Scots, but other features – the fact that Scotland has had its own separate legal system, education system and religious institutions throughout the period of political union – have helped to offset this. However the recipe for successfully nested nations involves more than just political integration plus cultural difference. Taking the Anglo-Scottish relationship as my example, and oversimplifying greatly what is a long and complex story, I shall suggest three other factors that have contributed to the formation of a single, but pluriform, nation in Britain. These factors are cultural overlap, mutual economic advantage and an interwoven history.

In referring to overlapping cultures, I am expressing the thought that English and Scottish cultures, although having distinct features overall, are sufficiently convergent that participants in each can readily understand the other, there is a good deal of mutual borrowing, individuals can relocate themselves fairly readily from one to the other, and so forth. I believe this holds both for the political cultures of the two peoples and for culture in the wider sense of literary, artistic, philosophical etc. traditions.

Speaking very generally and somewhat anachronistically, we can say that these are both liberal cultures in which ideas of religious freedom, personal independence and resistance to absolute monarchy have been paramount. The fact that the Scottish Reformation took place within a couple of decades of its English counterpart is a significant starting point. It meant that in the period following the Union of the Crowns in 1603 political argument in the two countries ran on roughly parallel tracks, with debates about the relationship between church and state, royal prerogative v. the supremacy of parliament and so forth. Political alliances formed naturally across the border, for instance between English Puritans and Scottish Presbyterians.[13] In both countries rival national histories were constructed in an effort to show that each author's preferred political programme had ancient antecedents – English narratives about Anglo-Saxon liberty and the Norman yoke were paralleled north of the border by competing stories about the relationship between Scottish monarchs and the nobility, going back as far as the legendary King Fergus in 330 BC.[14] Although the *dramatis personae* were different, the range of messages the stories were used to convey was much the same in both cases.

The convergence in political culture was not so great that the Union of Parliaments in 1707 which brought the British state proper into existence can be presented as a voluntary agreement on both sides. Although the Scottish parliament approved the Articles of Union, there was much dissent outside, and many ballads were written lamenting the loss of Scottish independence. Nevertheless there were good reasons internal to Scottish political culture for approving the Union, and some of these were expressed in the debates of the time, for instance by parliamentarians such as Seafield, Paterson and Seton who pointed out that the liberties of the Scots, and especially their religious liberty, could best be secured by the creation of a strong common parliament, and a unified state able to repel common enemies (by implication the Catholic powers of Europe). Alongside this there ran a clear appreciation of the advantages of free trade with England to the Scottish economy.[15]

It was in the century following the Union, however, that cultural convergence accelerated, allowing us to speak of a British national identity emerging over and above English and Scottish identities. This is particularly evident in the work of the leading figures of the Scottish Enlightenment, who not only saw themselves as writing for a general British audience, but contributed significantly to the transformation of English political culture through their reworking of Whig ideology. It has often been suggested that this required these writers to turn their backs on their Scottishness. Evidence for this of a somewhat trivial kind can be seen in their attempts to weed out distinctively Scottish verbal expressions from their writing, but more seriously in their repudiation of the Scottish historical past, which is regarded as distinctly murky by comparison to England's. (When Hume discusses Scottish affairs in his *History of England*, for example, there are frequent passing references to the disorderly character and political backwardness of Scotland by comparison with its southern neighbour. At one point he considers the charge against Edward I that he ordered the annals of Scottish history to be destroyed in order to remove the basis for claims to Scottish independence. However, says Hume, 'it is not probable, that a nation, so rude and unpolished, should be possessed of any history, which deserves much to be regretted'.)[16] Yet it is possible to interpret the achievement of these writers in a different way: their aim was to present the British constitutional settlement of 1689 as the best example available of a liberal regime, enshrining religious toleration, the liberties of subjects, parliamentary supremacy and so forth, and one therefore which the Scots, given their past history, should be glad to be part of, but without crediting the English specifically with a natural genius for liberty. As Kidd has put it, 'Hume and other Scottish writers aimed to educate the English to appreciate their liberties by replacing their vulgar exceptionalism with a pan-European historical perspective.'[17]

There was of course a rival political culture manifested in Jacobitism that presented a very different view of Scottish history. Here the martial glories and liberty of the past were contrasted with the fettering imposed by the Union. But Jacobitism was condemned to be either reactionary or nostalgic, and its appeal to Lowland Scots in particular was therefore rather limited. In the longer run, when Jacobitism as a political force was exhausted, the Stuarts, and especially the romantic figure of Bonnie Prince Charlie, could be rehabilitated as symbols of Scotland's colourful past by those whose political principles remained liberal and Unionist. This, it has often been pointed out, was the particular achievement of Sir Walter Scott, whose fictional reworking of Jacobite history combined a sympathetic portrayal of the participants themselves as Scottish patriots with a clear message that their cause was a doomed one and that the future of Scotland lay in a modernizing Britain.[18]

Broadly speaking this cultural pattern has been passed down to the present: my claim is not that English and Scottish cultures are identical, which would be patently absurd, but that there is a great deal of convergence, in political culture especially, and also that writers, philosophers, artists and others have been able to move easily between the two audiences. This is especially relevant in the light of Gellner's thesis that the rise of exclusive forms of nationalism in nineteenth-century Europe is to be explained by the barriers to social mobility facing educated members of outlying cultures within modernizing states.[19] In the case of the Scots, linguistic and cultural overlap meant that access to the wider cultural marketplace provided by Britain was easily available, and many Scots chose to take advantage of it.[20] This is the first factor making a dual-level Anglo-British or Scottish-British identity feasible.

The second factor is mutual economic advantage, the fact that both communities have benefited from the continuing existence of the Union. I am not suggesting here that we should treat national identities as epiphenomena of economic forces. Nevertheless it is clear that one factor that fuels nationalist sentiment in divided societies is a sense that you are being exploited by the other group or groups.

In the present case both English and Scots were culturally well-equipped to take advantage of the large market created by the Union and the liberal economic regime of eighteenth-century Britain. To the extent that Weber was right about the origins of the spirit of capitalism, the Calvinist ethos prevalent in Scotland should have provided a particularly good basis for economic take-off.[21] Scotland's failure to develop prior to Union is usually attributed to lack of investment capital and difficulties in gaining access to English and European markets. This was reversed following the Union, and particularly in the second half of the eighteenth century, when Scottish economic growth actually outstripped England's in certain respects, for instance in overseas trade. England meanwhile benefited from having a larger market in which to sell its manufactured goods, and from the influx of Scottish talent, engineers, architects and so forth.

With the passage of time the pattern of Scotland's economic development has come to mirror that of Britain as a whole: as David McCrone has shown, if one looks at indicators such as industrial structure or the percentages of people in different occupational groups, Scotland's position is close to the average for Britain as a whole, and in some cases significantly closer than that of particular English regions such as the North West.[22] So although living standards in Scotland have never caught up with those in the southern part of England, the claim that both parties to the Union have benefited from it economically seems to me irrefutable. In the recent period there has also of course been the particular benefit to the Scottish side that because of the way in which the formulae for government expenditure are defined, Scots receive on average something like £1.15 per head for every £1 per head spent on public services in England. (I do not mean to give the impression that this is necessarily unfair, because to a considerable extent it reflects the different conditions that prevail in Scotland, but it does underline the continuing economic advantage to Scots of remaining in the Union, an advantage which will continue now the Parliament is established.)[23]

The third element contributing to the formation of a common British nationality over and above English and Scottish ones is what I have called an interwoven history. This is not just a matter of the two peoples being locked together in the same state for several centuries, nor it is simply a question of the two peoples having impacted on one another's development, for this would also be true of rival nationalities, my second category of cases. What I am pointing to instead is active collaboration between members of both nations in determining the course of political change, and so in defining the historic identity of the whole. In the period following the Union Scots quickly grasped the opportunities open to them to participate in British political life, to the extent of provoking an English backlash in the later part of the eighteenth century, when, as Linda Colley has reminded us, John Wilkes and his followers railed against the political influence of Scotsmen, who were suspected not only of harbouring tyrannical tendencies – the legacy of Jacobitism – but of grabbing the best posts in government and administration.[24] As the Empire expanded through the nineteenth century, the interweaving increased. It has often been pointed out that the Scots played a disproportionate role in imperial government, in the armed forces which stabilized it, and in settling and colonizing the imperial lands – Canada is the outstanding example. To the extent that British national identity was shaped by the imperial experience, by the sense of mission that underlay it and the victories and defeats that inevitably accompanied it, the English and Scots are bound together in a community of memory.[25]

It is sometimes suggested that if the Empire played a central role in the consolidation of a common British identity, that identity must have begun to fade as the Empire shrank, or in other words that the historical interweaving I have described no longer exists in a post-imperial Britain. There is no question that the retreat from empire, along with other factors, has seriously disrupted British national identity.[26] But it is wrong to suggest that the influences that originally created and shaped a national identity must continue to operate indefinitely if the identity is to survive. Once formed, such identities have remarkable staying power, in part because of the multiple functions – both personal and political – that they perform for the people who adopt them. Moreover even without the Empire as their springboard Scots continue to play a prominent role in British domestic politics. In the present government four of the most senior posts (apart from the Scottish Secretary himself) – Chancellor of the Exchequer, Foreign Secretary, Defence Secretary and Lord Chancellor – are all held by Scots, and it is only because of the tragically premature death of John Smith that we do not now have a Scottish Prime Minister. In that sense the interwoven history I have briefly described continues apace.

How should nested national identities be expressed politically?

The purpose of this historical cameo has been to point to the conditions that lead naturally to the emergence of a split-level national identity in societies divided in the way that Britain is divided. My claim is not that such identities are cast in aspic and must persist indefinitely into the future: that would be absurd, and at odds with the historical evidence about the emergence of a British identity that I have just been drawing on. It is rather that the wider identity cannot be seen as detrimental to, or as artificially imposed upon, members of the sub-nations. On the contrary, enthusiasm for the larger identity has usually been greatest among members of the smaller nations: the Scots have been keener to describe themselves as Britons than the English have (even Robert Burns was sometimes happy to wear this badge).[27] And here we must confront one of the major difficulties facing nationally divided societies in which one component nation, because of its relative size, has played a dominant role: members of that dominant nation find it harder to distinguish between the two levels of identity. Nearly all Scots have a clear sense of how British identity differs from both Scottish and English identities, but on the English side there is often confusion: most Englishmen would find it hard to explain what it means to be English as opposed to being British. As I suggested earlier, it is even doubtful that there is such a thing as an English *national* identity in the proper sense: there is a cultural identity that finds expression in certain distinctive tastes and styles of life, but if we look for the hallmarks of national identity such as political culture and shared history, we would be hard put to find anything that is distinctively English as opposed to British.

This asymmetry causes difficulties. Given that nationality depends upon mutual recognition, one could say that the source of the problem with British national identity lies with the English, who fail to understand the differences between themselves and the other nationalities as national differences: the Scots are just English people with a different accent, quaint but appealing costume and a folk culture. Scottish people rightly resent this obliviousness. The proper response is to create a political structure that explicitly recognizes the nature of the difference between the two communities. The reason for creating a devolved parliament in Edinburgh with constitutionally-defined autonomous powers is not merely that it allows Scottish people some degree of control over their own cultural and social institutions, but that it gives expression to one-half of the dual national identity I have been describing. Its importance is symbolic as much as material. For that reason the question 'If Scotland gets a parliament, why doesn't England or why don't the English regions?' seems to me misplaced. Given the characteristic way in which English and British identities are blurred in the minds of the English, there is no distinct English national identity that demands political recognition. If there is a good case to be made out for regional assemblies in England, this would rest either on practical considerations having to do with the efficient delivery of public services, or on the general democratic argument that decisions should be made as near as possible to the people affected by them, not on any analogy with the Scottish or Welsh cases.

The same phenomenon can be observed in the Canadian and Spanish cases, where one cultural group dominates the other nested nationalities. It has often been pointed out that English Canadians outside Quebec largely think of themselves as Canadians-who-happen-to-speak-English, rather than as a distinct national group within Canada,[28] and this in turn makes it hard for them to regard the Québécois as a nation and not simply as French-speaking Canadians. In Spain, the Castilian-speaking majority have regional identities (to Andalucia, Navarre, Valencia and so forth), but unlike the Catalans and Basques their national identity is unambiguously Spanish. It is sometimes suggested that things would become easier if the dominant group began to think of themselves as a separate nation.[29] This proposal seems artificial, however, given that the institutions and history of the dominant group are largely identical with those of the nation as a whole. It is more plausible to ask of the dominant group that it should recognize the separateness of the nested nationalities, and give practical expression to this recognition in the shape of asymmetrical political arrangements (parliaments for Scotland, Wales, the Basque country and Catalonia, distinct society status for Quebec) while continuing to affirm its national identity at the level of the state as a whole.

At the same time the analysis I have given of nationality in divided societies tells against the break-up of those societies into separate states. Where people have nested national identities, their higher-level identities also demand recognition through institutions of political self-determination. But what if one community begins to demand the opposite? What if a majority of Scots come to favour Scottish independence? Two issues arise here. The first is that we cannot treat a demand for independence (for instance a majority vote in that direction in a referendum) as decisive evidence that Scottish identity has become detached from British. The demand has to be interpreted: it might, for instance, be motivated largely by perceived economic advantage, or by indignation at some slight delivered by the English people or their representatives. But even if we treat the vote as an expression of political identity, it is still possible that the majority verdict is on this occasion wrong. The vote expresses a judgement: it says, in effect, 'the way that we now understand ourselves as a people requires that we should form a separate state'.[30] Just as we might say of an individual who tries not merely to reinterpret but to jettison the identity he has been brought up to have that he probably doesn't understand himself, we can say that for Scots to renounce their higher-level British identity would in one way be to fail to understand who they are, what makes them the people they are today.

In reply to this it might be said that such an interpretation seems to trap people in their own past: their inherited identities are being made to take precedence over their current sense of who they are. I agree that national identities are always in flux, and that independence votes by nested nations have to be treated as evidence that their identities are being reshaped in opposition to the larger nation of which they have up to now formed a sub-unit. If such votes are repeated, and if the majorities are substantial, then the evidence for this conclusion becomes strong. But I still want to insist that what is at stake is essentially a judgement about which political arrangement best expresses the complex set of national

and other political identities that most people in contemporary democracies possess, and that such judgements are not self-validating.

However this argument might not seem decisive by itself. To use a
somewhat misleading analogy, we think individual people should be free
to divorce even when doing so is a mistake in the sense that they're giving
up a valuable relationship for something that is less valuable. So the fact
that the Scots would be denying an important part of their identity in
opting for independence might not seem a conclusive reason for denying
their wish. But there is also a second consideration. The British people
taken together have established a valid claim to control the whole territory of Britain, and this claim would be infringed by a unilateral secession.
Claims to exercise territorial authority arise when people sharing a
common national identity form a political community, and occupy
territory over a substantial period of history.[31] Thus the English too
now have a stake in Scottish lands, a stake that arises from the process
that I described earlier, namely the emergence of a common national
identity from overlapping cultures, mutually advantageous economic
co-operation and an interwoven history. Unless and until there arises
some kind of radical discontinuity such that these historical factors
cease to affect contemporary political identities, the English majority
have a right to resist unilateral secession, and for the reasons I have
given they would be justified in doing so.[32]

The truth of this argument is sometimes obscured in contemporary
political debate by the popularity of the doctrine that political boundaries
should be decided by majority vote, so that if the inhabitants of any
particular territory vote for independence in a referendum, that territory
should be granted independence forthwith. The British government may
appear to have signalled its assent to this doctrine when it said that it had
no inherent interest in the territory of Northern Ireland, so that if at some
future point there should be a majority in that territory favouring union
with Ireland, their wish should be granted. It may have been necessary to
say this to get the peace process under way, but the doctrine itself is
wrong. It might seem to follow naturally from liberal and/or democratic
principles, but in fact it doesn't. If we try to settle boundaries by appeal to
liberal principles of consent alone, then we end up potentially with an
infinite regress with each individual person claiming sovereignty over the
piece of territory he happens to be standing on.[33] Equally majority voting
as a way of implementing democratic principles applies only once the
boundaries of the relevant constituency have been determined. A majority
vote cannot be used to fix these boundaries, since the outcome of such a
vote will itself depend on who is included in and who excluded from the
electorate that takes the initial vote. Because of this indeterminacy, it is
tempting to use existing administrative boundaries to define the public

among whom an independence vote will be held. But this is defensible only if these boundaries already enclose a political community with common interests and a shared identity.[34] We cannot, therefore, escape making qualitative judgements about national identities, and how far smaller group identities can nest comfortably within them. Only when it is established that the people living in region R do indeed constitute a separate nationality with a strong claim to self-determination, can a referendum in R then serve as a procedural device to legitimate their secession from existing state S.[35]

Nationalists of all kinds need to be true to their core belief, that where a group of people form a community with a common national identity, it is of very great importance that they should be able to exercise political self-determination. But this must apply universally and to identity at all levels. So where a political community includes nested nationalities, each layer of identity must be given proper recognition. That is the reason for seeking a constitutional settlement which devolves appropriate powers to the sub-nations, but it also reveals why majority voting alone cannot decide what is the appropriate structure of authority: a unilateral English vote to annul Scottish devolution ought to be given no more weight than a unilateral Scottish vote for independence. It is tempting for sub-nation nationalists to believe that by repeatedly demanding referendums on independence they will one day get the answer that they want, but in yielding to this temptation they abandon the principles that make nationalism an ethically appealing creed in the first place.

Conclusion

To return from this argument about the use and abuse of referendums to the general theme of this chapter, I have proposed that if we want to apply the principle of nationality to culturally divided societies, we must draw some qualitative distinctions: specifically between ethnic divisions, rival nationalities and nested nationalities. Politically speaking these cannot be treated in the same way: a political arrangement that might work for an ethnically plural state won't work for one inhabited by rival nationalities. I have been exploring particularly the phenomenon of nested nationalities, and trying to show how genuinely split-level national identities may arise, and how best to respond to their existence. Whether the factors that I cited to explain the emergence of a common British identity among the English and the Scots apply also in the case of Belgium, Canada, Spain, Switzerland and other societies with nested national identities remains to be seen. Cultural overlap may be less evident in linguistically divided societies; an interwoven history may be easier to achieve where the overarching nation-state emerged from a compact between its component nationalities rather than from a conquest; and so on. Such historical differences will determine how comfortable it is for present-day citizens in these societies to embrace split-level identities. My aim has simply been to explain how nested national identities are possible at all, and to draw some practical implications for the idea of national self-determination.

9

Is Deliberative Democracy Unfair to Disadvantaged Groups?

Over the last ten years or so, many democratic theorists have been drawn towards the idea of deliberative democracy. This is not because they believe that existing liberal democracies already conform to their conceptions of how an ideal deliberative democracy would work: no one could sensibly maintain that. But there appears now to be something of a consensus that if we want the real world systems that we call democracies to become more truly democratic, we should be looking for ways of propelling them towards the deliberative ideal.[1] What, then, is this ideal? A democratic system is deliberative when the decisions it takes are arrived at through a process of open discussion to which each participant is able to contribute freely, but is equally willing to listen to and consider opposing views; as a result, the decisions reached reflect not simply the prior interests or prior opinions of the participants, but the judgements they make after reflecting on the arguments made on each side, and the principles or procedures that should be used to resolve disagreements.[2] Such an ideal democracy promises to meet at least the following three conditions: it is *inclusive*, in the sense that each member of the political community in question takes part in decision-making on an equal basis; it is *rational*, in the sense that the decisions reached are determined by the reasons offered in the course of deliberation, and/or the procedures used to resolve disagreement in the event that no consensus can be found; and it is *legitimate*, in the sense that every participant can understand how and why the outcome was reached even if he or she was not personally convinced by the arguments offered in its favour.

Critiques of deliberative democracy

These are bold promises to make, and we need to put deliberative democracy under the microscope to see whether it can really live up to the
claims that have been made on its behalf. Moreover, although deliberative
democracy has won favour among many democratic theorists, it has not
escaped powerful criticism. I shall just mention two kinds of criticism
before coming to a third kind that forms the main subject of this chapter.
The first set of critics are realists who point to the huge and seemingly
unbridgeable gap between the deliberative ideal and the practice of
existing democracies.[3] How is it possible for large and complex societies
to be governed by deliberative assemblies which in their nature must be
small, slow-moving bodies? Deliberative democracy might have suited
the ancient Athenians, who could listen to and reflect upon the orations
of Pericles, Alcibiades and the rest before deciding whether to send out a
fleet to attack the Peloponnese, but how could it function in a world in
which not only military but many other decisions – financial decisions,
for example – have to be made in minutes rather than days, leaving no
time for popular consultation let alone deliberation? Furthermore, even
where deliberative assemblies might have a feasible role to play in decision-making, why should we believe that the participants will adhere to
the norms of deliberation sketched above, and not merely manipulate the
institution to their own advantage? Deliberative democracy requires a
high degree of social responsibility on the part of each participant: yet
everything we know about politics suggests that it attracts people with
Machiavellian dispositions and rewards those who act on them to greatest effect.

The second critical assault on deliberative democracy comes from
social choice theory. Here it is said that whereas deliberative democracy
assumes that something like a general will can emerge from the deliberative process, social choice theory tells us that this must be an illusion.[4]
Arrow's Impossibility Theorem and its descendants prove that there is no
method of reaching a collective decision from an array of individual
preferences that conforms to a set of conditions that we would expect a
democratic procedure to respect. Since we cannot assume that public
discussion will always result in unanimity, deliberative democracy must
finally employ a decision procedure which might, for instance, be majority voting among the body in question. But social choice theory reveals
the indeterminacy and arbitrariness of procedures such as majority voting, and so undermines both the rationality and the legitimacy claims of
deliberative democracy. If the decision made depends upon arbitrary
features of the procedure used to reach it (such as the order in which

alternatives are put to the vote) then its success is not simply a reflection of the weight of the reasons offered to support it; and equally there seems to be no strong reason why those who end up on the losing side should regard the decision as a legitimate one.

So deliberative democracy has to withstand both the empirical criticism of the realists and the formal criticism of the social choice theorists. Now I believe that on both fronts good defences can be offered, but I don't propose to try to offer them here.[5] I have introduced these critiques mainly to distinguish and contrast them with a third critique that has emerged more recently and from a quite different quarter. This third critique challenges deliberative democracy's credentials as a fair method of reaching collective decisions in a plural society; it claims that deliberative democracy is biased against groups that historically have been disadvantaged – the poor, ethnic minorities, women and so forth. Deliberation is not a neutral procedure, but one that works in favour of people with certain cultural attributes, and especially white middle-class males. This is a serious challenge because it directly contests one of the main claims advanced in support of deliberative democracy, namely that it is capable of reaching decisions that are more socially just than those reached in existing liberal democracies, where the distribution of political power tends to reflect the distribution of wealth and other forms of social advantage. According to deliberative democrats, what should count in deliberative settings are reasons and arguments, not the colour of one's skin or the size of one's bank balance. This ideal may never be fully realized, but to the extent that it is, democratic procedures can serve as a counterweight to the inequalities generated in a society in which capitalists dominate workers, men dominate women, and whites dominate blacks and other ethnic groups. But the critics dispute this, or at least wish to qualify it severely. And in so doing, they also put in question the claims about inclusion, rationality and legitimacy that I sketched earlier. Deliberative democracy may be formally inclusive, in the sense that everyone is permitted to enter and speak in democratic forums, but if the debate by its very nature favours some groups at the expense of others, it is not inclusive in a substantive sense. Similarly if the reasons that prove to count in deliberative settings are not reasons for everyone, but only reasons for particular groups or coalitions of groups, then the outcome cannot be described as rational in a sense that transcends group membership. If the rationality claim falls, so does the legitimacy claim, for why should the disadvantaged groups accept as legitimate a procedure that relies upon methods of argument and reasons that they cannot share?

So there is much at stake here, and we must look more closely at the substance of the third critique, as it has been articulated by authors such as Lynn Sanders and Iris Young.[6] I distinguish two aspects of this critique, the second raising deeper and more difficult issues than the first.

Inequality in deliberative institutions

Sanders and Young both argue that there is inequality within deliberative institutions between advantaged and disadvantaged groups. This goes beyond the problem of access to such institutions. Currently, as we well know, disadvantaged groups tend to be underrepresented in political forums – they vote less often, play a smaller role in most pressure groups, have fewer elected representatives and so forth. From the standpoint of deliberative democracy this is unacceptable, since deliberation cannot be inclusive, and therefore cannot be expected to produce fair outcomes, unless the composition of the deliberating body reflects with reasonable accuracy the composition of the whole body of citizens to whom its decisions will apply. How this state of affairs is to be rectified is the subject of ongoing debate: in particular there is disagreement about whether in the case of representative institutions there should be quotas to ensure proportional representation of women and ethnic minorities.[7] This controversy about the best policy to ensure inclusion should nevertheless not obscure the underlying agreement between deliberative democrats and their critics about the need for disadvantaged groups to have access to democratic institutions on an equal footing with other citizens. According to Young and Sanders, however, equal access is not sufficient, because it provides no guarantee that members of disadvantaged groups will be treated as equals once they are inside the institutions. They may, for instance, be reluctant to engage in political argument, feeling that they have no right to speak or that others will not take their interventions seriously. Sanders cites evidence about the behaviour of men and women on juries, and about school groups made up of whites and blacks, which suggests that men in one case and white students in the other contribute disproportionately to group discussion.[8] Assuming, as seems reasonable, that there is a connection between the volume of argument behind a position and the likelihood of its prevailing, the implication is that in cases where men and women or whites and ethnic minorities had different concerns and interests in a deliberative forum, the disadvantaged groups would tend to lose out because of their reluctance to state their case in public.

Even Sanders concedes, however, that the position is more complex than my brief summary has suggested. As she says, 'it appears that some styles of group discussion are more likely to elicit the views of all group members than are others'.[9] In the case of juries, she makes use of a contrast between 'verdict-driven deliberation' and 'evidence-driven delib-eration' which was first introduced in an empirical study of jury beha-viour.[10] The evidence-driven style of deliberation encourages a wide range of views to be expressed, and therefore tends to draw more of the participants into the discussion; it also favours open-mindedness, in the sense of willingness to change position when fresh evidence is produced. It has been found that women tend to favour this style of deliberation more than men, and in particular that all-female groups are characterized by active attempts to draw the more silent members into discussion.[11] The lesson for deliberative democrats, therefore, is not that they should throw up their hands in dismay when it is pointed out that members of disadvantaged groups tend to participate less in collective deliberation, but that they should look for ways of ensuring that deliberation takes a form that corresponds to an evidence-driven jury, which means that instead of trying to move quickly to a yes/no decision, the arguments for and against different options should be explored without individual participants having to declare which they support. This, it seems to me, is what good political deliberation would in any case require. Where a decision has to be reached on an issue of some complexity, it is better for discussion to be open and exploratory at first, and it would be a mistake to require participants to signal at an early point which option they support, because the effect of doing so would be to encourage the deliberators simply to marshal the arguments that support their initial view, rather than to listen to and engage with all the perspectives put forward.

A similar point can be made concerning Iris Young's remarks about parliamentary debates and adversarial court procedures in which as she puts it 'Deliberation is competition. Parties to [the] dispute aim to win the argument, not to achieve mutual understanding.'[12] It may indeed follow that such contexts 'privilege those who like contests and know the rules of the game. Speech that is assertive and confrontational is here more valued than speech that is tentative, exploratory, or conciliatory' and that 'this privileges male speaking styles over female'. But this shows that parlia-mentary debates and adversarial courts, whatever their other virtues, are not good examples of deliberative democracy at work, and it is hard to imagine deliberative theorists saying otherwise. Deliberative democracy requires that political debate should be structured in such a way that, first, as wide a range of relevant views and arguments as possible should enter the debate, so that the ensuing discussion should genuinely reflect the concerns, interests and convictions of the members of the deliberating body; and second, that as the body attempts to move towards a solution to the issue that they confront, it should be the weight of the reasons offered in support of the different positions that counts. This means that participants, rather than trying to win, in the sense of ensuring that their initial preferences prevail, should be listening to and weighing up what others are saying, searching for the solution that has the strongest reasons behind it. That, of course, is an ideal description. But it can be approximated more or less exactly depending partly on the structure and partly on the ethos of the deliberating body. To give one example, studies of citizens' juries – small groups of randomly chosen citizens brought together to debate issues of current concern such as health policy – emphasize the importance of having moderators whose job it is to ensure that everyone has a chance to contribute to the discussion, and that different points of view get properly explored and critically scrutinized.[13] Now, in so far as these conditions for good deliberation correspond to forms of speech and argument that Young characterizes as typically female rather than typically male – speech that is 'tentative, exploratory, or conciliatory', speech used 'to give information and ask questions rather than state opinions or initiate controversy', a deliberative form of democracy should serve women far better than the institutions that she castigates for their male bias.[14]

Is deliberation biased against disadvantaged groups?

So far I have been addressing the claim that deliberative settings will inevitably be dominated by privileged groups at the expense of women and disadvantaged minorities, because the former will dominate the discussion; my reply is that there are ample reasons stemming from the deliberative ideal itself to favour forms of debate in which this does not happen. But I said there was also a deeper issue here, and that is the issue whether the very idea of deliberation – the idea that decisions be made through a process of reasoned argument in which the weightier arguments finally prevail – is not biased against disadvantaged groups. This indeed is Young's claim when she says that deliberation privileges speech that is 'formal and general', speech that is 'dispassionate and disembodied' and speech that 'proceeds from premise to conclusion in an orderly fashion that clearly lays out its inference structure'.[15] Sanders, likewise, asserts that deliberation requires talk that is 'rational, contained, and oriented to a shared problem' as opposed to talk that is 'impassioned, extreme, and the product of particular interests'.[16] Both maintain that these norms of acceptable speech discriminate against women and ethnic minorities, whose perspectives and demands need to be presented in other ways. It is not simply that the speech of members of the disadvantaged groups tends to be more 'excited and embodied', using physical gestures and forms of emotional expression that are lacking in the speech of white middle-class men, but that prevailing norms of deliberation are inherently unsuited to the presentation of their concerns. According to Young and Sanders, what disadvantaged groups need is not deliberation at all, but other forms of political interaction in which their distinct perspectives and distinct concerns can emerge more clearly.

What, then, are these alternative modes of political communication? Young mentions three – greeting, rhetoric and storytelling – and Sanders mentions one – testimony – which corresponds roughly to what Young means by storytelling.[17] Greeting refers to the various formal and informal ways in which parties to political discussion recognize one another prior to and during the discussion. Rhetoric refers to forms of speech and argument that identify the speaker with a particular audience, and which evoke particular symbols or cultural values that resonate with this audience; rhetoric also serves to engage and motivate the audience not merely to think but also to act in certain ways. Storytelling, finally, refers to speech in which someone presents a personal narrative – their life-story, so to speak – as a way of explaining what it means to occupy a certain place in society and/or to dramatize the injustice suffered by a certain group. Young gives the example of wheelchair users describing the obstacles they have faced in getting around, and Sanders suggests that the position of American blacks may remain incomprehensible to the white majority unless blacks can describe their historical experience through forms of personal testimony.

Now it would be very easy – too easy – to respond to these proposals by saying that greeting, rhetoric and storytelling can all be added to the deliberative pot by treating them as additional forms of dialogue that deliberative democrats have no reason to reject. That response is too easy because it overlooks the fact that deliberation is one method of reaching political decisions among others, with particular virtues that distinguish it from its rivals and that are unlikely to be preserved if all forms of political interaction are allowed to count indiscriminately as 'deliberation'. For instance, deliberation must exclude forms of bargaining where groups capitalize on the advantages they enjoy along particular dimensions to secure outcomes that lean as far as possible in their direction. Bargaining certainly involves political communication, and even one could say forms of argument – along the lines 'If you opt for X, then I'm sorry to say that I'll have to do Y' – but this is quite different from the kind of argument required by deliberation.[18] But we have not yet established precisely which forms of communication and reasoning are consistent with the deliberative ideal, and so we cannot yet say whether greeting, rhetoric and storytelling should be included as legitimate elements in deliberation. Nor can we say whether these alternative forms of communication are likely to serve the interests of disadvantaged groups better than familiar styles of deliberation. We need first to establish how deliberation proper is supposed to proceed, and then ask whether there is any reason to think that this method of reaching political decisions is biased against disadvantaged groups.

Unfortunately supporters of deliberative democracy have given rather different accounts of the modes of reasoning required by the deliberative ideal. One view, inspired by the work of John Rawls, and presented most eloquently in a series of essays by Joshua Cohen, describes the ideal deliberative procedure as involving 'public reasoning'.[19] This requires participants in deliberation to confine themselves to arguing for the proposals they favour in a certain way: they must put forward reasons that they believe others must accept, their differing personal commitments notwithstanding. As Cohen puts it:

> it will not do simply to advance reasons that one takes to be true or compelling: such considerations may be rejected by others who are themselves reasonable. One must instead find reasons that are compelling to others, acknowledging those others as equals, aware that they have alternative reasonable commitments, and knowing something about the kinds of commitments that they are likely to have – for example, that they may have moral or political commitments that impose what they take to be overriding obligations.[20]

According to this view, then, deliberation must proceed by presenting arguments that everyone has reason to accept, arguments in other words that appeal to common ground – to shared principles of justice, or to ideas of the common good. Equally there must be a high probability of arriving at a consensus – if everyone appeals only to reasons that everyone else can accept, it is hard to see how there can be substantive disagreement about what should be done. Cohen escapes this conclusion by pointing out that there could be disagreement about the relative *weight* of considerations that passed the public reason test, and so there may still have to be a majority vote at the end of deliberation. But still, on this view, everyone would endorse the reasons that lay behind the decision reached; it's just that some would have weighted them differently, and come to a different practical conclusion.

Clearly the Rawls–Cohen view passes with flying colours the tests of rationality and legitimacy that I referred to at the beginning of the chapter. Deliberative decisions will be rational in the sense that they are justified by reasons that everyone in the relevant community has in common, and their legitimacy flows directly from the same source. But at the same time it seems highly vulnerable to the critique launched by authors such as Sanders and Young. For it requires disadvantaged groups in putting forward their case to restrict themselves to arguments that are also compelling to advantaged groups. Or to be more precise, although they are not formally barred from presenting arguments that make sense only from their particular perspective, they have to be prepared to switch to public reasoning if they are to count as reasonable, and therefore as people who meet the conditions for inclusion in the deliberation.

I believe, however, that this view of deliberation is too restrictive: it offers too monolithic an account of the type of reasoning that must lie behind a decision if it is to pass the test of democratic legitimacy. To begin with, unless we are going to confine deliberative democracy to a small sub-set of the decisions that a democratic political community may have to take, deliberative procedures have to be flexible enough to cope with many different kinds of issue. In the case of some issues, the scope for reason-giving in the Rawls–Cohen sense is very limited. Some questions, for instance, require first of all that people should simply state their preferences.[21] Suppose that as members of a local community we have to choose between various possible sites for our new public library: here the main role for democratic deliberation will be to discover who mainly uses the library and then which location they will find most convenient. We may also believe, of course, that we should pay special attention to the needs of certain groups, say the elderly or the disabled, in which case we will need to give extra weight to the preferences expressed by members of these groups. In that sense our final decision will be informed by a principle as well as by expressed preferences. But the primary information that we need in reaching a decision in a case such as this is information about what most people prefer, at this point consulting only their own convenience. It may be that one site is so overwhelmingly preferred that there is no need for further deliberation. If, on the other hand, there is substantial disagreement, we may need to settle on a procedure to resolve it (for instance we might ask participants to rank the sites in numerical order and then use a Borda count to select a preferred site). In that case, there would have to be a reasoned argument as to why *that* procedure is the appropriate one to use for *this* issue. But the point is that participants do not have to offer substantive reasons in support of the site they favour in a case like this; it may be enough that they state their preferences and agree on a fair procedure for reaching a decision. There is no need for people to move to the moral high ground and present only reasons that pass the Rawls–Cohen test.

In other cases the problem may be that people move on to the moral high ground too quickly, in the sense that they find themselves arguing from incompatible moral premises that they nevertheless take to be fundamental. The debate over the legalization of abortion is often taken as an example here. The difficulty is that, if we apply the Rawls–Cohen test, then both sides are reduced to silence because they know that the arguments they want to make will not be compelling to those who disagree. Thus pro-life advocates will typically rest their arguments on religious assumptions about the sanctity of life that they cannot reasonably expect their secular opponents to share. If deliberation is to proceed here, it must take the form of looking for solutions that neither side finds completely abhorrent. In an illuminating discussion of the issue, Gutmann and Thompson speak of 'an economy of moral disagreement'.[22] This involves first of all showing that you respect the reasons advanced by your opponents even though you do not share them – you recognize the depth and the sincerity of their commitments. Then it involves finding practical solutions that do not blatantly offend these commitments.[23]

Sometimes deliberation will indeed involve appealing to substantive principles that everyone (or almost everyone) in the political community holds in common. Thus in a debate about educational policy, it may turn out that a principle of equal opportunity is universally endorsed – everyone agrees that children should have the same opportunities to learn no matter what their sex, class or ethnic background. But rather than this principle being invoked because it passes the reasonable rejection test, it may be applied simply because it turns out in the course of discussion that this is indeed a principle that everyone endorses. In other words, people begin by arguing about education from a variety of perspectives, some tightly bound up with their personal values or religious beliefs, but they realize as discussion progresses that the arguments they are making have little appeal to others. Thus a Muslim might argue in favour of state-supported Muslim schools by claiming that it is vitally important that a child's religious background should be reinforced by his or her school, but quickly discover that this view was not shared by others, indeed that many people held precisely the opposite opinion. But this line of argument having run into the sand, he might argue instead that Muslim children would in many cases not flourish academically unless they were sent to schools where the teaching reflected their cultural values, and this argument invokes a principle of equal opportunity that can appeal to many others in the deliberating body – not because it reflects some universal standard of rationality, but simply because as a matter of fact it forms part of the underlying ethos of the community in question. Rather than deliberation being legitimate only when the deliberators confine themselves to public reasoning in the Rawls–Cohen sense, the suggestion here is that the search for agreement will itself act as a filter on the kinds of reason that prevail in the discussion, sectarian reasons being weeded out precisely because it becomes apparent to their supporters that they are not going to command wide assent. It is unnecessary to specify in advance what kinds of reason will be permitted to determine policy; we should rely instead on the process of deliberation to select reasons that are generally accepted.[24]

It might be said by way of criticism here that deliberative democracy only requires that a *majority* should be convinced of the rightness of a certain policy: unanimity may be the ideal, but we know that in most cases this is unrealizable, so decisions will have to be made by majority vote. By the same token, the principles that survive the deliberative filter need only be principles that attract majority support – if I can see that most of my audience are nodding in agreement when I invoke principle P, I need not be concerned by the fact that others are rolling their eyes and grinding their teeth, so long as my concern is just that my arguments should prevail in the debate. If we apply the Rawls–Cohen criterion, by contrast, I am obliged to find reasons that are compelling to everyone, and this is a stronger constraint on deliberation than the one I am offering.

Well, I agree that democratic deliberation must include more than just searching for whatever arguments will bring a majority of your fellow-deliberators on to your side. The deliberative process must aim to discover the policy outcome that enjoys the widest possible support, even though it is unrealistic to suppose that strict unanimity will ever be achieved. Thus if it turns out that 51 per cent of the deliberating body will support outcome O, but that 80 per cent will support outcome O', which is not radically different from O, but omits elements that many of the 29 per cent find quite objectionable, then good deliberation should culminate in choosing O'. What motivates this choice is first of all respect for one's fellow-deliberators. They have sincerely-held reasons for rejecting O, reasons which I do not share, but which I can recognize as reasons for them. If there is an alternative such as O' which accommodates these reasons without requiring me to give up a great deal, then I should favour that. Moreover I should do so not only out of respect for those I disagree with, but in order to promote a general atmosphere of trust inside the deliberating body. Next time round I may turn out to be in a minority that has strong and sincere reasons for objecting to the policy that commands majority support, and I will want my reasons listened to and if possible accommodated.[25]

My proposal, then, is that we should understand deliberation not as requiring that we restrict ourselves to offering reasons and arguments that must commend themselves to all members of the deliberating body, but as requiring only that we should seek agreement on terms that respect our fellow-deliberators and their convictions.[26] This requirement, I have suggested, will itself serve as a filter that eliminates certain arguments in the course of the debate without disqualifying them *a priori*. Armed now with this more accommodating understanding of how deliberation is supposed to work, let's return to the challenge posed by Young and Sanders, which as you will recall holds that deliberation is inherently biased against disadvantaged groups, who must use other forms of communication – greeting, rhetoric and testimony/storytelling – if their perspectives and concerns are to receive proper attention. And let's consider the charges against deliberation first, and then the merits of the proposed alternatives.

Among the charges levelled at deliberation by Young and Sanders are that it privileges speech that is rational and dispassionate at the expense of speech that is emotional and passionate; that it privileges formal and abstract reasoning at the expense of the concrete concerns of particular groups; and that it privileges speech that is 'moderate' at the expense of speech that is 'extreme'. Consider the first charge. To me this seems to rely on a false dichotomy between reason and emotion – false in the sense that all political speech and argument must convey the feelings and commitments of the speaker, but also give reasons either positively for some proposal, or negatively against some alternative (which might just be the status quo). A cry of pain is not a political intervention, unless it is implicitly or explicitly linked to some proposal for relieving the pain. It's true that speakers sometimes say, in effect, 'this state of affairs is intolerable', and show why it is intolerable, but this makes sense only in a context in which other speakers have remedies to suggest. As we move from protest or outrage towards solutions, standard canons of rationality must apply – it would clearly be unreasonable to propose as a solution a policy that actually made matters worse for the affected group, or that subjected some other group to precisely the kinds of suffering or deprivation that inspired the original protest. Emotional speech is important because it demonstrates to others how strongly the group in question feel about the situation they find themselves in, but rational speech is important too, because of the need to convince others that the remedy you propose is indeed a remedy.[27] It seems to me, in fact, rather insulting to disadvantaged groups to suggest that norms of argumentative rationality are loaded against them, because it implies that they cannot give coherent arguments for the changes they want to bring about.

Next, we have the charge that deliberation favours 'speech that is formal and general' and in that way discriminates against speakers who want to draw attention to some concrete injustice or the concerns of a particular group. Once again I believe this creates a false dichotomy. Very often political argument takes the form of connecting the situation in which a particular group finds itself to some general principle that has been applied in the past to other groups and that now commands widespread assent. Thus wheelchair users may want to describe in some detail the way that their mobility opportunities are reduced by thoughtless town planning or building design. But the relevance of these descriptions is that they bring the group under the rubric of a more general principle, namely the principle that those with special needs should be granted the resources that allow them to enjoy the same set of basic opportunities as other citizens. It is true that in moving from the particular case to the more general principle we lose something of the specificity of the particular – by classifying wheelchair users as people with special needs we are putting them into the same general category as blind people, people suffering from certain diseases and so on – but this may not be to their disadvantage. They may attract more sympathy and support precisely because we now see them alongside others whose needs may be seen as more urgent still. The claim 'we are like the Xs whom everyone agrees should be given special treatment' is a powerful claim to make in political argument, but its logic is to advance a particular claim under the umbrella of a general principle.

Finally, we have the charge that deliberation favours moderate speech over extreme speech, which I am taking here to be an observation not about the *manner* of speech that is favoured but about its *substance*; the charge, in other words, is that radical demands and proposals are disfavoured, and middle-of-the-road, compromise proposals favoured. In one way, I believe, this charge is indeed true. Take an issue like affirmative action on which people hold a wide spectrum of views – at one extreme there is the view that employers should be totally free to employ whomever they like, even if they are sexually or racially prejudiced; at the other extreme there is the view that justice requires us to apply strict ethnic, racial and sexual quotas to ensure that in every branch of employment each group is represented in exact proportion to its size; in between there are a number of positions that we could describe as moderate. Suppose the members of our political community hold views that are evenly distributed across this spectrum. The outcome of (good) deliberation is likely to be one of the moderate views, for reasons that should be clear from my earlier account of the deliberative process – people will abandon arguments that they find command little general support, they will search for a solution that does not blatantly offend the commitments of others, and so forth. But then it might be said that this is exactly what democracy requires in such a case. To complain that one of the extreme views – say the strong quotas view, which might indeed attract the support of some members of disadvantaged racial groups – has not been adopted, is to complain about democracy itself, and not about deliberation as a procedure. Sanders says, at one point, 'In settings where there are gross inequities in power and status, calling for compromise may be perilously close to suppressing the challenging perspectives of marginalized groups. Such suppression, when it occurs, is not democratic.'[28] But there is a crucial difference here between *suppressing* a perspective – not allowing it to enter the democratic debate, or ignoring it when it is introduced – which is indeed undemocratic, and *not following* it when a final decision is reached. Except in cases where everyone has the same preferences, or can be brought to concur with the same set of judgements, democracy cannot help but be a process of compromise in which participants give up some part of their initial demands for the sake of reaching agreement. The claim made on behalf of deliberative democracy is that it allows each perspective to be considered and weighed in the course of deliberation, without of course being able to guarantee that any particular perspective will prevail in the final outcome.[29]

Alternatives to deliberation

Let me turn now from the critical charges levelled against deliberation to the alternatives proposed by Young and Sanders. I do not propose to spend much time either on greeting or on rhetoric. I think that Young is perfectly right to say that greeting rituals may perform a significant function within political communities, particularly perhaps when the community is being enlarged to include new members. But the role of greeting here is only to create an atmosphere in which deliberation or other forms of politics can proceed, making people feel at home, and giving them some confidence that their arguments will be listened to. Indeed one might say that greeting may be impossible unless there is already some degree of sympathetic recognition between the parties concerned – witness the difficulties encountered in getting hardened enemies to shake hands or sit down at the same table. Greeting is as much symptomatic of trust as it is generative. But the main point here is that greeting surely cannot substitute for deliberative or other procedures that move a political body towards a collective decision.

As to rhetoric, while one can say that it is a powerful motivating force when people are united in their aims, it is equally clearly a divisive force in situations of conflict, because the rhetoric used by one group may be more alienating to the others than the concrete policies it is used to support. In 1968, the proposal that some restrictions should be put on immigration into Britain would have commanded widespread assent, even among ethnic groups who were themselves recent immigrants, but when Enoch Powell justified this by saying that he saw 'the River Tiber foaming with much blood' if (non-white) immigration were allowed to continue, the effect of his rhetoric was severely to inflame relations between whites and ethnic immigrants. This also underlines the point that no group has a monopoly on rhetoric. Indeed insofar as historically advantaged groups are better placed than disadvantaged groups to engage in political *argument*, one would also expect them to be better placed to produce political *rhetoric*, having at their disposal the resources of the established culture to draw upon for their symbols and analogies (in Powell's case, a classical education gone to waste). So when rhetoric enters political discourse there is no reason to think that disadvantaged groups will benefit, and one might go further and say with Benhabib that Young's proposal 'would limit rather than enhance social justice because rhetoric moves people and achieves results without having to render an account of the bases on which it induces people to engage in certain courses of action rather than others'.[30] In other words, because rhetoric conceals rather than reveals the grounds on which decisions are taken, it is less likely than reasoned argument to produce socially just policies.

A better case, I believe, can be made on behalf of 'testimony' or 'story-telling'. It may be difficult for people who have not experienced certain kinds of oppression or deprivation to understand the predicament of those who have without this being brought to life by personal testimony. So it has a legitimate role to play in the process of deliberation. Yet as a mode of political communication, it suffers from two limitations.[31] First, it is difficult to know how reliable or how representative one person's life-story is unless this is being used to corroborate and illuminate a more impersonal (for instance sociological) account of the general position of the group he or she belongs to. Young says 'because everyone has stories to tell... and because each can tell her story with equal authority, the stories have equal value in the communicative situation'.[32] But this is surely false. Stories can be treated merely as expressions of personal feeling, but if they are supposed to be more than that, their value depends first on their veracity and second on their capacity to capture the experience and the perspective of a wider group. In a later paper Young acknowledges this: 'valid generalities about people and groups of course must be supported by well known methods of inductive inference, including relying on many cases.'[33]

Second, it is unfortunately not the case that by adding together the testimony of many different individuals, we can arrive at an overall perspective which provides a solution to the problems that the various stories are highlighting.[34] A multiplicity of perspectives is just that: a multiplicity. Young sometimes speaks as though the perspectives of the various groups were complementary, so that we can get an accurate overall picture of how our society looks by allowing each group to fill in one part of the canvas from its own perspective. She speaks of 'comprehensive social knowledge' emerging from interaction between groups with different stories to tell about the social world.[35] But the perspectives may give rise to *conflicting* accounts, in which case the only way to get at the truth will be to bracket off all perspectives and call in the social scientists. For example: it is well known that rich people and poor people tend to have conflicting perceptions of the opportunity structure of liberal societies – the rich seeing these societies as meritocratic (where people end up on the social ladder depends largely on their own talents and efforts), the poor seeing them as unmeritocratic (where people end up depends largely on factors outside of their control such as family background and connections). Juxtaposing these two perspectives doesn't tell us much except perhaps that people are always inclined to rationalize their own position. To discover which perception is nearer to the truth – and therefore what we need to do, assuming that we value equality of opportunity as an ideal – we have to go beyond subjective experience and begin looking systematically at the evidence about relative rates of social mobility and the factors that might explain them.[36]

I am also very doubtful about Young's claim that the effect of introducing competing perspectives into political discussion is to encourage the participants 'to express their proposals as appeals to justice rather than expressions of mere self-interest or preference'.[37] It is common ground between us that political discussion can proceed to a legitimate conclusion only if this process occurs – if discussants present reasons for their proposals that go beyond narrow self-interest and sectarian conceptions of value and appeal to conceptions of justice and other principles that others may share or at least find acceptable. The question is whether introducing new perspectives through personal testimony and the like will have such an effect. Young's idea, I think, is that being confronted with a new and radically different perspective on some issue will force participants to question the assumptions from which they have been arguing up to now. Suppose there is some convenient way of selecting people to hold special offices that most of us have up to now regarded as uncontentious (a seniority rule, for instance). When the effects of this practice on a particular minority group are pointed out, we are forced to ask whether the rule we have been using is really fair, or whether it has not served merely to perpetuate the position of well-established groups. So far, so good: we can imagine this happening in certain cases. But now consider another possible effect of introducing unfamiliar perspectives into democratic debate: by widening the perceived social distance between groups, it may weaken each group's commitment to deal justly with the others.

In suggesting this I am relying on research undertaken by social psychologists which shows that the boundaries of the moral community within which people are willing to apply principles of justice to fellow-members are affected by perceptions of similarity and common identity.

In these studies, each subject's degree of identification with a range of social groups is measured, and then the subject is asked whether he or she is willing to extend justice to the group in the form, for example, of respecting its members' civil rights, or providing resources to support its activities.[38] It turns out that there is a strong correlation between identification and justice, even among subjects whose political attitudes are generally liberal. Other studies have shown that people who identify exclusively with their ethnic sub-group as opposed to embracing a more inclusive identity alongside it are less willing to accept the authority of procedures that may be used to resolve disputes or allocate resources, and become more concerned about how well or how badly they have fared personally in the outcome – in other words their thinking tends to be instrumental rather than justice-driven.[39] Now deliberative legitimacy depends upon participants being motivated to find principles of justice that can be shared by all members of the political community in question, and being willing to accept the outcome of deliberative procedures as fair even if they are required to give up a substantial part of what they had initially demanded, or initially enjoyed. Highlighting radical differences between groups within the community may erode these motivational conditions.

In consequence, as I have argued elsewhere, democratic deliberation that serves the cause of social justice is most likely to occur in a community whose members share a common identity that transcends their group-specific identities – which in practice means a shared national identity.[40] My focus here, however, is on how to proceed in democratic deliberation if you want your fellow-deliberators to deal with you fairly – to assess and act on your claims in terms of principles of justice that command wide support in the deliberating body. The answer, I think, is that you must strike a fine balance between emphasizing what you have in common with other members of your audience, so as to win their sympathy and motivate them to see you as someone to whom justice is owed, and emphasizing the ways in which you are different, and which mean that you have special needs or suffer special disadvantages.[41] So returning now to the question of testimony, this may form an effective mode of communication so long as the content of the testimony, and the form in which it is presented, is not so alien to the audience as to raise barriers between the group the testifier is trying to represent and the rest of the community, so inducing hostility rather than a concern for justice. When Sanders, for example, cites approvingly the claim that rap music may be an effective form of testimony for young blacks, she seems to see the testimony only through the eyes of the blacks themselves; it is difficult to envisage this being a persuasive means of communication with citizens generally. But perhaps this does not concern her. She says, 'There's no assumption in testimony of finding a common aim, no expectation of a discussion oriented to the resolution of a community problem.'[42]

This statement may serve to highlight a difference in perspective between deliberative democrats and their critics in the third camp, a difference which is concealed within the title of this chapter. If we ask 'Is deliberative democracy unfair to disadvantaged groups?', we may be asking 'Is deliberative democracy *materially* fair?', meaning 'Does it give minority groups a fair chance to influence the outcome, thereby also delivering policies that address their needs and interests in a fair way?' This is how I would understand the question, and also I believe how other deliberative democrats such as Cohen would understand it. But the critics might understand it differently, as the question 'Does deliberative democracy give adequate recognition to the perspectives of disadvantaged groups?', a question that places the emphasis on giving everyone a chance to speak politically in their own authentic voice. As we have seen, the assumption here is that every story is of equal value. As Sanders puts it, 'testimony is also radically egalitarian: the standard for whether a view is worthy of public attention is simply that everyone should have a voice, a chance to tell her story'.[43] By contrast, the deliberative ideal requires that we should endeavour to put forward views and arguments that commend themselves to our fellow deliberators, on grounds of their intrinsic cogency, or because they invoke reasons and principles that are widely shared – a standard that involves discrimination between expressed views, and that is therefore not egalitarian in Sanders' sense.

What concerns me, however, is that fairness in this expressive sense may come at the expense of fairness in the material sense. Consider the position of disadvantaged groups in contemporary liberal democracies, especially ethnic minorities with a history of material and cultural disadvantage. Their members typically have fewer resources and fewer opportunities than people in the mainstream. They have comparatively little economic bargaining power, nor do they have much political clout if they form conventional pressure groups and engage in lobbying. Threats to engage in political disruption or violence are largely empty: when minority groups take to the streets they usually inflict more damage on their own communities than on outsiders. For groups in this position, democracy on the deliberative model seems to provide the best chance of using political power to counteract social disadvantage. Yet even here their only real resource is their capacity to invoke the sense of justice of their fellow-citizens, and use this to win policies that work in their favour. If a democratic forum is reduced to a talking shop in which each person has their own story to tell, but discussion is not constrained by the need to find practical solutions that are acceptable to all, then the strongest weapon a disadvantaged minority has – indeed almost the only weapon that it has – is blunted. Individuals may have the satisfaction of hearing their stories voiced on a public stage, but nothing is done to compensate for the huge inequalities of wealth and power that disfigure liberal democracies.

10

National Self-Determination and Global Justice

The Problem

In this final chapter I want to explore what appears to be a deep tension between two values that many of our contemporaries hold in high regard: national self-determination and global justice. To feel the force of the problem, let me begin by setting it out in fairly simple terms. Global justice, I will assume for purposes of argument, means distributive justice on a global scale (in the same way as social justice means justice within the boundaries of a particular society). If justice is to be done globally, then this must mean, so it is widely believed, that the rights and resources available to someone should depend only on characteristics of that particular person.[1] For instance, if someone is in need, then what justice requires is that resources should be available to them to meet that need, the quantity of resources being determined only by the extent of need. This immediately entails that geographical factors such as location and political membership must be regarded as irrelevant from the perspective of global justice. If someone needs medication to remedy a disabling condition, then her claim on it does not depend on whether she lives in country A or country B, under political regime X or political regime Y. More generally justice requires that each person should get what is due to them, and what is due to a person depends only on personal features such as the actions someone has performed or the choices they have made or the physical condition they find themselves in – the precise specification varying from one theory of justice to the next. But there would seem to be no theory that makes belonging to one or other society itself a relevant consideration in deciding what is due, particularly in light of the fact that such memberships are for the most part unchosen. Most Bangladeshis are simply born and raised in Bangladesh, so how can it be just for their access to resources to depend on that morally arbitrary fact?

What now of national self-determination? The principle of national self-determination tells us that where the people who inhabit a continuous piece of territory form a national community, they have a right to determine their own future, through establishing political institutions of self-government to control that territory and living according to decisions reached in those institutions. In other words, they are entitled to a form of collective autonomy: being different in certain respects from neighbouring communities, they are entitled to live according to their own particular values, and it is a serious form of oppression if they are forced to comply with the dictates of some foreign power. In many cases this will be best achieved by having their own independent state. National self-determination requires that the government should be democratically accountable to the members of the community in question, so that what it does in their name genuinely reflects their aspirations and ideals. Moreover the government must have sufficient latitude to put those ideals and aspirations into practice. It must enjoy genuine, and not merely nominal, autonomy, at least in so far as this is consistent with other nations enjoying a comparable level of self-determination.

It is this last requirement in particular that seems to generate a fundamental conflict between national self-determination and global justice. For it seems inconceivable that in a world that includes many separate nation-states exercising the kind of autonomy that national self-determination entails, the rights and resources available to individuals should not vary according to their membership of one or other of these states. The decisions that governments make are not trivial; they do not just concern the colour of the national flag or who should be the manager of the national football team. They concern very basic questions such as the choice of economic system (capitalism or socialism), the nature and extent of the welfare state (if there is one), the rate of population growth or decline, whether religious codes of behaviour should be enforced, how to use or safeguard the natural world, and so forth. Decisions reached on these questions are certain to have a fundamental impact on the kinds and quantities of resources to which members have access. In a culturally plural world there is no reason to expect that different national communities would all decide such matters in the same way, or even in closely similar ways. So it would be nothing short of a miracle if it turned out that people whose rights and opportunities were chiefly determined by decisions reached at national level all enjoyed the same level of rights and opportunities, or more precisely sets of rights and opportunities that varied only according to personal characteristics such as need or choice, which is what global justice appears to demand.

That is the issue I intend to address in this final chapter. I shall not attempt to cover all of its many dimensions. In particular, I shall not consider the charge that national self-determination is impossible to achieve, and therefore of no genuine value, in the world we inhabit. This charge may be supported by different observations. One is that we do not in practice find political communities with shared national identities inhabiting continuous and neatly bounded territories; instead we find a hotchpotch of ethnic and other groups whose members are intermingled on the ground, and who make incompatible claims to exercise authority over territory. Another observation is that the choices open to nation-states are heavily constrained by the decisions made by other nation-states, and especially by the workings of the global market, so that the idea that people in any place can actually decide how their society is going to develop turns out to be a chimera. The first observation says that (genuine) nation-states don't and can't exist; the second says that even if they can, they cannot be self-determining in the face of outside forces. I believe that good replies can be given to these sweeping observations, and have tried in earlier chapters in this book to respond to the first in particular.[2] As to the second, I should just remark that, even if the observation were to be true, it is likely to be no more palatable to the defender of global justice than to the defender of national self-determination. If we are all at the mercy of the world market or the uncontrollable actions of other states, then there seems no prospect that the global allocation of rights and resources can be made to match criteria of distributive justice – unless perhaps one is the kind of libertarian who thinks that justice simply means having those rights and resources that one can win in market competition. Leaving such libertarians aside, to try to resolve the conflict between national self-determination and global justice in favour of the latter by appealing to a strong globalization thesis would indeed be to win a Pyrrhic victory.

I shall make the more modest assumption that nation states, acting singly or in collaboration, can take decisions that significantly affect the distribution of resources, both within their boundaries and across them. They can, for instance, constrain the economic market in ways that will alter the shares of resources going to different groups of actors within it, and they can use their powers of taxation to supply goods and services on a non-market basis to those who are considered to have a just claim to receive them. They can also alter the international distribution of resources, either through direct transfers (foreign aid, etc.) or through altering the terms of international trade. Such policies will almost certainly incur costs, and beyond a certain point attempts to pursue them may prove self-defeating; nevertheless states still have enough leeway to make debate about the ethics of national and international redistribution a fruitful exercise.[3] Such an assumption about national autonomy, let me repeat, must be made both by advocates of domestic social justice and by advocates of global justice. If the domestic distribution of resources is governed by the iron laws of economics, then speculation about the principles of just distribution becomes pointless, and so equally for the international distribution of resources.

The value of national self-determination

Let us assume, then, that national self-determination is not merely an illusion – that states have sufficient power to alter the distribution of resources inside and outside their borders to make the relationship between self-determination and global justice a matter of ethical concern. But to say that national self-determination is possible is not to say that it is valuable. One rather obvious way to resolve the conflict identified at the beginning of the chapter is to deny that national self-determination has any intrinsic value – to say, for example, that it is valuable only to the extent that its exercise leads to greater justice in the world. It is not, I think, in dispute that national self-determination is highly valued in practice, especially perhaps by peoples who are denied its enjoyment, but we need to say more to show that this valuation is justified.

Why, then, might national self-determination be considered intrinsically valuable?[4] In general, self-determination for groups is valuable in much the same way as self-determination for individuals. Just as individual people want to be able to shape their circumstances to suit their aims and ambitions, so groups want to be able to decide how to organize their internal affairs and to dispose of their resources. Of course, as a member of such a group, I cannot guarantee that my preferences will prevail when the group makes such decisions. But so long as I have a chance to make my views known, and so long as there is sufficient consensus over aims and purposes within the group that broadly speaking its decisions reflect my values, then it is valuable to me that the group is autonomous. The group as a whole can achieve much more than I as an individual can achieve, so by belonging I have a smaller say over a bigger range of issues than I have as a private person. If we think of an association such as a tennis club, then it is hardly controversial to say that the members should enjoy collectively a wide measure of autonomy over such questions as how the club will be organized, how big it should be, how courts will be allocated and so forth. We may believe that this autonomy should be exercised only within certain limits, but the actual value of self-determination in such a case is almost self-evident.

If we try to extend the argument to nations, however, for many people the self-evidence disappears. Why is this? One reason is that whereas the members of our tennis club really do have a good deal in common – primarily that they all wish to play enjoyable tennis – it is not so clear that this is true of the people who are thrown together as compatriots. Critics point out that national boundaries are arbitrary in the sense that frequently they stem from historical contingencies such as peace treaties drawn up between rival overlords several centuries back, or lines drawn on the map by colonial administrators, which then serve to demarcate the people who are to become 'the nation'. They point out too that claims about 'national character' – that is, the distinctive traits alleged to be carried by the members of a particular nation – are falsified as soon as we observe the huge range of cultural and political differences that can be found inside those political communities commonly identified as nations. Another reason is that national memberships are for the most part involuntary. Whereas the members of the tennis club have demonstrated their commitment to the aims and purposes of the club by choosing to join, the great majority of the people are simply born and raised in the community that becomes their nation. So why should we suppose that they share the beliefs and values that are supposed to constitute national identity?

These criticisms are less than decisive. Even if the shape of some nations has been determined by arbitrary actions such as those just described, what matters is whether the people who *now* constitute the would-be nation sufficiently share an identity and a set of values to make nationhood and the idea of a national will – the notion that a decision reached or an action taken reflects common understandings of what ought to be done in the circumstances in question – more than mere hyperbole.[5] Moreover to push the arbitrariness claim too far would make nonsense of the fact that we see all around us claims for national self-determination being made by people who for centuries have resisted being incorporated into larger states. If nations could be conjured into existence merely by the stroke of a pen or the flight of an arrow, the world would be a much tidier place, and national self-determination would be both far easier to achieve, and far less important, than it is in our world. Whatever their ultimate origins, national identities once created are remarkably tenacious, and often remarkably resistant to being reshaped to fit existing political boundaries.

As to the point that people do not choose their national membership but have it thrust upon them, this cuts both ways. It certainly creates a problem for the person who develops culturally and ethically in such a way that she finds herself alienated from the surrounding community, but it also means that people are very often deeply attached to their national identities in a way that they are not to their jobs or their hobbies, for instance. This is sometimes expressed by saying that national identities are *constitutive* of the self, but I shall avoid the difficulties and ambiguities surrounding this idea by treating the depth of attachment simply as a psychological fact – for a great many people it matters a great deal that they belong to a particular nation, that the nation should continue to exist and that it should enjoy self-determination. No doubt this psychological fact is largely a product of contingent social processes that have operated from the day of someone's birth onwards, not a necessary feature of human existence. But given that it obtains, the case for national self-determination remains strong, even in the face of dissenters who would like the political community to be following a different path from the one it is currently taking.

The case is at its strongest when three conditions are met. The first is that the community's political institutions should approximate as closely as possible to the ideal of deliberative democracy. It should reach its political decisions through a process of open discussion to which each member is able to contribute freely, but is equally willing to listen to and consider opposing views. Under these circumstances, and assuming good will on all sides, the outcome will reflect not simply the prior interests or prior opinions of the participants, but the judgements they make after reflecting on the arguments made on each side, and the principles or procedures that should be used to resolve disagreements.[6] A deliberative democracy not only allows dissenting views about the future direction of the political community to be heard, but also exposes its prevailing principles and practices to critical scrutiny. Second, the standard range of civil and political rights should be constitutionally entrenched, so as to afford protection to those who may find themselves in a minority on any given occasion. They may not succeed in getting the community to embrace their beliefs and aspirations, but at least they have a protected sphere of liberty in which to put those ideals into partial effect through forms of private life and civil association. Third, there should be a legal right of emigration for those who find it intolerable to have to live in the way that their nation chooses. It is, I think, part of what it means to belong to a nation that one recognizes a moral obligation to remain a member and not to leave merely for the sake of financial advantage, say, but this can and should be combined with a legal right of exit. So, to conclude, national self-determination seems *prima facie* valuable, particularly when the institutions of self-determination incorporate deliberative democracy, protected civil and political rights, and the right to emigrate.

The demands of justice

I now want to consider an apparently appealing solution to the conflict we are considering. This says, simply, that national self-determination is valuable *so long as it remains within the bounds laid down by justice*. In other words, justice imposes certain requirements on political communities: so long as their decisions and their practices conform to those requirements, national self-determination may be a perfectly good thing, but it ceases to be so the moment it oversteps those boundaries. An analogy might be drawn here with individuals, or associations of individuals, acting within the system of justice created by a state. It is a widely-held and reasonable view that personal autonomy and group autonomy should be limited by the requirements of justice that are imposed impartially across individuals. It is valuable for me to choose the way of life that best satisfies my underlying ideals, but only in so far as this does not involve injuring or constraining or depriving other individuals who have an equally strong claim to enjoy the range of opportunities and benefits that a political society creates. By analogy we might think that national autonomy is valuable only in so far as it is consistent with justice, in particular with the just claims of other peoples who are exposed to the consequences of national self-determination. This solution resolves our original conflict by giving global justice priority. Self-determination must be exercised within the limits imposed by our principles of global justice.

What this solution implies in practice is going to vary a great deal according to the conception of justice that gives it substantive content. Some conceptions of justice may be so demanding that they appear to leave nations very little room for discretion in choosing their policies – not much more, indeed, than deciding the colour of the national flag. Other conceptions will impose some fairly basic requirements and leave a great deal open for national political communities to decide. But rather than reviewing the list of possible candidates, I want to challenge the proposed solution more directly. I want in particular to suggest that the analogy with individuals and groups acting within a regime of domestic justice is misleading. This analogy leads us astray because it overlooks the fact that nation-states are also engaged in the pursuit of an important form of justice – social justice – among their own members. Whereas in the individual case, justice features only on one side of the balance, in the case of conflicts between national self-determination and global justice it features on both sides. Nations prevented from exercising self-determination may also be prevented from practising justice among their members. Immediately it ceases to be clear that global justice must take priority in such cases.

Now it might seem that this challenge rests on a mistake. For what is social justice if it is not global justice pursued on a smaller scale, within the boundaries of a national society as opposed to across the world as a whole? So how can there be a basic conflict between the two ideals? Someone who offers this response must, I believe, have a picture of the following sort in mind. Justice is a matter of what each person can rightfully claim as his due. Suppose that we have a person with feature A (certain needs, say) as a result of which he can rightfully claim resources R. Social justice within his society then demands that the state ensures that he has access to resources R. But equally global justice demands that the ensemble of states (together with international organizations of various kinds) should ensure that he has access to R. The two ideals ultimately impose the same requirements. At most there might be a short-term divergence between them (should state S give priority to making sure that its own citizens with feature A have access to R or should it give equal weight to the claims of everyone with feature A regardless of citizenship?). And since social justice and global justice are ultimately one and the same, national self-determination that remains within the bounds of justice cannot be exercised at the expense of global justice.

Such a picture, I shall argue, is fundamentally misleading. It assumes that we can give a thick specification of the demands of justice in advance of the articulation of those demands within the many different political communities that make up the world we inhabit. In contrast, it is more reasonable to expect that conceptions of justice will take different forms in different cultural milieux, and therefore that where the conditions for national self-determination sketched earlier are met, each nation-state will implement policies for social justice that differ more or less radically from those of its neighbours. Justice, as Pascal once memorably said, will mean one thing on this side of the Pyrenees and something else on the other, but not because (as he thought) human justice is merely conventional.[7] The reason is rather that our understanding of the demands of justice forms part of our wider world-view, something that is expressed in the whole culture of the society to which we belong. Since, globalization notwithstanding, societal cultures still differ markedly from each other, conceptions of justice will diverge too.

There are three main reasons for this divergence. First justice, in its distributive guise, has to do with the way in which valued goods (and disvalued burdens) are allocated among persons. But how these goods are to be conceived – in other words, how the *subject-matter* of justice is to be understood – will vary to some degree from one society to the next. One can miss this point by thinking only of the most basic of goods – food, shelter and clothing. But justice also has to do with the distribution of goods such as money, work, honours, status and political power, and (as

Michael Walzer in particular has emphasized[8]) the meaning of such goods is socially constituted. Whether work, for example, is regarded as a burden to be borne, or as a valuable opportunity for self-realization, will depend upon the underlying world-view of the society in which it is performed. Even a good such as medical care, whose meaning may appear to be fixed by its physical relationship to human health, turns out on closer inspection to have a significant (and variable) cultural content.

The second reason concerns the *criteria of just distribution*. If we ask what principles are used to determine whether a distribution of goods to persons is just or not, then once again it appears on the surface as though these principles are universal and invariant across societies. For instance, almost all societies discriminate between persons on grounds of merit or desert, holding that some members deserve a larger share of valued goods than others. But as we begin to look more closely at what this principle means, its invariance vanishes. In different societies, different qualities are held up as meritorious; equally, what it is that people deserve by virtue of their merit varies from one place to the next (is it money, or political office, or heavenly grace?). There are important variations, too, in the tightness of the link that is drawn between desert and the idea of personal responsibility. In some cultures, people are judged meritorious for possessing qualities or performing deeds for which they are not, in the sense familiar to us, responsible, whereas in contemporary liberal societies we find a marked tendency to think that people can be judged deserving only to the extent that they are fully responsible for the performances that form the basis of desert.[9]

Somewhat similar considerations apply to *need* as a criterion of distributive justice. In a general sense we can understand needs as those conditions in the absence of which a person cannot lead a minimally decent life in the society to which she belongs.[10] Although some of these conditions have a biological basis, and will therefore be universal, in other cases needs will depend on social norms that determine what counts as living a minimally decent life, and these may be expected to vary from one society to the next, in line with variations in overall world-view.

The third reason has to do with the *contexts* in which different criteria are applied. Very often, people's judgements about which principle of justice they should apply in order to determine what counts as the just distribution of some good depends on the context in which the distribution is taking place. It is true that there are some goods whose social meaning entails a criterion of distribution independently of context – honours, awards and prizes are examples. Something cannot *be* an honour or a prize unless it is given to those regarded as displaying the relevant kind of merit. But for many other goods, it is possible to envisage different criteria of distribution being used. Money, for example, can be allocated on the basis of need, or desert, or contractual rights, or through a lottery. My claim is that we judge which criterion is the just criterion by considering the social context – by considering the kind of relationship that obtains between the people among whom the distribution will be made. What seems fair in one context – a family, say – will not seem fair in a different context – a workgroup, say. Indeed we may be able to produce a typology of contexts and explore how different principles of justice are used in each.[11]

Rather than elaborating here on this idea, I want to underline the point that contexts of justice are likely to vary from one society to the next, again in line with underlying world-views. Take as an example the organization of work. How should we understand the relationship between those who work together in a productive enterprise? In contemporary liberal societies, such enterprises are predominantly seen as made up of individuals whose relationship with one another is instrumental and/or competitive. People go to work in order to take home a salary and advance their careers. They are expected to contribute as effectively as possible to the enterprise's performance so long as they are employed by it, but they are free to look for a better job elsewhere at any time, and no one blames them for disloyalty if they take up an offer of this kind. In this context, the primary criterion for distributing income fairly will be desert, as measured by each member's estimated contribution to the overall productivity of the enterprise.

But work could be, and has often been, organized very differently. Work units could be understood as communities whose membership is expected to be permanent and whose ethos is co-operative rather than competitive. Each member would see herself as forming part of a unified team, and her role at work as that of helping the team carry out its task most effectively. In this context, different norms of justice will come into play. Less emphasis will be placed on desert (if people are differentially rewarded at all, this may be done symbolically rather than materially) and greater emphasis placed on competing principles such as equality and need.

Different understandings of work, and of the nature of productive enterprises, lead in the way I have sketched to different understandings of social justice. I am not suggesting that societies have a free hand in deciding how to arrange the social contexts in which distributive justice is practised. It may, for instance, be the case that technological developments will propel all societies in the contemporary world into adopting the first of the two models of work organization outlined above. My point is only that where the contexts differ – whether because the societies in question are at different levels of economic development, or because their underlying philosophies of human life are different, or for some other reason – so too will conceptions of social justice. To conclude, therefore, we have found three sources of likely divergence in these conceptions – different understandings of the *goods* whose distribution is at stake; different understandings of the *principles* that should govern distribution; and different understandings of the *social contexts* in which these principles are to be applied

The argument I have been advancing should not be interpreted as a form of subjectivism about justice. I am not claiming that there is no right answer to the question 'What is social justice for society S at time T?' ('What is social justice for Britain at the beginning of the twenty-first century?'), but I am claiming that the right answer must draw upon shared meanings and shared understandings in such a way that it will not serve as an answer for all societies. In saying this I am assuming that the relevant shared meanings and understandings do in fact exist. I do not mean that we always find spontaneous agreement in people's judgements about what is just and what is not, but that there is sufficient underlying agreement – about the general criteria of distributive justice, for instance – to make debate about particular instances of justice fruitful, and the notion of a right answer meaningful. Whether this agreement exists is, of course, an empirical question. Elsewhere I have tried to present the evidence that supports an affirmative answer.[12] So I want to describe my understanding of social justice as contextualist rather than as sub-jectivist. It does not imply that any interpretation of justice (for society S at time T) is as good as any other.

But how are we to go about finding this best interpretation of social justice? From one perspective, we can see it as the job of sociologically-literate philosophers to develop theories of justice that systematize people's judgements and the principles they apply when making those judgements, removing inconsistencies and correcting errors that arise, for instance, from misperceptions of empirical reality. From a different per-spective, it is one of the virtues of deliberative democracy that it encourages ordinary citizens to enlarge their understanding of social justice, through having to listen to the claims and arguments of groups who have different interests and different needs, and through having to present their own claims in terms that will attract widespread support in the political community in question.[13] It is not the *purpose* of deliberative democracy to generate a widely-shared conception of social justice; its purpose is to take practical decisions on issues facing the community. But it may be a *side-effect* of a well-functioning deliberative democracy that it does just this, by inducing participants to revise their original judgements about what's fair when confronted by fellow-citizens who hold different views.

This point also brings out more clearly the connection between national self-determination and social justice. If the arguments that I have given for seeing nations as the optimal sites for large-scale deliberative democracy are valid, and if it is also true that deliberative democracy helps to bring it about that a shared conception of social justice will emerge and be implemented, then we have good reason to favour nation-states as forms of political organization.[14] National self-determination matters not only for the reasons given earlier, having to do with the value of collective autonomy, but also because it creates the conditions under which people can live together on terms of justice.

Against global egalitarianism

But now we must return to *global* justice and ask what that idea can mean, given what has already been said about the contextual character of social justice. It should immediately be clear that global justice cannot require that people everywhere should enjoy the same resources and advantages regardless of their membership in particular political communities. For if the demands of social justice vary from one community to the next, as argued above, then it should be obvious that membership must make a relevant difference to what anyone can claim as a matter of justice. In one society, the public honouring of artists and musicians may be seen as a matter of justice; in another, religious instruction may be considered a need and provided free of charge from the public purse. But if I live in a society which understands justice differently, and as a result does neither of these things, I cannot point to these other societies and demand equal treatment with their members. Of course if I decide to leave my state and become a citizen of one of these, then *ceteris paribus* it will be unfair if I do not qualify for artistic awards or religious instruction. But that is a different matter.

You might think that my argument holds only because I have focused on specific goods like jobs and honours, and that global justice as a form of equal treatment can be salvaged by presenting its requirements in more abstract terms. For instance you might think that global justice requires that everyone should have equal access to 'advantage' in some generalized sense that is consistent with the advantage taking different forms in different places, in the same way as the diners in a communal restaurant have an equal entitlement to food that is consistent with some of them taking their entitlement in the form of hamburger and chips and others in the form of quiche and salad. But this suggestion is not sustainable, because of the radical heterogeneity of the things that together might constitute 'advantage' from the perspective of global justice. It is not merely that the list itself is long; it is also that the items on the list will have a different significance in different communities: for instance, whether being without a job *in itself* constitutes a form of deprivation, aside from the loss of income that accompanies it, will vary from one community to the next. My argument here is not that the goods that may appear on the list are radically incommensurable, in the sense that we cannot make consistent trade-offs between them; my argument is that the trade-offs can only be made, intelligibly, within communities with sufficient cultural cohesion that their members can come to a broad agreement about how each item on the list should be valued in relation to the others.

It is true that in the world we inhabit there are many millions of people who are disadvantaged relative to others in an across-the-board sense, scoring lower on every measure that corresponds to a significant good – they have less money, poorer housing and health care, enjoy fewer civil and political rights, and so on.[15] So even if it is wrong to see global justice as requiring equal access to 'advantage', it might at least require the elimination of across-the-board disadvantage. Those who advocate global distributive justice by analogy with social justice nearly always seem to be thinking of people who are deprived in this sense. But it is then important to be clear whether the injustice to be rectified consists in the *inequality* between the relatively advantaged and the relatively disadvantaged, or in the absolute position of the disadvantaged. If Tanzanians, say, are victims of global injustice, is this because nearly all of them have *less* (of all significant goods) than nearly all Germans, or because their level of access to money, health care, education and so on falls below what we and they both regard as an acceptable minimum? In other words, is inequality the problem, or poverty?

As I have argued at greater length elsewhere, I believe it is wrong to see the problem as a problem of inequality *per se*.[16] This is partly because, as suggested above, we cannot even specify what equality between people everywhere would mean in a world where conceptions of social justice – understandings of goods, principles of distribution, etc. – are always local. We can say that people are unequally placed only where there is across-the-board disadvantage. And this will restrict the application of the principle to comparisons between members of societies that are quite affluent, and members of societies that are very poor. In other words, we can only use a weak principle of equality whose scope (in the kind of world we inhabit) will not be materially different from a principle of poverty. It will point, in practice, to the injustice suffered only by those who are absolutely as well as relatively deprived.

Beyond this lies the deeper issue of whether egalitarian principles of justice are the right principles to apply at global level, supposing the problem raised in the last paragraph could be resolved. Some philosophers have thought that justice and equality are one and the same – that the demands of justice can always be expressed in terms of a suitably formulated principle of equality. It would follow from this that global justice must be understood as requiring some form of global equality. I hold the contrary view that justice assumes the form of a principle of equality only in certain contexts, and here the relationship between citizens of a nation-state is especially important as a context in which substantial forms of equal treatment can be demanded as a matter of justice.[17] In the absence of a politically-organized global community, this context cannot be stretched in such a way as to make global inequalities unjust merely by virtue of their being inequalities.

Global justice

So what, positively, *are* the requirements of global justice? Rather than thinking about this question with the help of analogies drawn from the practice of social justice within states, it is better to begin by asking the basic ethical question: what does each of us, individually, owe to other human beings, regardless of their cultural make-up, or their citizenship, or their place of residence? How must we treat them if we are not to be accused of injustice? The first and most fundamental answer, I suggest, is that we must respect the conditions that are universally necessary for human beings to lead minimally adequate lives. These conditions are both negative and positive. We know that injuring people, or physically confining them, or abusing them in ways that destroy their self-respect, makes it impossible for them to live adequate lives no matter what their particular aims and values turn out to be. So we are required not to treat people in these ways. Equally we know that people must have access to certain basic resources to pursue any set of aims, and so we have an obligation to ensure that food, medical aid and so forth are available. To verify this, I ask the reader to imagine herself coming across a complete stranger from a different culture in some remote place, and to ask herself what it would clearly be unjust to do to this person, and also what the stranger could legitimately ask of her if he turns out to be in need (as distinct from what it would be generous to offer). The first requirement of global justice, I suggest, is simply that this individual-to-individual obligation should be observed universally, that is to say by states and other collectivities as well as by private persons.

This requirement is often spelt out in terms of a list of basic human rights, the protection of which becomes the first imperative of global justice. Although it is not essential to spell the requirement out in this way, and some would argue that the language of rights is inappropriate here because of difficulties in identifying the bearers of the obligations that correspond to the alleged rights,[18] it is clearly a powerful form of expression, particularly in liberal societies which have learnt to regard the protection of rights as an overriding ethical and political imperative. The familiar challenge here is to identify a definitive list of basic human rights, and then to justify that list in a manner that is genuinely culturally neutral and not merely, for instance, an expression of Western liberal values.[19] This problem has been widely discussed, and since I have nothing original to contribute to the discussion, I shall simply assume that the challenge can be met, and that we can identify the first requirement of global justice as a respect for the basic human rights of people everywhere, by individuals, states and other collectivities.[20]

The second requirement of global justice is that individuals and collectivities should refrain from exploiting those who are vulnerable to their actions. As a general phenomenon, exploitation occurs when a powerful agent uses its power to transact with a weaker agent on unfair terms – terms that the weaker agent would not accept were it not dependent on the first agent, or vulnerable in some other way.[21] The most commonplace example of exploitation is an exchange conducted between a person who is in desperate need and a second person who can supply that need but chooses to do so at an inflated price. Pervasive global inequality means that opportunities for international exploitation are legion, whether this takes the form of states imposing onerous conditions on the governments of poorer countries in return for (economically vital) access to investment and markets, or corporations employing workers in these countries on terms that would be wholly unacceptable in developed societies. Again the challenge is to provide criteria for identifying exploitative transactions that are neutral as between different societal cultures. These could then generate a code of practice to regulate dealings between governments, corporations and individuals so that international trade and investment, and other forms of interaction, are conducted on terms that represent a fair division of benefits between the parties involved.

Global justice in the form of non-exploitation is primarily a negative requirement for the political community as a whole – the obligation is to refrain from engaging in exploitative transactions – though at the same time it imposes positive obligations on governments to ensure that multinationals and other institutions under their jurisdiction also respect that requirement. But now we come to the third, and most problematic, requirement of global justice, which can be characterized as the obligation to ensure that all political communities have the opportunity to determine their own future and practise justice among their members.[22]

STRANMILLIS
UNIVERSITY COLLEGE
BELFAST

The basis of this obligation is not itself especially problematic. If we defend national self-determination, as I have done, by pointing to the considerable value people attach to collective autonomy – to determining their own future along with others they identify as compatriots – and also to the value in living according to laws and policies that correspond to the local understanding of social justice, then we must defend it not just for ourselves but for everyone. We have a particularly strong reason to defend the self-governing rights of our own people, but when these are secure, we also have a reason to aid others in their quest for self-determination. This is now widely accepted in the case of people struggling to escape from alien rule. What is more controversial is whether the obligation extends to an obligation to provide the resources needed to achieve justice internally – justice as seen by the political community in question. This, we may assume, would go well beyond the level of provision required by basic human rights.

In thinking about this question, we are pulled in two different directions. On the one hand, there are political communities that seem to have little chance to achieve justice and a worthwhile life for most of their members, because of resource deficiencies, because of their (dependent) economic relationship to other communities, because of internal divisions that make political co-operation difficult, or for other reasons. On the other hand, political decisions taken within states may have negative or even disastrous effects from the point of view of social justice within those states, and then we want to say that political communities should be treated as responsible for the results of the decisions they reach: we cannot value self-determination, and at the same time seek to nullify its effects whenever it leads to outcomes that appear to us mistaken. The issue is further complicated by the fact that in many cases the decisions at stake will have been made not by formally democratic methods, but by political elites who claim, with some justification, that they speak on behalf of the people. How far is it reasonable in these cases to say that ordinary people must bear the resulting injustice because in some sense they share in the responsibility for it?

Because of these conflicting impulses, we should construe the third element of global justice as an obligation to provide political communities with the *opportunity* to achieve justice internally, where this means ensuring that they have an adequate resource base, and a tolerable economic environment, against which to make their decisions. This entails, for example, helping to set the borders of states in such a way that they enclose viable economic units (in cases of secessionist conflicts, for instance); going to the aid of states that suffer catastrophically as a result of climatic change; offering some protection to states that have become dependent on producing for a particular market (such as

Caribbean islands which rely almost entirely on the export of bananas), at least as long as it takes them to diversify into other areas; and so on. It does not entail providing states with resources to compensate for errors of economic management, or for making expenditure choices that detract from the pursuit of justice (for instance to stockpile large quantities of armaments). The guiding principle is that political communities should assume responsibility for their decisions, but should not be expected to cope with every eventuality that may arise in an interdependent world. If we value justice and self-determination, then we owe it to other political communities to create the conditions under which they too can achieve these goals.

So the demands of global justice, for purposes of the present analysis, can be summed up under three heads: the obligation to respect basic human rights world-wide; the obligation to refrain from exploiting vulnerable communities and individuals; and the obligation to provide all political communities with the opportunity to achieve self-determination and social justice. The final question to ask is how far these obligations set limits to national self-determination within our own community. It seems clear to me that the first two obligations do indeed set such limits. In particular, the domestic pursuit of social justice must be conducted in such a way as not to require the violation of basic rights or the exploitation of outsiders. We might in our community wish to have an extensive national health service that provides a high level of medical care to every citizen. But if the only way in which we can afford to provide this is by exploiting the members of another political community – for instance forcing a community that is poorer than ours to make unilateral transfers in our direction, or engaging in exploitative trading relationships with a nation that is dependent on us for vital resources – then it is wrong to do so. Just as individuals are prohibited from performing certain kinds of action even in cases where those actions promise to yield great benefits, so a political community's right to self-determination, including its aspiration to achieve social justice, is subject to moral limits – and the first two requirements of global justice as I have stated them are a prime example of such limits.

As to the third requirement, it seems legitimate for nation-states to give priority to creating regimes of justice among their own citizens before undertaking whatever actions may be necessary to create such regimes elsewhere. This simply expresses the special moral responsibility that compatriots have to one another. But there are other national projects to which it would be hard to attach this kind of priority – building a national football stadium, or a Millennium Dome, for instance. It does not seem justifiable to claim that projects such as this should take priority over, for example, helping to rebuild the economy of a foreign nation that has been shattered by foreign invasion or civil war. So here global justice is not a requirement that sets absolute limits to self-determination, but rather a factor that needs to be balanced against it.

There is a further complication that must be mentioned here, even though I cannot hope to address it properly. Global justice, plainly, imposes obligations on all nations with the capacity to comply with its requirements – whether the negative capacity to injure or exploit, or the positive capacity to provide resources which protect basic rights and allow social justice to be pursued. Very often global injustice arises because of the wilful or unwitting failure of other states to meet those obligations. In such circumstances, what responsibility does our nation have to make good the injustice that has been perpetrated, either by intervening to prevent rights-violations or exploitation, or by supplying additional resources to make good the shortfall caused by the failure of other nations to contribute their fair share? Beyond a certain point, plainly, the burdens imposed by global justice may become very heavy, if we assume that they include such actions as these.

A proper answer to this question will need to draw upon our general ethical understanding of the responsibility of individual agents in situations where there is a collective duty to generate some outcome. Let me simply signal that there are two answers that I take to be wrong. One answer is that the failure of others to discharge their obligations of global justice relieves us of our corresponding obligations too. We need only behave as justly as others are behaving. The other answer is that we have as much responsibility to rectify the injustices perpetrated by others as we have to pursue justice ourselves – for instance as much responsibility to combat rights-violations by third parties as we have to avoid committing rights-violations ourselves. We are charged with compensating fully for the injustices inflicted by others, so far as it is within our power to do so. Just as the first answer demands too little of us, this second answer surely demands too much; the truth must lie somewhere in between. But formulating a principle of limited responsibility that gives the intuitively right answer in all cases is no easy matter.[23]

Conclusion

I have tried in this chapter to give accounts of the value of national self-determination and of the demands of global justice which show that there is no such basic tension or conflict between these values as might at first appear. As the last paragraphs have indicated, there may indeed be cases in which we have to balance the pursuit of some national objective against our obligations to other communities, but in general the requirements of global justice, once these are properly understood, leave considerable space for national communities to pursue their own projects and objectives. I have highlighted especially the pursuit of social justice within national boundaries, arguing that conceptions of social justice are likely to vary markedly from one community to the next, and also that one virtue of political self-determination, especially where it is exercised through institutions that approximate to the ideal of deliberative democracy, is that it allows members of each community to reach a shared understanding of what justice requires internally. Global justice, by contrast, must be spelt out in terms that do not rely on these thicker local understandings, and I have suggested what these terms might be. We can then envision a world in which nations independently pursue their own conceptions of social justice, as well as other aims and goals, while at the same time respecting basic rights, both internally and externally, and avoiding exploitation of individuals or of other communities. To create such a world, very different from our own, would be an achievement of the highest order.

Notes

Chapter 1   Deliberative Democracy and Social Choice

I should like to thank Joshua Cohen, David Held, Iain McLean, William Riker and Albert Weale, as well as the participants in the *Political Studies* conference on Alternatives to Liberal Democracy, for their very helpful comments on earlier versions of this chapter.

1   This is how liberal democracy, *qua* regulative ideal, will be understood for the purposes of the chapter. Some liberals may protest at this appropriation of the term. However, although my interpretation only fastens upon one strand of liberalism – the importance it attaches to individual preferences and their expression – I take it to be an important strand. It is also the strand that prevails in contemporary liberal societies, where democracy is predominantly understood as involving the aggregation of independently-formed preferences.

2   The ideal of deliberative democracy has recently been advocated and discussed by a number of political theorists. The most incisive presentation is probably J. Cohen, 'Deliberation and Democratic Legitimacy' in A. Hamlin and P. Pettit (eds), *The Good Polity* (Oxford, Blackwell, 1989). See also B. Manin, 'On Legitimacy and Political Deliberation', *Political Theory*, 15 (1987), 338–68; J. Drysek, *Discursive Democracy* (Cambridge, Cambridge University Press, 1990); and my own earlier discussion in *Market, State, and Community* (Oxford, Clarendon Press, 1989), ch. 10.

3   This point is well made in J. Elster, *Sour Grapes* (Cambridge, Cambridge University Press, 1983), ch. I.5.

4   See J. Coleman and J. Ferejohn, 'Democracy and Social Choice', *Ethics*, 97 (1986–7), 6–25 for this view.

5 See H.P. Young, 'Condorcet's Theory of Voting', *American Political Science Review*, 82 (1988), 1231–44.

6 See B. Barry, 'The Public Interest' in A. Quinton (ed.), *Political Philosophy* (London, Oxford University Press, 1967); B. Grofman and S.L. Feld, 'Rousseau's General Will: A Condorcetian Perspective', *American Political Science Review*, 82 (1988), 567–76.

7 Some of the ambiguities are brought out in the exchange between D. Estlund, J. Waldron, B. Grofman and S.L. Feld, 'Democratic Theory and the Public Interest: Condorcet and Rousseau Revisited', *American Political Science Review*, 83 (1989), 1317–40.

8 This is not to deny that deliberation tends to improve the quality of decisions. It may indeed be part of the process of reaching a decision that alternatives which initially find favour with some people are eliminated because these preferences rest on empirical misapprehensions which discussion exposes (I give an example of this later on). But it is wrong to suppose that this is the only or in many cases the main purpose of deliberation.

9 J.A. Schumpeter, *Capitalism, Socialism and Democracy*, 5th edn (London, Allen and Unwin, 1976); R.A. Dahl, *A Preface to Democratic Theory* (Chicago, University of Chicago Press, 1956). Schumpeter wrote before Arrow had stated his theorem, but I believe it is informally anticipated in some of Schumpeter's remarks. Dahl refers explicitly to Arrow.

10 W.H. Riker, *Liberalism Against Populism* (San Francisco, W.H. Freeman, 1982).

11 K.J. Arrow, *Social Choice and Individual Values*, 2nd edn (New York, Wiley, 1963).

12 See Riker, *Liberalism Against Populism*, ch. 4.

13 This is the so-called Gibbard–Satterthwaite theorem after A. Gibbard, 'Manipulation of Voting Schemes: A General Result', *Econometrica*, 41 (1973), 587–601 and M. Satterthwaite, 'Strategy-Proofness and Arrow's Conditions', *Journal of Economic Theory*, 10 (1975), 187–217.

14 Coleman and Ferejohn, 'Democracy and Social Choice', p. 22. See also the discussion in J. Cohen, 'An Epistemic Conception of Democracy', *Ethics*, 97 (1986–7), 26–38, esp. pp. 29–31.

15 The literature of social choice theory may give the impression that voters' preferences are taken as immutable, with apparent changes being explained in terms of changes in the choice set. But in fact a social choice theorist can quite readily concede that preferences vary, are subject to social influences and so forth, so long as for any particular decision or set of decisions they are taken as fixed and identifiable. The shift of approach occurs when we see preferences as altering within the process of decision-making itself, so that individuals end up making judgements which do not necessarily correspond to their initial preferences.

16 Riker, *Liberalism Against Populism*, p. 117. Arrow himself, however, concedes that the condition may be too strong, and indeed in his original proof of the Possibility Theorem used a somewhat weaker version; see *Social Choice and Individual Values*, pp. 24–5 and 96–7.

17 R. Goodin, 'Laundering Preferences' in J. Elster and A. Hylland (eds), *Foundations of Social Choice Theory* (Cambridge, Cambridge University Press, 1986).

18 G. Brennan and P. Pettit, 'Unveiling the Vote', *British Journal of Political Science*, 20 (1990), 311–33.

19 Jon Elster argues along similar lines in *Sour Grapes*, p. 36.

20 See J. Davis, M. Stasson, K. Ono and S. Zimmerman, 'Effects of Straw Polls on Group Decision-Making: Sequential Voting Pattern, Timing and Local Majorities', *Journal of Personality and Social Psychology*, 55 (1988), 918–26.

21 J.M. Orbell, A. van der Kragt and R. Dawes, 'Explaining Discussion-Induced Co-operation', *Journal of Personality and Social Psychology*, 54 (1988), 811–19.

22 This idea was first introduced and explored in D. Black, *The Theory of Committees and Elections* (Cambridge, Cambridge University Press, 1958).

23 Suppose the alternatives are coal, gas and oil and they are arranged from left to right in that order. For single-peakedness to obtain, each voter must rank them in one of the four following ways: (1) coal, (2) gas, (3) oil; (1) gas, (2) coal, (3) oil; (1) gas, (2) oil, (3) coal; or (1) oil, (2) gas, (3) coal; conversely, no voter may have (1) coal, (2) oil, (3) gas or (1) oil, (2) coal, (3) gas. The requirement is not that voters should agree, but that there should be a certain logic to their disagreement.

24 Arrow himself accepts that if decisions are made on impartial, rather than self-interested grounds, voting cycles are less likely to occur. 'If voters acted like Kantian judges, they might still differ, but the chances of coming to an agreement by majority decision would be much greater than if voters consulted egoistic values only' (K.J. Arrow, 'Tullock and an Existence Theorem' in *Collected Papers of Kenneth J. Arrow*, vol. I (Oxford, Blackwell, 1984), p. 87).

25 The majority position on the two dimensions may still be defeated when run against the minority position on both. Thus suppose the first issue is whether to have coal- or oil-fired stations and the second is whether to fit pollution filters or not. Majorities may judge that coal is preferable to oil and that filters are desirable; yet if we were to take a vote between coal-with-filters and oil-with-no-filters, the latter might still win by attracting the support of enough people strongly committed to oil together with people strongly opposed to filters. In my view we should still regard coal-with-filters as the majority choice in these circumstances.

26 This is so even where their support for that alternative is based on ethical beliefs: convictions as well as interests may give people a motive to manipulate democratic procedures.

27 M. Dummett, *Voting Procedures* (Oxford, Clarendon Press, 1984), p. 142.

28 The assumption here is that we have an issue about which reasonable people may disagree, but on which some collective decision is needed: in such a case the decision with the greatest democratic legitimacy will be that which follows the will of the majority, which points us towards the Condorcet

criterion. If, however, we took the epistemic view – i.e. we thought that there was indeed a right answer to the question being posed, and justified democratic decision-making as the most likely means of finding it – then with more than two options on the table the best method will probably be to take a Borda count. See Young, 'Condorcet's Theory of Voting' for this result.

29 This is not the only way in which deliberative institutions might be created, and advocates of deliberative democracy disagree to some extent about the best institutional setting for their ideal. Tocqueville, one of the founders of this tradition, pointed to voluntary associations as well as to town meetings as sites of public debate. Others have emphasized the role of political parties as institutions within which policies are put together in coherent packages, enabling ordinary voters to arrive at more rational decisions. See Manin, 'On Legitimacy and Political Deliberation' and J. Cohen and J. Rogers, *On Democracy* (New York, Penguin, 1983), ch. 6 for the latter view.

30 For a good discussion, see I. McLean, *Democracy and New Technology* (Cambridge, Polity Press, 1989).

Chapter 2   In Defence of Nationality

An earlier version of this chapter was read to the Nuffield Political Theory Workshop and was given as the Conference Address at the Society for Applied Philosophy's 1992 annual meeting, The Isle of Thorns, Sussex. I should like to thank both audiences for their helpful comments. I am especially grateful to Jerry Cohen, Tariq Modood and Andrew Williams for discussion of some of the issues it addresses.

1 K. Grahame, *The Wind in the Willows* (London, Methuen, 1926), pp. 16–17.

2 D. Hume, *A Treatise of Human Nature*, ed. L.A. Selby-Bigge, 3rd edn revised P.H. Nidditch (Oxford, Clarendon Press, 1978), p. 272.

3 I have attempted the second especially in 'The Ethical Significance of Nationality', *Ethics*, 98 (1987–8), 647–62. I am mainly concerned with the first in the present chapter.

4 See for instance T. Nagel, *Equality and Partiality* (New York and Oxford, Oxford University Press, 1991) whose organizing idea is the contrast between personal and impersonal ethical standpoints.

5 A. MacIntyre, 'Is Patriotism a Virtue?' (Lawrence, University of Kansas, Department of Philosophy, 1984).

6 G. Orwell, *The Road to Wigan Pier* (Harmondsworth, Penguin, 1962), p. 160.

7 I speak of 'nationality' rather than 'nationalism' because the latter term usually carries with it unwelcome assumptions about what nations are entitled to do to advance their interests; however there is no alternative to 'nationalist' as an adjective. An alternative approach would be to follow Neil MacCormick in distinguishing different conceptions of nationalism; like MacCormick's, the conception I want to defend includes the condition that in supporting my nation's interests, I should respect others' national identities (and the claims that follow from them) as well. See N. MacCormick, 'Nation

and Nationalism' in *Legal Right and Social Democracy* (Oxford, Clarendon Press, 1982) and N. MacCormick, 'Is Nationalism Philosophically Credible?' in W. Twining (ed.), *Issues of Self-Determination* (Aberdeen, Aberdeen University Press, 1991).

8 E. Renan, 'What is a Nation?' in A. Zimmern (ed.), *Modern Political Doctrines* (London, Oxford University Press, 1939).

9 Ibid., p. 203.

10 D. Hume, 'Of National Characters' in *Essays Moral, Political, and Literary*, ed. E. Miller (Indianapolis, Liberty Classics, 1985), pp. 197–8.

11 'It is only when you meet someone of a different culture from yourself that you begin to realize what your own beliefs really are' (Orwell, *Wigan Pier*, p. 145).

12 Renan, 'What is a Nation?', p. 190.

13 I should make it clear that this consideration could not be put forward as a reason for having or adopting a national identity. A national identity depends upon a prereflective sense that one belongs within a certain historic group, and it would be absurd to propose to the subjects of state X that because things would go better for them if they adopted a shared national identity, they should therefore conjure one up. The argument points to benefits that national allegiances bring with them as by-products. Others who have defended nationality in this way include B. Barry, 'Self-Government Revisited' in D. Miller and L. Siedentop (eds), *The Nature of Political Theory* (Oxford, Clarendon Press, 1983), reprinted in B. Barry, *Democracy, Power and Justice* (Oxford, Clarendon Press, 1989); and Nagel, *Equality and Partiality*, ch. 15.

14 I have argued this with specific reference to socialism in 'In What Sense Must Socialism Be Communitarian?', *Social Philosophy and Policy*, 6 (1988–9), 51–73; but I believe the point holds more generally.

15 See especially L. Colley, 'Whose Nation? Class and National Consciousness in Britain 1750–1830', *Past and Present*, 113 (1986), 97–117.

16 See E.J. Hobsbawm, *Nations and Nationalism since 1780* (Cambridge, Cambridge University Press, 1990).

17 It is also true, however, that conservatives of a different persuasion may embrace national identities as a source of social cohesion and authority; see in particular R. Scruton, 'In Defence of the Nation' in *The Philosopher on Dover Beach* (Manchester, Carcanet, 1990). In chapter 6 I look more closely at what distinguishes this kind of conservative nationalism from other forms of communitarianism.

18 E. Kedourie, *Nationalism* (London, Hutchinson, 1966); K. Minogue, *Nationalism* (London, Batsford, 1967).

19 Minogue, *Nationalism*, p.148.

20 There is a fine and suitably controversial example of this in Margaret Thatcher's recent attempt to present her political views as the logical outcome of British history and national character.

I always said and believed that the British character is quite different from the characters of people on the Continent – quite different. There is a great sense of fairness and equity in the British people, a great sense of individuality and initiative. They don't like being pushed around. How else did this really rather small people, from the times of Elizabeth on, go out in the larger world and have such an influence upon it? ...

I set out to destroy socialism because I felt it was at odds with the character of the people. We were the first country in the world to roll back the frontiers of socialism, then roll forward the frontiers of freedom. We reclaimed our heritage ... (M. Thatcher, 'Don't Undo My Work', *Newsweek,* vol. 119, no.17, 27 April 1992, p. 14)

21 Lord Acton, 'Nationality' in *The History of Freedom and Other Essays,* ed. J.N. Figgis (London, Macmillan, 1907).
22 T. Modood, 'Establishment, Multiculturalism and British Citizenship', *Political Quarterly,* 65 (1994), 64–5.
23 D. Miller, 'Socialism and Toleration' in S. Mendus (ed.), *Justifying Toleration* (Cambridge, Cambridge University Press, 1988); *Market, State and Community* (Oxford, Clarendon Press, 1989), ch. 11.
24 One can find it expressed, for example, in Kedourie, *Nationalism,* chs 6–7.
25 See, for instance, H. Beran, 'A Liberal Theory of Secession', *Political Studies,* 32 (1984), 21–31 – though Beran would deny the consequence I wish to infer from this doctrine.
26 If this is allowed, it follows that there can be no simple answer to the question 'How many nations are there in area A?'. Nations are not discrete and easily counted entities like billiard balls. The criteria that I have offered to define them admit of degree, and that is why it is possible to have a smaller nationality nesting within a larger one.
27 The conditions given are intended to be necessary rather than sufficient. I have addressed the issue of justified secession at greater length in 'The Nation-State: A Modest Defence' in C. Brown (ed.), *Political Restructuring in Europe: Ethical Perspectives* (London, Routledge, 1993) [see also ch. 7 below].

Chapter 3 Citizenship and Pluralism

This chapter was originally written for the workshop on Citizenship and Plurality at the ECPR Joint Sessions, Leiden, 2–7 April 1993. Subsequently it has been presented to a seminar in the Department of Government, University of Uppsala, to the Israeli Forum for Legal and Political Philosophy in Jerusalem and to the Nuffield Political Theory Workshop. I am very grateful to the participants in each of these seminars for their helpful comments, which have been incorporated into the present version.

1 I have not been able to find an extended statement of this argument, but the brief presentations by Douglas Hurd and others are usefully threaded together by Ruth Lister in *The Exclusive Society: Citizenship and the Poor* (London, CPAG, 1989), part I.

2 This view is very well put in R. Plant 'Social Rights and the Reconstruction of Welfare' in G. Andrews (ed.), *Citizenship* (London, Lawrence and Wishart, 1991).

3 P.J. Conover, I.M. Crewe and D.D. Searing, 'The Nature of Citizenship in the United States and Great Britain: Empirical Comments on Theoretical Themes', *Journal of Politics*, 53 (1991), 800–32.

4 This threefold division is inspired by Adam Swift's discussion in *For a Sociologically Informed Political Theory* (D.Phil. thesis, University of Oxford, 1992), part III, though what I call the libertarian conception in particular is presented in a way that departs somewhat from the first conception in Swift's analysis.

5 For an alternative typology, see G. Parry, 'Conclusion: Paths to Citizenship' in U. Vogel and M. Moran (eds), *The Frontiers of Citizenship* (London, Macmillan, 1991).

6 T.H. Marshall, *Citizenship and Social Class*, ed. T Bottomore (London, Pluto Press, 1992) (originally published 1950).

7 Marshall, *Citizenship*, p. 24.

8 It has also been argued that Marshall's conception of citizenship marginalizes women. See U. Vogel, 'Is Citizenship Gender-Specific?' in Vogel and Moran, *The Frontiers of Citizenship*.

9 J. Rawls, 'The Domain of the Political and Overlapping Consensus', *New York University Law Review*, 64 (1989), pp. 234–5. Cf. J. Rawls, *Political Liberalism* (New York, Columbia University Press, 1993), pp. 216–17.

10 J. Rawls, 'The Idea of Overlapping Consensus', *Oxford Journal of Legal Studies*, 7 (1987), pp. 5–6. The reading of Rawls that follows attempts to present the main outlines of his view of citizenship, although it has to be said that the later Rawls, in attempting to accommodate all possible lines of criticism, has become almost infinitely malleable. In particular, as noted below, he appears at times to make substantial concessions to the republican view of citizenship, especially when presenting his account of public reason.

11 This is made explicit in J. Rawls, 'Justice as Fairness: Political not Metaphysical', *Philosophy and Public Affairs*, 14 (1985), pp. 240–2. Cf. Rawls, *Political Liberalism*, pp. 30–2.

12 Rawls, *Political Liberalism*, p. 206. Rawls claims that his position is not incompatible with 'classical republicanism', but to make good this claim he is obliged to dilute the latter essentially to the claim that 'the safety of democratic liberties requires the active participation of citizens who possess the political virtues needed to maintain a constitutional regime' (p. 205). On this reading Benjamin Constant, for instance, would have to be counted as a 'classical republican'.

13 Rawls, 'Justice as Fairness: Political Not Metaphysical', p. 241. Cf. Rawls, *Political Liberalism*, p. 30.

14 Rawls, 'Justice as Fairness: Political Not Metaphysical', p. 241. Rawls, *Political Liberalism*, p. 31.

15 W. Kymlicka, 'Two Models of Pluralism and Tolerance', *Analyse und Kritik*, 13 (1992), 33–56.

16 This is more or less the strategy advocated by Brian Barry in 'How Not to Defend Liberal Institutions' in B. Barry, *Liberty and Justice* (Oxford, Clarendon Press, 1991).

17 A way round this which has attracted some libertarians is for the state to issue vouchers on an equal basis to all citizens which can be used to purchase, e.g. educational places or medical services. Note, however, that for such a scheme to be possible there must already be agreement on what the vouchers are to be used for, and what the value of each kind of voucher is to be – in other words there must already be substantive agreement that each citizen is to be entitled to so much education, so much health care, etc. For this reason voucher schemes cannot cope with radical pluralism in the form of deep disagreement about what goods the state ought to provide to all its citizens in common.

18 For reasons why a system of private charity cannot be relied upon to provide minimum levels of welfare, see my analysis in *Market, State and Community: Theoretical Foundations of Market Socialism* (Oxford, Clarendon Press, 1989), ch. 4.

19 As one might expect there is a body of economic literature exploring the efficiency arguments for and against this policy. The classic statement of the case in favour is C. Tiebout, 'A Pure Theory of Local Expenditures', *Journal of Political Economy*, 64 (1956), 416–24. For discussion see W.E. Oates, 'An Economist's Perspective on Fiscal Federalism' in W.E. Oates (ed.), *The Political Economy of Fiscal Federalism* (Lexington, Mass., D.C. Heath, 1977) and D.C. Mueller, *Public Choice* (Cambridge, Cambridge University Press, 1979), ch. 7.

20 Once again there is no definitive statement in the recent literature, but variations on the republican theme can be found in H. Arendt, *The Human Condition* (Chicago, University of Chicago Press, 1958); B. Barber, *Strong Democracy* (Berkeley, University of California Press, 1984); R.N. Bellah et al., *Habits of the Heart* (Berkeley, University of California Press, 1985); Michael Walzer, *Spheres of Justice* (Oxford, Martin Robertson, 1983). The tradition as a whole is surveyed in A. Oldfield, *Citizenship and Community: Civic Republicanism and the Modern World* (London, Routledge, 1990) and, much more briefly, in M. Walzer, 'Citizenship' in T. Ball, J. Farr and R.L. Hanson (eds), *Political Innovation and Conceptual Change* (Cambridge, Cambridge University Press, 1989).

21 I.M. Young, *Justice and the Politics of Difference* (Princeton, Princeton University Press, 1990), p. 117.

22 Compare the careful discussion of impartiality and its preconditions in S. James, 'The Good-Enough Citizen: Citizenship and Independence' in G. Bock and S. James (eds), *Beyond Equality and Difference* (London, Routledge, 1992).

23 I have explored this point at somewhat greater length in 'Deliberative Democracy and Social Choice', ch. 1 above.

24 Young, *Justice and the Politics of Difference*, p. 186. For a better and clearer account of the way in which political participation forces us to relate our

demands to public standards of justice, see H.F. Pitkin, 'Justice: On Relating Private and Public', *Political Theory*, 9 (1981), section V.

25 It is a major weakness of Young's argument that she does not consider how agreement is to be reached under the form of politics that she favours. She is preoccupied with the question of how oppressed groups are to find their authentic voice, and she does not ask what will happen when the (authentic) claims of some groups are confronted by the equally authentic but conflicting claims of others. There seems to be an unstated premise that when the groups she identifies as oppressed make their case, this case will overwhelm the opposition. As an understanding of politics, this seems naive in the extreme.

26 On the politics of recognition, see the very interesting essay with that title by Charles Taylor in A. Gutmann (ed.), *Multiculturalism and 'The Politics of Recognition'* (Princeton, Princeton University Press, 1992).

27 It is difficult to decide how far the republican view should go in supporting formal mechanisms to ensure 'presence', for instance reserving seats in legislatures for women or ethnic minorities. It is clear that political dialogue is only genuinely democratic to the extent that all significant points of view and demands are represented in the deliberating body; on the other hand republicans will want to avoid 'freezing' people into predefined identities, which may perhaps be the danger posed by reservation schemes. There is a very good discussion of this question in A. Phillips, 'Dealing with Difference: A Politics of Ideas or a Politics of Presence?', *Constellations*, 1 (1994), 74–91. Phillips gives reasons why reservation of political positions for women poses fewer problems than might arise in the case of other hitherto-excluded groups.

28 See for example the essays in J. Elster and R. Slagstad (eds), *Constitutionalism and Democracy* (Cambridge, Cambridge University Press, 1988).

29 Miller, *Market, State and Community*, chs 9–11; 'The Ethical Significance of Nationality', *Ethics*, 98 (1987–8), 647–62; 'In Defence of Nationality', ch. 2 above; *On Nationality* (Oxford, Clarendon Press, 1995), chs 4 and 5.

Chapter 4   Group Identities, National Identities and Democratic Politics

An earlier version of this chapter was presented to the Morrell Conference on Toleration, Identity and Difference, University of York, September 1995, and to the Anglo–French Seminar on Political Philosophy, Collège Internationale de Philosophie, Paris, November 1995. I am very grateful to both audiences for their comments, and especially to John Horton for his very helpful suggestions.

1 I shall use these phrases more or less interchangeably in the chapter, as also a third phrase, 'the politics of difference', which is favoured by the political theorist whose work I shall chiefly discuss, Iris Marion Young.

2 This is the liberal multiculturalism defended by writers like Raz and Kymlicka. See J. Raz, 'Multiculturalism: A Liberal Perspective', *Dissent*, 41(1)

(Winter 1994), 67–79, reprinted in J. Raz, *Ethics in the Public Domain* (Oxford, Clarendon Press, 1994); W. Kymlicka, *Multicultural Citizenship* (Oxford, Clarendon Press, 1995), ch. 5.

3 I.M Young, *Justice and the Politics of Difference* (Princeton, Princeton University Press, 1990), p. 116.

4 The issues here are best discussed by Anne Phillips in *The Politics of Presence* (Oxford, Clarendon Press, 1995).

5 Young, *Justice*, p. 167.

6 Ibid., p. 184.

7 Young addresses a similar critique to recent theories of deliberative democracy in 'Communication and the Other: Beyond Deliberative Democracy' in S. Benhabib (ed.), *Democracy and Difference* (Princeton, Princeton University Press, 1996).

8 Young, *Justice*, p. 119.

9 Ibid., p. 97.

10 D. Miller, 'Citizenship and Pluralism', ch. 3 above.

11 Note, however, that this point cuts both ways. Supporters of identity politics generally assume that there are relevant similarities between the positions of women, blacks, Jews, etc., as the passage from Young I have just quoted illustrates. If we decide that there are big differences in both the nature and the political significance of these various group identities, then this puts the general case for a politics of recognition in question, as well as my challenge to it. There is a good critique of Young on this issue in N. Fraser, 'Recognition or Redistribution: A Critical Reading of Iris Young's *Justice and the Politics of Difference*', *Journal of Political Philosophy*, 3 (1995), 166–81.

12 I draw here on the research presented in T. Modood, S. Beishon and S. Virdee, *Changing Ethnic Identities* (London, Policy Studies Institute, 1994).

13 M.C. Waters, *Ethnic Options: Choosing Identities in America* (Berkeley, University of California Press, 1990).

14 These examples come from Waters, *Ethnic Options*, pp. 23–5.

15 Waters studied Catholics, among whom Irish or Italian identities, for instance, were rated more highly than Scottish or German identities – so people of mixed ancestry would be more likely to choose to identify themselves as Irish or Italian.

16 For the idea of symbolic ethnicity, see H.J. Gans, 'Symbolic Ethnicity' in J. Hutchinson and A.D. Smith (eds), *Ethnicity* (Oxford, Oxford University Press, 1996).

17 See, for instance, David Hollinger's argument that the 'ethno-racial pentagon' around which much American social and cultural policy is built is presenting an increasingly distorted image of a society in which cross-bloc marriage has become widespread (D.A. Hollinger, *Postethnic America* (New York, Basic Books, 1995), ch. 1).

18 See also here Appiah's discussion of the dangers to personal autonomy that the politics of recognition may pose in K.A. Appiah, 'Identity, Authenticity, Survival' in C. Taylor, *Multiculturalism: Examining the Politics of Recognition*, ed. A. Gutmann (Princeton, Princeton University Press, 1994).

19   Young, *Justice*, p. 172. In fairness to Young I should say that in other places she
     gives a somewhat less voluntaristic account of group membership, referring to
     groups differentiated by 'cultural forms, practices, or ways of life' (p. 43).
20   The depth of the gulf separating traditionalist from feminist views of the
     family is well brought out in J. Exdell, 'Feminism, Fundamentalism and
     Liberal Legitimacy', *Canadian Journal of Philosophy*, 24 (1994), 441–64.
21   This is not a hypothetical example. Hizb ut-Tahrir, the Islamic Liberation
     Party, is according to the *Observer* (13 August 1995) the fastest-growing
     Muslim group in Britain. Its declared objective is to make Britain into an
     Islamic state.
22   Charles Taylor has made a similar point about the demand that we should
     value other *cultures* equally with our own. 'It makes sense to demand as a
     matter of right that we approach the study of certain cultures with a pre-
     sumption of their value . . . But it can't make sense to demand as a matter of
     right that we come up with a final concluding judgement that their value is
     great, or equal to others'. That is, if the judgement of value is to register
     something independent of our own wills and desires, it cannot be dictated by
     a principle of ethics. On examination, either we will find something of great
     value in culture C, or we will not. But it makes no more sense to demand that
     we do so than it does to demand that we find the earth round or flat, the
     temperature of the air hot or cold' (C. Taylor, *Multiculturalism and 'The
     Politics of Recognition'*, ed. A. Gutmann (Princeton, Princeton University
     Press, 1992), pp. 68–9).
23   Here I both draw upon and expand arguments made in *On Nationality*
     (Oxford, Clarendon Press, 1995), ch. 5.
24   Young, *Justice*, pp. 110–11.
25   Ibid., pp. 179–80.
26   Ibid., pp. 178–81.
27   It is true that under this arrangement there is still some incentive for the users
     of the non-public languages to assimilate to the public language, and that this
     may eventually lead to the minority languages dying out. But that incentive
     always exists: in any society that is not strongly segmented, there will be
     some economic advantage in speaking the majority language, and this may
     mean that, over time, there is a spontaneous tendency towards linguistic
     homogeneity.
28   I argue this more fully, and supply some supporting evidence, in *On Nation-
     ality*, pp. 135–9. See especially the study of American immigrants in J. Harles,
     Politics in the Lifeboat (Boulder, Co., Westview, 1993).
29   Similar worries about an unrestrained politics of difference are expressed in
     C. Sypnowich, 'Some Disquiet about "Difference"', *Praxis International*, 13
     (1993), 99–112, esp. pp. 104–5.
30   Young, *Justice*, p. 167.
31   Ibid., p. 190.
32   Including 'In What Sense must Socialism be Communitarian?', *Social Philo-
     sophy and Policy*, 6 (1989), 51–73; *Market, State and Community* (Oxford,
     Clarendon Press, 1989), ch. 10; *On Nationality*, ch. 4.

33 See the very thoughtful discussion of this question in M.S. Williams, 'Justice towards Groups: Political not Juridical', *Political Theory*, 23 (1995), 67–91. Williams writes: 'To understand the justice claims of those whose perspectives and experiences are radically different from ourselves, we must engage in the work of putting aside our own interests and attempt to understand how justice looks from the other's point of view. But this requires a characteristic which is an attribute of will more than mind. There is no point in engaging in the difficult work of articulating justice from your point of view on the margins of society unless those who are listening have a will to treat you justly' (pp. 85–6).

34 This latter error is not unique to the politics of recognition. Liberals of a more conventional kind also very often disparage or dismiss national identities, not appreciating the role they have played (and continue to play) in supporting liberal institutions. Historically this was not so: contemporary liberals should be made to read, alongside the famous first chapter of Mill's *On Liberty*, the less famous sixteenth chapter of his *Considerations on Representative Government*, headed 'Of Nationality, as Connected with Representative Government'. I have looked more closely at Mill's defence of nationality in 'Nationalism and Political Liberty' (forthcoming).

35 See for instance W. Kymlicka, *Liberalism, Community and Culture* (Oxford, Clarendon Press, 1989); Kymlicka, *Multicultural Citizenship*; C. Kukathas, 'Are There Any Cultural Rights?', *Political Theory*, 20 (1992), 105–39, and the exchange between Kukathas and Kymlicka in Ibid., pp. 140–6 and 674–80; J. Waldron, 'Can Communal Goods be Human Rights?' in *Liberal Rights: Collected Papers 1981–91* (Cambridge, Cambridge University Press, 1993).

36 If possible this should be done by indirect means rather than through a formal system of minority group representation. The danger with proposals of the latter kind is that, on the one hand, they encourage fluid group identities to crystallize, as I have already argued, and on the other, they encourage the representatives who are chosen to behave simply as group spokesmen, rather than as citizens with concerns that reach right across the political agenda. See further my brief discussion in *On Nationality*, pp. 150–4, and the much fuller one in Phillips, *The Politics of Presence*.

Chapter 5 Bounded Citizenship

Earlier versions of this chapter were read to audiences in Edinburgh, Locarno, Brighton and Aberystwyth, and I should like to thank everyone who attended those meetings for helpful criticisms and comments.

1 I have tackled this issue in 'Justice and Global Inequality' in A. Hurrell and N. Woods (eds), *Inequality, Globalization, and World Politics* (Oxford, Oxford University Press, 1999). [See also ch. 10 below.]

2 For more on this contrast see my paper 'Citizenship and Pluralism', ch. 3 above.

3 T.H. Marshall, *Citizenship and Social Class*, ed. T.B. Bottomore (London, Pluto, 1992); J. Rawls, *Political Liberalism* (New York, Columbia University Press, 1993).

4 For clarity of exposition I have drawn a fairly sharp contrast between liberal and republican conceptions of citizenship, but in practice there are a number of intermediate positions one may hold. It is also the case that historically many liberals have incorporated republican ideas into their thinking. For a persuasive attempt at a synthesis, see P. Pettit, *Republicanism: A Theory of Freedom and Government* (Oxford, Clarendon Press, 1997).

5 See P.J. Conover, I.M. Crewe and D.D. Searing, 'The Nature of Citizenship in the United States and Great Britain: Empirical Comments on Theoretical Themes', *Journal of Politics*, 53 (1991), 800–32.

6 See P.J. Conover, 'Citizen Identities and Conceptions of the Self', *Journal of Political Philosophy*, 3 (1995), 133–65.

7 See H.-D. Klingemann and D. Fuchs (eds), *Citizens and the State* (Oxford, Oxford University Press, 1995).

8 J.J. Mansbridge, *Beyond Adversary Democracy* (Chicago, University of Chicago Press, 1983).

9 J. Elster, 'The Market and the Forum' in J. Elster and A. Hylland (eds), *Foundations of Social Choice Theory* (Cambridge, Cambridge University Press, 1986), p. 115.

10 J.-J. Rousseau, *The Social Contract* in *Rousseau's Political Writings*, ed. A. Ritter and J.C. Bondanella (New York, Norton, 1988), p. 143.

11 Ibid., p. 149.

12 J.-J. Rousseau, *Discourse on Political Economy* in *Rousseau's Political Writings*, p. 70.

13 J.-J. Rousseau, *Considerations on the Government of Poland* in Rousseau, *Political Writings*, ed. F. Watkins (Edinburgh, Nelson, 1953), p. 176.

14 See M. Viroli, *For Love of Country* (Oxford, Clarendon Press, 1995), pp. 90–4.

15 I argue this at greater length in *On Nationality* (Oxford, Clarendon Press, 1995), esp. ch. 4.

16 E.J. Sieyès, *What is the Third Estate?* (London, Pall Mall Press, 1963).

17 See, for instance, R. Brubaker, *Citizenship and Nationhood in France and Germany* (Cambridge, Mass., Harvard University Press, 1992). These two models have informed the historical development of citizenship policy in the respective countries, although recent German legislation reveals a shift towards a more inclusive conception of citizenship.

18 E. Weber, *Peasants into Frenchmen* (London, Chatto and Windus, 1979).

19 I have explored this option more fully in 'Secession and the Principle of Nationality', ch. 7 below.

20 Some critics have regarded it as a fatal objection to my argument that the world is not neatly divided up into nation-states. My response to this objection is twofold. First, it is implicit in the argument that we should aim to create a world that comes closer to the nation-state model, partly by encouraging the growth of inclusive national identities in states which do not

already have them, partly by creatively redrawing existing lines of political authority so that they correspond more closely to the pattern of national allegiances as we find them. Second, it does not detract from any political ideal that it has preconditions that are not fulfilled everywhere; it is a matter of regret that there are societies in which the ideal cannot be realized, but that does not invalidate it. This is equally true of liberty, or democracy, or the rule of law, as it is of the idea of republican citizenship I am defending.

21 In its familiar form the argument is almost certainly overstated. There is a salutary critique of crude globalization theses in P. Hirst and G. Thompson, *Globalization in Question* (Cambridge, Polity Press, 1996).

22 C. Beitz, *Political Theory and International Relations* (Princeton, Princeton University Press, 1979), part 3, sect. 3.

23 See especially J. Rawls, 'The Law of Peoples' in S. Shute and S. Hurley (eds), *On Human Rights* (New York, Basic Books, 1993); C. Beitz, 'Cosmopolitan Ideals and National Sentiment', *Journal of Philosophy*, 80 (1983), 591–600.

24 D. Held, *Democracy and the Global Order* (Cambridge, Polity Press, 1995); R. Falk, *On Humane Governance* (Cambridge, Polity Press, 1995).

25 Held, *Democracy and the Global Order*, p. 273.

26 Falk, *On Humane Governance*, pp. 211–12.

27 I am indebted here to Andrew Hurrell's unpublished paper 'International Society, Coercive Enforcement and Global Governance'.

28 For instance over the issues of equal pay for women and of differences in the retirement age for men and women. For a discussion see E. Meehan, 'European Citizenship and Social Policies' in U. Vogel and M. Moran (eds), *The Frontiers of Citizenship* (London, Macmillan, 1991), or E. Meehan, *Citizenship and the European Community* (London, Sage, 1993), chs 6–8.

29 As late as the mid-nineteenth century Ruskin could comment 'The words "countryman . . . villager" still signify a rude and untaught person, as opposed to the words "townsman" and "citizen"' (*Oxford English Dictionary* (Oxford, Clarendon Press, 1989), vol. III, p. 250).

Chapter 6   Communitarianism: Left, Right and Centre

1 See, in particular, A. Gutmann, 'Communitarian Critics of Liberalism', *Philosophy and Public Affairs*, 14 (1985), 308–22, reprinted in S. Avineri and A. de-Shalit (eds), *Communitarianism and Individualism* (Oxford, Oxford University Press, 1992).

2 For its guiding ideas, see A. Etzioni, *The Spirit of Community* (London, Fontana, 1995).

3 S. Holmes, *The Anatomy of Antiliberalism* (Cambridge, Mass., Harvard University Press, 1993), p. 178.

4 C. Taylor, 'Cross-Purposes: The Liberal–Communitarian Debate' in *Philosophical Arguments* (Cambridge, Mass., Harvard University Press, 1995); M. Walzer, 'The Communitarian Critique of Liberalism', *Political Theory*, 18 (1990), 6–23.

5   A. MacIntyre, 'A Partial Response to My Critics' in J. Horton and S. Mendus (eds), *After MacIntyre* (Cambridge, Polity Press, 1994), p. 302.

6   M. Sandel (ed.), *Liberalism and its Critics* (Oxford, Blackwell, 1984); M. Sandel, *Democracy's Discontents* (Cambridge, Mass., Belknap Press, 1996).

7   Charles Taylor draws a rather similar distinction between 'ontological issues' and 'advocacy issues' in 'Cross Purposes'. See also S. Caney, 'Liberalism and Communitarianism: A Misconceived Debate', *Political Studies*, 40 (1992), 273–89, and A. Buchanan, 'Assessing the Communitarian Critique of Liberalism', *Ethics*, 99 (1988–9), 852–82.

8   For this argument, see, for instance, M. Sandel, *Liberalism and the Limits of Justice* (Cambridge, Cambridge University Press, 1982), ch. 1.

9   This claim is developed in, for instance, C. Taylor, *Sources of the Self* (Cambridge, Cambridge University Press, 1989), part 1.

10 A. MacIntyre, *After Virtue* (London, Duckworth, 1981), esp. chs 1–5.

11 R. Nozick, *Anarchy, State and Utopia* (Oxford, Blackwell, 1974); J. Rawls, *A Theory of Justice* (Cambridge, Mass., Harvard University Press, 1971); R. Dworkin, 'Liberalism' in *A Matter of Principle* (Oxford, Clarendon Press, 1986).

12 See J. Raz, *The Morality of Freedom* (Oxford, Clarendon Press, 1986), chs 14–15; J. Raz, 'Multiculturalism: A Liberal Perspective' in *Ethics in the Public Domain* (Oxford, Clarendon Press, 1994); W. Kymlicka, *Liberalism, Community and Culture* (Oxford, Clarendon Press, 1989), chs 7–9; W. Kymlicka, 'Liberal Individualism and Liberal Neutrality', *Ethics*, 99 (1988–9), 883–905 (partially reprinted in S. Avineri and A. de-Shalit (eds), *Communitarianism and Individualism* (Oxford, Oxford University Press, 1992)).

13 See the debate on these questions between Chandran Kukathas and Will Kymlicka: C. Kukathas, 'Are There Any Cultural Rights?', *Political Theory*, 20 (1992), 105–39; W. Kymlicka, 'The Rights of Minority Cultures: Reply to Kukathas', *Political Theory*, 20 (1992), 140–6; C. Kukathas, 'Cultural Rights Again: A Rejoinder to Kymlicka', *Political Theory*, 20 (1992), 674–80.

14 See R. Scruton, *The Meaning of Conservatism* (Harmondsworth, Penguin, 1980); 'In Defence of the Nation' in *The Philosopher on Dover Beach* (Manchester, Carcanet, 1990).

15 Scruton, 'In Defence of the Nation', p. 310.

16 I have explained the idea of equality of status more fully, and explored some of its empirical preconditions, in 'Complex Equality' in D. Miller and M. Walzer (eds), *Pluralism, Justice and Equality* (Oxford, Oxford University Press, 1995). See also D. Miller, 'What Kind of Equality Should the Left Pursue?' in J. Franklin (ed.), *Equality* (London, IPPR, 1997).

17 M. Walzer, *Spheres of Justice* (Oxford, Martin Robertson, 1983), ch. 2.

18 I have argued this at greater length in *On Nationality* (Oxford, Clarendon Press, 1995), ch. 5.

19 In *On Nationality*, chs 4–5, and in 'Bounded Citizenship', ch. 5 above.

20 K. Marx, 'On the Jewish Question' in T.B. Bottomore (ed.), *Karl Marx: Early Writings* (London, Watts, 1963).

21 Walzer, *Spheres of Justice*, ch. 1; I have tried to expand upon and defend Walzer's idea in 'Complex Equality'.

22 There is a large and growing literature on deliberative democracy which includes: B. Manin, 'On Legitimacy and Political Deliberation', *Political Theory*, 15 (1987), 338–68; J. Cohen, 'Deliberation and Democratic Legitimacy' in A. Hamlin and P. Pettit (eds), *The Good Polity* (Oxford, Blackwell, 1989); J. Drysek, *Discursive Democracy* (Cambridge, Cambridge University Press, 1990); J. Fishkin, *Democracy and Deliberation* (New Haven, Yale University Press, 1991); D. Miller, 'Deliberative Democracy and Social Choice', ch. 1 above; A. Gutmann and D. Thompson, *Democracy and Disagreement* (Cambridge, Mass., Belknap Press, 1996).

23 A. Etzioni, 'Common Values', *New Statesman and Society*, 8(352), 12 May 1995, p. 25.

24 See Etzioni, *The Spirit of Community*, part 3.

Chapter 7 Secession and the Principle of Nationality

An earlier version of this chapter was presented to the Roundtable on National Self-Determination and Secession, American Political Science Association Annual Meeting, San Francisco, 28 August–1 September 1996. I am grateful to the participants in that meeting for their comments, and also to Michel Seymour for writing to me at some length about the case of Quebec.

1 A. Buchanan, *Secession* (Boulder, Colo., Westview Press, 1991), p. 49.

2 Under international law, regions within the main body of a state have for some time been regarded differently from geographically separate territories, such as colonies. The 'right of self-determination' that international bodies such as the UN sometimes proclaim has only been taken to support independence movements in the latter case. In the case of a territorially compact state, it does not imply a right of secession for any part of the state, but the right of the population as a whole to determine its form of government. See J. Crawford, *The Creation of States in International Law* (Oxford, Clarendon Press, 1979), esp. ch. 3.

3 Most fully in *On Nationality* (Oxford, Clarendon Press, 1995). See also 'In Defence of Nationality', ch. 2 above, and 'On Nationality', *Nations and Nationalism*, 2 (1996), 409–21.

4 See Buchanan, *Secession*, ch. 4 and W. Norman, 'The Ethics of Secession as the Regulation of Secessionist Politics' in M. Moore (ed.), *National Self-Determination and Secession* (Oxford, Oxford University Press, 1998).

5 A. Buchanan, 'Theories of Secession', *Philosophy and Public Affairs*, 26 (1997), 31–61.

6 I have given a fuller account of nationality in *On Nationality*, ch. 2.

7 I have drawn here on the discussion of Catalonia in M. Keating, *Nations Against the State: The New Politics of Nationalism in Quebec, Catalonia and Scotland* (Basingstoke, Macmillan, 1996), ch. 5.

8   See D. McDowall, *The Kurds: A Nation Denied* (London, Minority Rights
     Group, 1992); P.G. Kreyenbroek and S. Sperl (eds), *The Kurds: A Contem-
     porary Overview* (London, Routledge, 1992).

9   It should also be said that some Kurds have chosen the route of assimilation,
     forgoing their Kurdish identity in favour of a Turkish one. The important
     contrast with the Catalan case is that a Kurd in Turkey is more or less forced
     to make a choice between these two identities, whereas for a Catalan in Spain
     a hyphenated identity is easily available, and indeed a large majority of
     Catalans describe themselves in these terms (for instance as ' Equally Spanish
     and Catalan', 'More Catalan than Spanish', etc. – see Keating, *Nations
     Against the State*, pp. 129–34).

10   Nor is it to say that secession is only justified when there is a sharp conflict of
     national identities: national groups may decide to separate by mutual con-
     sent, as the Norwegians and the Swedes did in 1905, and here the depth of
     the antagonism between them is largely irrelevant. I am considering the much
     more common case where the Xs wish to secede but the majority Ys oppose
     this.

11   See, for example, K. Nielsen, 'Secession: The Case of Quebec', *Journal of
     Applied Philosophy*, 10 (1993), 29–43; D. Gauthier, 'Breaking Up: An Essay
     on Secession', *Canadian Journal of Philosophy*, 24 (1994), 357–72.

12   According to Hillel Steiner, for instance, 'since nations' territories are aggre-
     gations of their members' real estate holdings, the validity of their territorial
     claims rests on the validity of those land titles' (H. Steiner, 'Territorial Justice'
     in S. Caney, D. George and P. Jones (eds), *National Rights, International
     Obligations* (Boulder, Colo., Westview Press, 1996), p. 146).

13   Buchanan, *Secession*, pp. 107–14.

14   If one group occupies the territory previously held by another, then, *ceteris
     paribus*, the strength of its claim to exercise authority will increase with time.
     At a certain point – impossible to specify exactly – it will have a stronger title
     than the original inhabitants. This may sound uncomfortably like a version
     of 'might makes right', but I cannot see any reasonable alternative to the view
     that it is the occupation and transformation of territory which gives a people
     its title to that territory, from which it follows that the competing claims of
     the present and original inhabitants increase and diminish respectively with
     the passage of time.

15   This brings into play questions about distributive justice which I shall address
     later.

16   Though note the qualification recorded in n. 10 above.

17   Margaret Moore argues for the relevance of numbers in 'On National Self-
     Determination', *Political Studies*, 45 (1997), 900–13 and in 'Miller's Ode to
     National Homogeneity', *Nations and Nationalism*, 2 (1996), 423–9. I am
     not sure, however, that she would endorse the criterion I am discussing in
     its crude form because she also speaks about 'utilitarian calculations'
     which suggests taking into account intensities of feeling as well as the sheer
     numbers who are satisfied or dissatisfied with a proposed boundary
     redrawing.

18 D.L. Horowitz, 'Self-Determination: Politics, Philosophy, and Law', in I. Shapiro and W. Kymlicka (eds), *Nomos XXXIX: Ethnicity and Group Rights* (New York, New York University Press, 1997), and in M. Moore (ed.), *National Self-Determination and Secession* (Oxford, Oxford University Press, 1998).

19 See, for instance, D. Philpott, 'In Defense of Self-Determination', *Ethics*, 105 (1994–5), 352–85. 'In a heterogeneous candidate territory, the decision [to secede] rests with the majority of the territory's inhabitants, with the qualification that under the new government, minority rights – including Kymlickan cultural rights – are guaranteed' (p. 380).

20 Perhaps the most interesting example of an exchange of this kind occurred between Greece and Turkey in the 1920s. Under the terms of a formal agreement between the two states, some 200,000 people of Greek descent living in Turkey were required to emigrate to Greece, and about 350,000 Turks were required to move from Greece to Turkey. Alongside the formal exchange, however, much larger numbers of Greeks – perhaps about one million – emigrated to Greece either voluntarily or as a result of Turkish oppression, and a further 100,000 Turks moved in the opposite direction. There is not a great deal of hard evidence about the overall impact of the transfer on the people who experienced it, but, focusing on the Greek side, the following four statements appear to be true. (1) Materially speaking the infrastructure and investment provided by the internationally funded Refugee Settlement Commission allowed large numbers of immigrants to settle and flourish in their new places of residence. (2) The exchange appears also to have had a strongly positive effect on the overall economic prosperity and sense of national identity in Greece. (3) The refugees experienced psychological difficulties in adjusting to their forcible translation and continued to harbour hopes of a return to their birthplaces at least up until World War II. (4) Over the same period there were significant social divisions between natives and refugees in Greek towns and villages. To arrive at a balanced assessment, these pluses and minuses would need to be set against the likely fate of the minorities, particularly at the hands of the Turkish authorities, if the transfer had not occurred. For descriptions of the exchange, see S.P. Ladas, *The Exchange of Minorities: Bulgaria, Greece and Turkey* (New York, Macmillan, 1932); D. Pentzopoulos, *The Balkan Exchange of Minorities and its Impact upon Greece* (Paris, Mouton, 1962); J.A. Petropulos, 'The Compulsory Exchange of Populations: Greek–Turkish Peacemaking, 1922–1930', *Byzantine and Modern Greek Studies*, 2 (1976), 135–60.

21 Including Buchanan, *Secession*, ch. 3; Gauthier, 'Breaking Up: An Essay on Secession'; C.H. Wellman, 'A Defense of Secession and Political Self-Determination', *Philosophy and Public Affairs*, 24 (1995), 142–71.

22 Buchanan, *Secession*, pp. 114 ff.

23 I have set this argument out more fully in 'The Limits of Cosmopolitan Justice', in D.R. Mapel and T. Nardin (eds), *The Constitution of International Society: Diverse Ethical Perspectives* (Princeton, Princeton University Press, 1998) and in 'Justice and Global Inequality' in A. Hurrell and

N. Woods (eds), *Inequality, Globalization, and World Politics* (Oxford, Oxford University Press, 1999).

24 These two grounds do not necessarily coincide, as the Scottish case illustrates. In recent years many Scots have felt that their public culture and sense of social justice is increasingly at odds with the Thatcherite ideas that have infected some parts of British central government and administration. On the other hand, Scotland has for some while been a net beneficiary of the British system of public finance, so it would be hard for Scots to claim that they are victims of discriminatory treatment.

25 There may be cases – Blacks in America come to mind – in which groups suffer from injustice at the hands of the majority without having or developing a separate sense of national identity. But where a minority group is territorially concentrated, the experience of injustice has a strong tendency over time to foster such a separate identity, so that once again the cause of justice and the cause of national self-determination are fused.

26 Gauthier, 'Breaking Up: An Essay on Secession', section III.

27 Wellman, 'A Defense of Secession and Political Self-Determination', pp. 161–2.

28 So, for example, I think that the Slovenian secession from Yugoslavia could not be condemned on the grounds that it made the achievement of liberal democracy in Yugoslavia as a whole less likely. We ought indeed to try to promote liberal and democratic ideals externally, but I don't think that our duty in this respect is so strong as to oblige us to remain in political association with groups whose culture or identity we find uncongenial.

Chapter 8   Nationality in Divided Societies

Earlier versions of this chapter were presented to audiences at the University of Newcastle, the University of Edinburgh and Arizona State University; it was also presented to the Conference 'In Search of Justice and Stability: A Comparative and Theoretical Analysis of Canada, Belgium, Spain and the United Kingdom' organized by the Research Group on Multinational States, McGill University, March 1998, and to a panel on 'Liberalism and Nationalism' at the American Political Science Association Annual Conference, Boston, September 1998. I should like to thank all those who spoke at these meetings for their helpful comments, and especially Alain Gagnon and Dominique Arel for their written suggestions.

1 My general defence of national self-determination can be found in D. Miller, *On Nationality* (Oxford, Clarendon Press, 1995), esp. ch. 3.

2 Will Kymlicka has underlined the importance of distinguishing between ethnic groups and national minorities if we wish to develop a political theory of multiculturalism, in *Multicultural Citizenship* (Oxford, Clarendon Press, 1995), esp. ch. 2. I depart from his position first by distinguishing between two kinds of national minorities, as indicated in the text, and second by placing less emphasis on the immigrant status of ethnic groups. Although immigration is a major source of ethnic pluralism, it is not the only source,

and my own account of ethnicity does not treat it as a defining feature. In part, this may reflect a contrast between North American and European perspectives.

3   I am also not sure that my categorization is exhaustive. If we consider the position of aboriginal groups such as native Americans or Australian aborigines, then as Kymlicka has emphasized it is wrong to treat them simply as ethnic groups, but on the other hand they do not fit easily into either of my categories of national minority. Their social and political structure is not sufficiently developed for them to constitute integral nations rivalling the dominant national groups in the states to which they belong; but because of the way in which they were incorporated historically into nation-states, it is also difficult for their identities to nest comfortably within the overarching national identity. (The reasons why they cannot be treated as nested nationalities will become clearer as we proceed.) Perhaps then we should treat aboriginal groups as a fourth category when discussing the implications of the principle of nationality.

4   I have looked at responses to ethnic pluralism in 'Group Identities, National Identities and Democratic Politics', ch. 4 above, and at different ways of responding to the demands made by rival national groups in 'Secession and the Principle of Nationality', ch. 7 above.

5   A recent television report from Bosnia showed a reporter standing in a classroom of small children (the education system is now a divided one). He asked, 'How many of you think of yourselves as Bosnians?' No hands went up. 'How many of you think of yourselves as Serbs?' Every hand went up.

6   See chapter 7 for a fuller discussion.

7   The idea that people can sustain social and political identities at different levels without significant internal conflict is now fairly familiar. Anthony Smith spoke of 'concentric loyalties' in *The Ethnic Revival* (Cambridge, Cambridge University Press, 1981), p. 164, and this idea was taken up and applied in an illuminating way to the Scottish case by T.C. Smout in 'Perspectives on the Scottish Identity', *Scottish Affairs*, 6 (1994), 101–13. Two further points are worth noting. If we use the metaphor of concentric circles of identity, this is only to indicate the wider or narrower spatial range of the various identities that a person may bear (Smout starts with the family and ends with supranational groupings); it is not to say anything about the relative *importance* of these identities. Moreover in some cases we should think not just in terms of concentric circles but also of overlapping circles, where people identify to some degree with neighbouring communities as well as with more inclusive ones. (A Scottish Catholic living in Glasgow may feel some affinity with Irishmen across the water as well as with Scotland, Britain, Europe, etc.) I am grateful to Zenon Bankowski for emphasizing this latter point.

8   For evidence supporting my claim that national identities in these states typically exhibit such a duality, see, for Belgium, K.D. McRae, *Conflict and Compromise in Multilingual Societies: Belgium* (Waterloo, Wilfrid Laurier

University Press, 1986), esp. ch. 3, and B. Maddens, R. Beerten and J. Billiet, 'The National Consciousness of the Flemings and the Walloons. An Empirical Investigation' in K. Deprez and L. Vos (eds), *Nationalism in Belgium: Shifting Identities, 1780–1995* (Basingstoke, Macmillan, 1998); for Canada, J. Webber, *Reimagining Canada* (Kingston and Montreal, McGill-Queen's University Press, 1994), esp. ch. 6, and K. McRoberts, *Misconceiving Canada* (Toronto, Oxford University Press, 1997), esp. ch. 10; for Spain, M. Keating, *Nations Against the State* (London, Macmillan, 1996), ch. 5, and J.D. Medrano, *Divided Nations: Class, Politics, and Nationalism in the Basque Country and Catalonia* (Ithaca and London, Cornell University Press, 1995), esp. ch. 11; for Switzerland, K.D. McRae, *Conflict and Compromise in Multilingual Societies: Switzerland* (Waterloo, Wilfrid Laurier University Press, 1983), esp. ch. 3, and J. Steinberg, *Why Switzerland?*, 2nd edn (Cambridge, Cambridge University Press, 1996), esp. ch. 7.

9   See Keating, *Nations Against the State*, p. 130.

10   The idea that one must belong exclusively to a single nation is linked to the idea that national loyalty must take precedence over all other ethical demands to which one may be subject. Clearly, if one's supreme duty is to act as the interests of one's nation require, it makes no sense to suppose that one might belong simultaneously to two nations. But the ethical doctrine is untenable, and once that is abandoned, it is not difficult to think of a person balancing her loyalties to a larger and to a smaller country, particularly where, as I shall try to show in the Anglo-Scottish case, the two identities dovetail reasonably well.

11   There are historical precedents for using 'nationality' to identify the smaller community and 'nation' to identify the inclusive community: this terminology is used in, for instance, the Spanish Constitution of 1978 which prepared the way for regional autonomy for Catalonia and the Basque Country.

12   Miller, *On Nationality*, p. 141.

13   The religious background to the Act of Union is highlighted in A.V. Dicey and R.S. Rait, *Thoughts on the Union between England and Scotland* (London, Macmillan, 1920). They point out, for instance, that the King James Bible, published in 1611, 'was read, and has been constantly read by every English and Scottish Protestant sufficiently educated to read any book. ... The religious, the moral, the social, and the political effects of such a Bible hardly admit of exaggeration. It made Englishmen and Scotsmen ultimately speak, read, and write one and the same language, and it linked together the religious ideas of all British Protestants' (p. 333).

14   See C. Kidd, *Subverting Scotland's Past: Scottish Whig Historians and the creation of an Anglo-British identity, 1689 – c. 1830* (Cambridge, Cambridge University Press, 1993), ch. 2.

15   See P.H. Scott, *1707: The Union of Scotland and England* (Edinburgh, Chambers, 1979). See also G.S. Pryde, *The Treaty of Union of Scotland and England, 1707* (London, Nelson, 1950) which includes the text of the Treaty of Union.

16 D. Hume, *The History of England* (Indianapolis, Liberty Classics, 1983), vol. II, p. 113.
17 Kidd, *Subverting Scotland's Past*, p. 211.
18 For the historical trajectory of Jacobitism, see M.G.H. Pittock, *The Invention of Scotland: The Stuart Myth and the Scottish Identity, 1638 to the present* (London, Routledge, 1991).
19 E. Gellner, *Nations and Nationalism* (Oxford, Blackwell, 1983), esp. ch. 5. For a much more elaborate account along these general lines of why Scottish nationalism failed to develop in a way parallel to that of other peripheral European nations, see T. Nairn, 'Scotland and Europe' in *The Break-Up of Britain* (London, New Left Books, 1977).
20 To take one example: Allan Ramsay, arguably the most accomplished portrait painter Scotland has produced, based himself in London while continuing from time to time to undertake commissions in Edinburgh. He was appointed Painter-in-Ordinary to George III in 1760. His well-known portrait of Hume, now hanging in the Scottish National Portrait Gallery, was almost certainly painted in London.
21 See the detailed analysis in G. Marshall, *Presbyteries and Profits: Calvinism and the Development of Capitalism in Scotland, 1560–1707* (Edinburgh, Edinburgh University Press, 1992).
22 D. McCrone, *Understanding Scotland: The Sociology of a Stateless Nation* (London, Routledge, 1992), esp. ch. 3.
23 The reasons for the disproportion are explained in I. McLean, 'The Semi-Detached Election: Scotland' in A King (ed.), *New Labour Triumphs: Britain at the Polls* (Chatham, NJ, Chatham House, 1998). McLean also examines nationalist claims about the offsetting effects of tax revenues from North Sea Oil.
24 L. Colley, *Britons: Forging the Nation 1707–1837* (New Haven and London, Yale University Press, 1992), ch. 3.
25 To take one example of many, when Wolfe defeated Montcalm on the Plains of Abraham, his left wing was commanded by Brigadier James Murray, a Scottish officer who went on to be Governor of Quebec and eventually of Canada as a whole.
26 I have explored this in *On Nationality*, ch. 6.
27 Here is one stanza from Burns that seems unlikely to be recited at Scottish National Party conventions (the SNP is strongly pro-European in outlook):

> Be BRITAIN still to BRITAIN true,
> Amang oursels united;
> For never but by British hands
> Must British wrongs be righted.

('The Dumfries Volunteers' from J. Kinsley (ed.), *Burns: Poems and Songs* (Oxford, Oxford University Press, 1971), p. 604)
For more on Burns see T.C. Smout, 'Problems of Nationalism, Identity and Improvement in Later Eighteenth-Century Scotland' in T.M. Devine (ed.), *Improvement and Enlightenment* (Edinburgh, John Donald, 1989).

28   See, for instance, Webber, *Reimagining Canada*, pp. 208–11, and W. Kym-
     licka, 'Multinational Federalism in Canada: Rethinking the Partnership' in
     R. Gibbins and G. Laforest (eds), *Beyond the Impasse: Towards Reconcilia-
     tion* (Montreal, Institute for Research on Public Policy, 1998), pp. 29–41.
29   This suggestion has been made in the Canadian context by Philip Resnick in
     Thinking English Canada (Toronto, Stoddart, 1994) and in the British con-
     text by Bernard Crick in 'The English and the British' in B. Crick (ed.),
     National Identities: The Constitution of the United Kingdom (Oxford,
     Blackwell, 1991).
30   In one sense it is true that nations are constituted by the will of their
     members. But this proposition needs careful analysis. Nations indeed only
     exist because the people who make them up continue to affirm their wish to
     remain associated (this is the truth in Renan's famous description of the
     nation as 'a daily plebiscite'). But the affirmation is grounded in beliefs
     about the shared history and shared cultural characteristics that make it
     appropriate for the people in question to live in association, and this second
     aspect of nationhood is equally important. As with all beliefs, these may be
     true, false, exaggerated, distorted, etc. Someone who says 'the Scots should
     separate from the UK: they have nothing in common with the English' is
     supporting his demand with an unwarranted assertion.
31   I have argued this at greater length in ch. 7, sect. 2.
32   I do not mean that they would be justified in using every means at their
     disposal to resist a secessionist movement in Scotland; in particular I do not
     think that physical force should be used. One reason is that the use of force to
     preserve the unity of a nation-state is likely to be self-defeating: the experi-
     ence of being subjected to physical coercion will destroy the sense of common
     national identity that allows us to speak of an overarching nation in the first
     place. In general, the means used to defend territorial claims have to be
     proportionate to the importance of those claims.
33   The regress can be stopped, but only by introducing further stipulations that
     make the outcome of applying the consent principle essentially arbitrary. See
     my critique of the consent theory of secession in *On Nationality*, ch. 3, sect. 3.
34   For further discussion of the limitations of using existing administrative
     boundaries to define the territory in which a secessionist vote will be held,
     see M. Moore, 'On National Self-Determination', *Political Studies*, 45
     (1997), 900–13, and M. Moore, 'The Territorial Dimension of National
     Self-Determination' in M. Moore (ed.), *National Self-Determination and
     Secession* (Oxford, Oxford University Press, 1998).
35   For a fuller discussion of the conditions under which secession is ethically
     justifiable, see ch. 7, sects 2–3.

Chapter 9   Is Deliberative Democracy Unfair to Disadvantaged Groups?

Earlier versions of this chapter were read to audiences at York University, Bristol
University, and Manchester University, and to the Nuffield Political Theory Work-

shop. I am very grateful for the many suggestions made on these occasions, and especially to John Drysek, Cécile Fabre and Amy Gutmann for their written comments on the penultimate draft.

1 The literature on deliberative democracy is now too extensive to be cited in full. Among book-length discussions see especially J. Drysek, *Discursive Democracy* (Cambridge, Cambridge University Press, 1990); J. Fishkin, *Democracy and Deliberation* (New Haven and London, Yale University Press, 1991); S. Chambers, *Reasonable Democracy* (Ithaca and London, Cornell University Press, 1996); A. Gutmann and D. Thompson, *Democracy and Disagreement* (Cambridge, Mass., Harvard University Press, 1996); J. Bohman, *Public Deliberation: Pluralism, Complexity and Democracy* (Cambridge, Mass., MIT Press, 1996). Recent edited collections addressing the topic include S. Benhabib (ed.), *Democracy and Difference: Contesting the Boundaries of the Political* (Princeton, Princeton University Press, 1996); J. Bohman and W. Rehg (eds), *Deliberative Democracy: Essays on Reason and Politics* (Cambridge, Mass., MIT Press, 1997); J. Elster (ed.), *Deliberative Democracy* (Cambridge, Cambridge University Press, 1998); J. Drysek, *Deliberative Democracy and Beyond* (Oxford, Oxford University Press, forthcoming).

2 This brief definition conceals some ambiguities over how deliberation is supposed to lead to decisions that command widespread if not universal consent. I return to these later in the chapter.

3 Among those who implicitly or explicitly criticize deliberative democracy from a realist perspective are G. Sartori, *The Theory of Democracy Revisited* (Chatham, NJ, Chatham House Publishers, 1987); A. Przeworski, *Democracy and the Market* (Cambridge, Cambridge University Press, 1991); D. Zolo, *Democracy and Complexity: A Realist Approach* (University Park, Penn., Pennsylvania State University Press, 1992).

4 See W.H. Riker, *Liberalism Against Populism* (San Francisco, W.H. Freeman, 1982); J. Coleman and J. Ferejohn, 'Democracy and Social Choice', *Ethics* 97 (1986), 6–25; J. Knight and J. Johnson, 'Aggregation and Deliberation: On the Possibility of Democratic Legitimacy', *Political Theory*, 22 (1994), 277–96; D. Van Mill, 'The Possibility of Rational Outcomes from Democratic Discourse and Procedures', *Journal of Politics*, 58 (1996), 734–52.

5 I have responded to the social choice critique in 'Deliberative Democracy and Social Choice', ch. 1 above. See also J. Johnson, 'Arguing for Deliberation: Some Skeptical Considerations' in Elster (ed.), *Deliberative Democracy* and J. Drysek and C. List, 'Deliberative Democracy and Social Choice Theory – A Reconciliation' (unpublished paper, 1998).

6 L. Sanders, 'Against Deliberation', *Political Theory*, 25 (1997), 347–76; I.M. Young, 'Communication and the Other: Beyond Deliberative Democracy' in Benhabib (ed.), *Democracy and Difference*; I.M. Young, 'Difference as a Resource for Democratic Communication' in Bohman and Rehg (eds), *Deliberative Democracy*; I.M. Young, 'Inclusive Political Communication: Greeting, Rhetoric and Storytelling in the Context of Political Argument' (paper

presented to Annual Meeting of the American Political Science Association, Boston, Mass., September 1998).

7 Vigorous arguments for and against can be found, respectively, in I.M. Young, *Justice and the Politics of Difference* (Princeton, Princeton University Press, 1990), ch. 6, and C. Ward, 'The Limits of "Liberal Republicanism": Why Group-Based Remedies and Republican Citizenship Don't Mix', *Columbia Law Review*, 91 (1991), 581–607. For more nuanced discussions, see C. Sunstein, 'Beyond the Republican Revival', *Yale Law Journal*, 97 (1988), 1539–89; W. Kymlicka, *Multicultural Citizenship* (Oxford, Clarendon Press, 1995), ch. 7; and especially A. Phillips, *The Politics of Presence* (Oxford, Clarendon Press, 1995).

8 Sanders, 'Against Deliberation' pp. 363–6.

9 Ibid., p. 366.

10 R. Hastie, S.D. Penrod and N. Pennington, *Inside the Jury* (Cambridge, Mass., Harvard University Press, 1983), ch. 8. Verdict-driven juries are those which take any early ballot to reveal the level of support for each possible verdict, and jurors then tend to act as advocates for one or other position, giving arguments that support that verdict. Evidence-driven juries try to form an agreed interpretation of the evidence presented to them, without individual members committing themselves to any particular verdict, and ballots are taken only late in the proceedings (or sometimes not until the very end, to confirm a consensus).

11 See N. Marsden, 'Gender Dynamics and Jury Deliberation', *Yale Law Journal*, 96 (1987), 593–612.

12 Young, 'Communication and the Other', p. 123.

13 See A. Coote and J. Lenaghan, *Citizens' Juries: Theory into Practice* (London, IPPR, 1997); G. Smith and C. Wales, 'Toward Deliberative Institutions: Lessons from Citizens' Juries' (paper presented to the ECPR Workshop on Innovation in Democratic Theory, 1999).

14 Young, 'Communication and the Other', p. 123.

15 Ibid., p. 124.

16 Sanders, 'Against Deliberation', p. 370.

17 See especially Young, 'Inclusive Political Communication', and Sanders, 'Against Deliberation'.

18 That deliberation and bargaining are mutually exclusive is standardly assumed in most discussions of deliberative democracy. See, for instance, J. Elster, 'The Market and the Forum: Three Varieties of Political Theory' in J. Elster and A. Aanund (eds), *The Foundations of Social Choice Theory* (Cambridge, Cambridge University Press, 1986). In his later work Habermas, by contrast, makes room for bargaining within a more pluralistic account of deliberation. He is careful to insist, however, that the bargaining has to be regulated to ensure fairness between the parties – each must have 'an equal opportunity to influence one another during the actual bargaining, so that all the affected interests can come into play and have equal chances of prevailing' (J. Habermas, *Between Facts and Norms: Contributions to a Discourse Theory of Law and Democracy* (Cambridge, Polity Press, 1996), pp. 166–7).

Whether 'bargaining' that is so constrained can properly be described as bargaining is moot. The general point is that deliberative theorists must be selective about what they will count as deliberation if the process is going to yield outcomes that meet the relevant ethical standards.

19 See J. Rawls, *Political Liberalism* (New York, Columbia University Press, 1993), Lecture VI; J. Rawls, 'The Idea of Public Reason Revisited', *University of Chicago Law Review*, 64 (1997), 765–807; J. Cohen, 'Deliberation and Democratic Legitimacy' in A. Hamlin and P. Pettit (eds), *The Good Polity* (Oxford, Blackwell, 1989), reprinted in Bohman and Rehg (eds), *Deliberative Democracy*; J. Cohen, 'Pluralism and Proceduralism', *Chicago-Kent Law Review*, 69 (1994), 589–618; J. Cohen, 'Procedure and Substance in Deliberative Democracy' in Benhabib (ed.), *Democracy and Difference* and in Bohman and Rehg (eds), *Deliberative Democracy*; and J. Cohen, 'Democracy and Liberty' in Elster (ed.), *Deliberative Democracy*.

20 Cohen, 'Procedure and Substance in Deliberative Democracy' in Benhabib (ed.), *Democracy and Difference*, p. 100.

21 I have developed this point with respect to environmental goods in D. Miller, 'Social Justice and Environmental Goods' in A. Dobson (ed.), *Fairness and Futurity: Essays on Environmental Sustainability and Social Justice* (Oxford, Oxford University Press, 1999).

22 Gutmann and Thompson, *Democracy and Disagreement*, ch. 2.

23 For instance in the case of abortion, they suggest that the state might introduce a scheme whereby those who favoured the state funding of abortion could indicate their consent to be taxed for this purpose, while those who objected could exempt themselves from paying this tax.

24 This conclusion needs qualification in one respect: certain reasons are ruled out by the requirements of deliberation themselves. Among such excluded reasons are those that challenge the equality of members of the deliberating body, e.g. racist arguments whose import is that some people should be deprived of equal rights of citizenship by virtue of their race, and those that involve the threat of violence or other forms of coercion. Where such reasons are presented, deliberation in the form of a free and open discussion among equals cannot proceed. In contrast, reasons that invoke personal ideals and values that others may not share need not be excluded. All that deliberation requires is a willingness to shift ground in the event that reasons of this kind turn out not to be persuasive.

25 This assumes, of course, that the deliberating body is an ongoing institution with a stable membership. Although this is not a necessary condition for successful deliberation – juries, including citizens' juries, provide a counter-example – I believe that, particularly where participants are being asked to make personal sacrifices in the name of reaching an agreement, it is strongly conducive to it. See further my argument in ch. 5 above about the link between responsible citizenship and continuity in the decision-making body.

26 This moral requirement applies only on condition that others reciprocate, by themselves seeking agreement on terms that respect *us* and *our* convictions. This means in particular that disadvantaged groups are not required to show

respect for the reasons advanced by members of advantaged groups unless they are reasonably confident that the latter will reciprocate, and not simply rely on their superior bargaining power to win the day. I am grateful to Amy Gutmann for insisting on this point.

27 For a good example of how emotional speech and rational speech can work together to promote deliberation, see the discussion of Carol Moseley Braun's opposition to the patenting of the Confederate flag in Gutmann and Thompson, *Democracy and Disagreement*, pp. 135–7.

28 Sanders, 'Against Deliberation', p. 362.

29 On an alternative reading of her claim, Sanders might be saying that a decision does not qualify as democratic unless it addresses the demands of marginalized groups. But this requires us to apply a substantive criterion of justice to the outcome and to count as democratic only those decisions that meet the criterion, no matter what procedure has been followed. There are familiar problems with this move. Even if we think that deliberative democracy is the political decision-procedure *most likely to* lead to just outcomes, it is a mistake to link the two conceptually in this way.

30 S. Benhabib, 'Toward a Deliberative Model of Democratic Legitimacy' in Benhabib (ed.), *Democracy and Difference*. I am not proposing a blanket ban on the use of rhetoric in democratic debate, which in any case would be impossible to enforce. Rhetoric which reaches across group boundaries to highlight shared aims and values undoubtedly plays a positive role. I am drawing attention, rather, to speech that uses rhetorical devices to promote causes favoured by particular groups, which invites counter-rhetoric from the opposition. It seems odd that authors such as Young who denounce the forms of argument found today in parliamentary debates and adversarial court proceedings should go on to defend the use of rhetoric by disadvantaged groups, which encourages precisely the confrontational style she elsewhere deplores.

31 In addition, one should take note of John Drysek's observation that each of the alternative forms of communication favoured by Young can have a coercive character: modes of greeting can serve to exclude or even intimidate outsiders; rhetoric can be used to discredit certain speakers; and storytelling can be constrained by norms of what constitutes a 'correct' storyline within a particular group. See Drysek, *Deliberative Democracy and Beyond*, ch. 3.

32 Young, 'Communication and the Other', p. 132.

33 Young, 'Inclusive Political Communication', p. 36.

34 Cf. Gutmann and Thompson, *Democracy and Disagreement*, p. 137.

35 Young, 'Difference as a Resource for Democratic Communication', pp. 403–4.

36 I do not mean to give the impression that this is an easy question to resolve. The difficulties are well explained in G. Marshall, A. Swift and S. Roberts, *Against the Odds? Social Class and Social Justice in Industrial Societies* (Oxford, Clarendon Press, 1997).

37 Young, 'Difference as a Resource for Democratic Communication', p. 402.

38 I draw here on two unpublished papers by Yuen J. Huo: 'Boundary Effects in Judgements of the Deservingness of Justice: Conflict, Identification and Values' and 'Justice and Exclusion: Exploring the Boundaries of Our Moral Community'. Some of the relevant evidence is reported in Y.J. Huo, 'Defining Moral Communities: Normative and Functional Bases of the Allocation of Social Goods', manuscript submitted for publication to the *Journal of Experimental Social Psychology*.

39 See T.R. Tyler, R.J. Boeckmann, H.J. Smith and Y.J. Huo, *Social Justice in a Diverse Society* (Boulder, Co, Westview Press, 1997), ch. 10.

40 D. Miller, *On Nationality* (Oxford, Clarendon Press, 1995), ch. 4; D. Miller, 'Group Identities, National Identities and Democratic Politics', ch. 4 above.

41 This brings to mind the famous passage from *The Merchant of Venice* in which Shylock protests against the calumnies he has suffered at the hands (especially) of Antonio by invoking the common humanity of Jews and Christians: 'Hath not a Jew eyes? hath not a Jew hands, organs, dimensions, senses, affections, passions? fed with the same food, hurt with the same weapons, subject to the same diseases, healed by the same means, warmed and cooled by the same winter and summer, as a Christian is? If you prick us, do we not bleed? if you tickle us, do we not laugh? if you poison us, do we not die?' (Act 3, Scene 1). Shylock goes on to couple this with a threat of revenge, but up to this point the passage says: 'How can it be fair for injustices to be heaped upon the head of one who shares so much with you?' This is the most emotionally and morally powerful appeal that a member of an oppressed minority can make, and Shakespeare as usual gives it perfect expression.

42 Sanders, 'Against Deliberation', p. 372.

43 Ibid., p. 372

Chapter 10   National Self-Determination and Global Justice

Earlier versions of this chapter were presented to a research seminar in All Souls College, Oxford, and to a symposium on 'Welfare Rights and International Duties' at the annual meeting of the American Philosophical Association, Central Division, New Orleans, 6–8 May, 1999. I am very grateful to both audiences for their comments, and especially to Jerry Cohen, Cécile Fabre, Richard Miller, Thomas Pogge and Michael Rosen for further discussion of the issues involved.

1 Among those who have understood justice as requiring some form of equality at global level are C. Beitz, *Political Theory and International Relations* (Princeton, Princeton University Press, 1979), part 3, section 2; B. Barry, 'Humanity and Justice in Global Perspective' in B. Barry, *Democracy, Power and Justice* (Oxford, Clarendon Press, 1989); T. Pogge, 'An Egalitarian Law of Peoples', *Philosophy and Public Affairs*, 23 (1994), 195–224; S. Caney, 'Nationality, Distributive Justice and the Use of Force', *Journal of Applied Philosophy*, 16 (1999), 123–38; C. Jones, *Global Justice: Defending Cosmopolitanism* (Oxford, Oxford University Press, 1999).

2 See especially chs 4, 7 and 8 above.

3 I have defended this claim at greater length with respect to social justice in *Principles of Social Justice* (Cambridge, Mass., Harvard University Press, 1999), ch. 12.

4 I hold national self-determination to have both intrinsic and instrumental value. It is instrumentally valuable because, *inter alia*, it provides the optimum conditions for the pursuit of social justice, and because it provides the conditions under which rich national cultures can flourish best, as I have argued in *On Nationality* (Oxford, Clarendon Press, 1995), ch. 4. These instrumental justifications may turn out in the end to be stronger than the intrinsic one that I sketch here. But I want to focus on the intrinsic justification first, to present the conflict between national self-determination and global justice in as clear a light as possible. Later on I return to the connection between self-determination and social justice.

5 See further *On Nationality*, ch. 2.

6 See my fuller discussion of this idea in chs 1 and 9 above.

7 B. Pascal, *Pensées*, ed. A.J. Krailsheimer (Harmondsworth, Penguin, 1966), p. 46.

8 M. Walzer, *Spheres of Justice* (Oxford, Martin Robertson, 1983), esp. ch. 1.

9 This contrast is sometimes marked by using 'desert' to describe the liberal idea linked tightly to responsibility, and 'merit' for the broader notion that identifies praiseworthy qualities without imputing responsibility. I have discussed this issue in greater depth in *Principles of Social Justice*, chs 6–7, and illustrated my claim about the variability of notions of merit in *Social Justice* (Oxford, Clarendon Press, 1976), ch. 8.

10 For a fuller account, see *Principles of Social Justice*, ch. 10.

11 I have attempted this in *Principles of Social Justice*, ch. 2.

12 See *Principles of Social Justice*, chs 3–4.

13 It may be objected here that when people deliberate with others in an effort to discover what justice requires, the principles that they invoke are regarded as principles of justice that are universally valid, not merely valid within their community. Now this may or may not be true as a matter of fact. The question of the final status of the principles that are invoked is not one that arises in deliberation, since all that concerns the participants is that they should be able to find principles which command the assent of their co-deliberators. But even if it turns out to be true that people engaged in deliberation standardly make the assumption in question, this raises no crucial difficulty *unless* it could be shown that deliberation would collapse without it – in which case my argument about local understandings of justice and their expression through deliberative democracy would have a self-defeating character. But I can see no reason why deliberation should collapse, since all that it requires is that there should be principles that members of the deliberating community regard as intersubjectively valid.

14 Let me emphasize that both of these are empirical claims. For the mechanisms linking nations to deliberative democracy, see *On Nationality*, ch. 4, and

chs 4–5 above. For the mechanisms linking deliberative democracy to social justice, see ch. 9 above.

15 Pedants might complain that we will always be able to discover some good in terms of which even the most deprived of the earth's inhabitants score highly. One may have no money, no job, no house, etc. but as a result have ample leisure time. But this would indeed be pedantry. Although I have stressed both the heterogeneity and the social constitution of the goods whose distribution is a concern of justice, I don't want to deny that there are many people in today's world whom any morally competent observer would judge to be deprived in an across-the-board sense. The argument in the paragraphs that follow nowhere relies on such a pedantic claim.

16 D. Miller, 'Justice and Global Inequality' in A. Hurrell and N. Woods (eds), *Inequality, Globalization, and World Politics* (Oxford, Oxford University Press, 1999).

17 See *Principles of Social Justice*, ch. 11, and 'Justice and Global Inequality'.

18 See especially Onora O'Neill, *Faces of Hunger: An Essay on Poverty, Justice and Development* (London, Allen and Unwin, 1986), ch. 6, and 'Hunger, Needs and Rights' in S. Luper-Foy (ed.), *Problems of International Justice* (London, Westview, 1988). For discussion, see Jones, *Global Justice*, ch. 4.

19 Among the more important recent attempts to address this problem are H. Shue, *Basic Rights: Subsistence, Affluence and US Foreign Policy* (Princeton, Princeton University Press, 1980); R.J. Vincent, *Human Rights and International Relations* (Cambridge, Cambridge University Press, 1986); J. Nickel, *Making Sense of Human Rights* (Berkeley, University of California Press, 1987); J. Donnelly, *Universal Rights in Theory and Practice* (Ithaca and London, Cornell University Press, 1989), parts 1–3; J.R. Bauer and D. Bell (eds), *The East Asian Challenge for Human Rights* (Cambridge, Cambridge University Press, 1999).

20 Note that this requirement entails more than just an obligation not to violate human rights oneself, whether negatively by injuring people, say, or positively by failing to provide vital resources. It is also an obligation to try to present the violation of human rights by third parties – say foreign governments that attempt to starve dissident minorities into submission. The difficult issue, which I cannot tackle here, is to decide how far this obligation extends – how far one agent must go, what costs the agent must bear, to prevent other agents from violating human rights. The growing literature on humanitarian intervention begins to address it.

21 I have elaborated on this definition in 'Justice and Global Inequality'.

22 I am looking in this chapter at international obligations of distributive justice, and trying to identify the basic principles that apply here. In a full account of global justice other questions would also need to be addressed, for instance questions about the rectification of historical injustices inflicted by one nation on another, questions about obligations of reciprocity that arise when states aid one another in various ways, questions about how the costs of environmental protection should be shared between states, and so forth.

23 For an illustration of this point, see the exchange between Liam Murphy and
    Tim Mulgan on what benevolence requires in a situation where the objective
    (the relief of third world poverty) is the joint responsibility of many indi-
    viduals. L. Murphy, 'The Demands of Beneficence', *Philosophy and Public
    Affairs*, 22 (1993), 267–92; T. Mulgan, 'Two Conceptions of Benevolence',
    Philosophy and Public Affairs, 26 (1997), 62–79; L. Murphy, 'A Relatively
    Plausible Principle of Beneficence: Reply to Mulgan', *Philosophy and Public
    Affairs*, 26 (1997), 80–6.

Index